CROSSINGS IN NINETEENTH-CENTURY AMERICAN CULTURE: JUNCTURES OF TIME, SPACE, SELF AND POLITICS

Interventions in Nineteenth-Century American Literature and Culture
Series Editors: Christopher Hanlon, Sarah R. Robbins, Andrew Taylor

Available
Liminal Whiteness in Early US Fiction
Hannah Lauren Murray

*Crossings in Nineteenth-Century American Culture: Junctures of Time,
Space, Self and Politics*
Edward Sugden (ed.)

Forthcoming
Melville's Americas: Hemispheric Sympathies, Transatlantic Contagion
Nicholas Spengler

The Aesthetics of History and Slave Revolution in Antebellum America
Kevin Modestino

Carlyle, Emerson and the Transatlantic Uses of Authority
Tim Sommer

*New Perspectives on Mary E. Wilkins Freeman:
Reading with and against the Grain*
Stephanie Palmer, Myrto Drizou and Cécile Roudeau

*Un(dis)covered Bodies: Science, Narrative, and the Female Body in
Feminist Medical Fiction*
Stephanie Peebles Tavera

www.edinburghuniversitypress.com/series/incal

CROSSINGS IN NINETEENTH-CENTURY AMERICAN CULTURE

Junctures of Time, Space, Self and Politics

Edited by
Edward Sugden

EDINBURGH
University Press

Edinburgh University Press is one of the leading university presses in the UK. We publish academic books and journals in our selected subject areas across the humanities and social sciences, combining cutting-edge scholarship with high editorial and production values to produce academic works of lasting importance. For more information visit our website: edinburghuniversitypress.com

Edinburgh University Press Ltd
The Tun – Holyrood Road
12(2f) Jackson's Entry
Edinburgh EH8 8PJ

Typeset in 10/12.5 Adobe Sabon by
IDSUK (DataConnection) Ltd, and
printed and bound in Great Britain.

A CIP record for this book is available from the British Library

ISBN 978 1 4744 7628 7 (hardback)
ISBN 978 1 4744 7630 0 (webready PDF)
ISBN 978 1 4744 7631 7 (epub)

CONTENTS

List of Figures   vii
Contributors   viii

Introduction   1
    Edward Sugden

Part I: Elsewheres
  1 Material/Immaterial: Frederick Douglass and the 'Moral Chemistry
     of the Universe', 1855   19
     Cody Marrs
  2 Earth/Atmosphere: The Leonid Meteor Shower, 1833   29
     Gordon Fraser
  3 Body/Spirit: Walt Whitman's Hicksite Quaker Poetics, 1855   41
     Rachel Heffner-Burns

Part II: Excess Identities
  4 Latinx/Confederate: Loreta Janeta Velazquez as a Cross-Dressing
     Soldier, 1861   59
     Leigh Johnson
  5 Philippines/United States: David Fagen Defects to the Filipino
     Army, 1899   71
     Spencer Tricker

6 White/Not-White: Robert Montgomery Bird's Racial
   Transformations, 1839   88
   Hannah Lauren Murray
7 Ecology/Radical Politics: Thoreau's Science of Civil
   Disobedience, 1849   101
   Michael Jonik

Part III: Chance Encounters
8 Mexico/Britain: A History of Julia Pastrana's Teeth, 1860–2013   123
   Marissa López
9 Matanzas, Cuba/Keswick, England: Maria Gowen Brooks
   Visits Robert Southey, 1831   146
   Erin C. Singer
10 England/New England: A British Quaker and a Fugitive from
   Slavery Encounter Each Other on a Train, 1850   158
   Bridget Bennett

Part IV: Impossible Systems
11 Slave Labour/Wage Labour: Reading Bartleby's Refusals, 1850   177
   Tomos Hughes
12 Antiquity/Modernity: An Issue of *Puck* Magazine, 1889   195
   Mark Storey
13 Democracy/State: James Fenimore Cooper on the Frontier,
   1826/1757   206
   Cécile Roudeau
14 Ulster, 1785/Pennsylvania, 1817/Ulster, 1845: James McHenry's
   Palimpsest of Anglo Settler Colonialism   222
   Jared Hickman

Index   246

FIGURES

8.1 Poster advertising appearances by Julia Pastrana at the Regent
     Gallery, London, singing romantic songs and performing
     'fancy dances'. Image courtesy of the Wellcome Library.   139

8.2 Miss Julia Pastrana, the embalmed nondescript: exhibiting at 191,
     Piccadilly. Image courtesy of the Wellcome Library.   140

8.3 Mari Hernandez as Julia Pastrana. Image courtesy of Mari
     Hernandez.   141

8.4 Mari Hernandez as Julia Pastrana. Image courtesy of Mari
     Hernandez.   142

8.5 Mari Hernandez as Julia Pastrana. Image courtesy of Mari
     Hernandez.   143

12.1 Front cover of *Puck*, 17 July 1889.   196

CONTRIBUTORS

Bridget Bennett is professor of American Literature and Culture at the University of Leeds. She has broad interests in US literary culture. Her publications include *Ripples of Dissent* (1996); *The Damnation of Harold Frederic* (1997); *Grub Street to the Ivory Tower* (1998); *Special Relationships: Anglo-American Affinities and Antagonisms, 1854–1936* (2002); *Twelve Months in an English Prison* (2003, two volumes); *Transatlantic Spiritualism and Nineteenth-Century American Literature* (2007) and two editions for the Macmillan Press, Walt Whitman, *Leaves of Grass and Selected Poems* (2019) and Willa Cather, *My Ántonia* (2019). She has also published a number of essays including '"The Silence Surrounding the Hut": Invisible Slaves and Vanished Indians in Wieland', *Early American Literature* (2018), which was awarded the 2019 Arthur Miller Prize. Her work has been supported by grants from the AHRC and British Academy and other bodies, and she was recently awarded a Leverhulme Major Fellowship for a project titled 'The Dissenting Atlantic: Archives and Unquiet Libraries, 1776–1865'.

Gordon Fraser is a lecturer and presidential fellow in American Studies at the University of Manchester, and he is the author of *Star Territory: Printing the Universe in Nineteenth-Century America* (Penn Press, 2021). His scholarship has appeared in numerous journals, including *PMLA*, *American Quarterly* and *J19*.

Rachel Heffner-Burns teaches composition and rhetoric in the Core Writing Program at Fairfield University. She is completing a manuscript on religion, embodiment, and social justice in nineteenth- and twentieth-century American poetry entitled *The Echo of Religious Influence in the Whitmanian Poetic Tradition*. She is also working on a transatlantic project that examines how science fiction and fantasy authors use theological ideas and imagery in their novels for young adult readers.

Jared Hickman is associate professor of English at Johns Hopkins University. He is the author of *Black Prometheus: Race and Radicalism in the Age of Atlantic Slavery* (Oxford, 2016) and the co-editor of *Abolitionist Places* (Routledge, 2013) and *Americanist Approaches to* The Book of Mormon (Oxford, 2019).

Tomos Hughes is a Leverhulme Early Career Fellow in the English and Comparative Literary Studies Department at the University of Warwick. He is completing a manuscript on the literature of the Reconstruction period and the revolutionary experience of emancipation, titled *America's Imagined Revolution: The Historical Novel of Reconstruction*. He is also working on a project that explores the interrelations between proslavery speculation and Black radical thought in nineteenth- and twentieth-century literature and culture.

Leigh Johnson is an associate professor of English at Marymount University, where she teaches courses in American literature, Latinx literature and gender studies. Her most recent work is on Latino masculinity, Ana Castillo's transvisionaria poetix, and women's friendships and forgiveness.

Michael Jonik teaches American literature and contemporary critical theory at the University of Sussex. He has published *Herman Melville and the Politics of the Inhuman* (Cambridge University Press, 2018), and he writes on pre-1900 American literature and philosophy. He is now editing the *New Cambridge Companion to Ralph Waldo Emerson* and co-editing *The Oxford Handbook of Herman Melville*. He is founding member of the British Association of Nineteenth-Century Americanists (BrANCA), and Reviews and Special Issues editor for the journal *Textual Practice*.

Marissa López is professor of English and Chicana/o Studies at UCLA, researching Chicanx literature from the nineteenth century to the present with an emphasis on nineteenth-century Mexican California. She has written two books: *Chicano Nations* (NYU, 2011) is about nationalism and Chicanx literature from the early 1800s to post-9/11; *Racial Immanence* (NYU, 2019) explores uses of the body and affect in Chicanx cultural production. She recently completed a year-long residency at the Los Angeles Public Library as a Scholars & Society fellow with the ACLS, where she worked to collaboratively develop a mobile app, 'Picturing Mexican America', that uses geodata to display images of Mexican California relevant to a user's location.

Cody Marrs is a professor of English at the University of Georgia. He is the author of *Melville, Beauty, and American Literary Studies* (Oxford, 2022), *Not Even Past: The Stories We Keep Telling About the Civil War* (Johns Hopkins, 2020) and *Nineteenth-Century American Literature and the Long Civil War* (Cambridge, 2015); the editor of *The New Melville Studies* (Cambridge, 2019); a co-editor of *Timelines of American Literature* (Johns Hopkins, 2019); and the General Editor of *Nineteenth-Century American Literature in Transition* (Cambridge, 2022). His work has also appeared in journals such as *American Literature* and *American Literary History*, and in several edited collections.

Hannah Lauren Murray is lecturer in American Literature at the University of Liverpool. Her monograph *Liminal Whiteness in Early US Fiction* (Edinburgh University Press, 2021) examines precarious and fluid whiteness in fiction from Charles Brockden Brown to Frank J. Webb. She has recently been published in *The Eighteenth Century: Theory and Interpretation*, *A New Companion to Herman Melville* and *The Oxford Handbook of Charles Brockden Brown*, and she sits on the steering committee for the British Association of Nineteenth-Century Americanists.

Cécile Roudeau is professor of American literature at Université de Paris, France. Her work focuses on the articulation between US literature and politics in the long nineteenth century and has appeared in *ESQ*, *William James Studies*, *Revue Française d'études américaines*, and the *European Journal of American Studies*. Her first book, *La Nouvelle-Angleterre: Politique d'une écriture* (Presses de la Sorbonne, 2012), read New England regionalism as a political mode of resistance. She is at work on two projects: 'Fictions of the Commons in 19th Century American Literature' and 'Beyond Stateless Literature: Practices of Democratic Power in Nineteenth-Century US Literature'.

Erin C. Singer is an assistant professor of American Literature at Louisiana Tech University. A scholar of nineteenth- and twentieth-century US and Latin American literature, her research specialty is poetry and poetics. You can read her work in *The Nathaniel Hawthorne Review*, *The Robert Frost Review* and elsewhere. She is at work on a book project about the hemispheric American epic after Walt Whitman.

Mark Storey is associate professor in the Department of English and Comparative Literary Studies at the University of Warwick. He is the author of the books *Time and Antiquity in American Empire* (Oxford University Press, 2021) and

Rural Fictions, Urban Realities: A Geography of Gilded Age American Literature (Oxford University Press, 2013), as well as essays on American literature that have appeared in *Modernism/modernity*, *Nineteenth-Century Literature* and *Studies in American Fiction*, amongst other venues. He is also the editor, with Stephen Shapiro, of the forthcoming *Cambridge Companion to American Horror*.

Edward Sugden is a senior lecturer in American Literature at King's College London. He is the author of *Emergent Worlds* (NYU Press, 2018). He is currently writing a biography of *Moby-Dick*.

Spencer Tricker is an assistant professor of English at Longwood University. His research focuses on nineteenth- and early twentieth-century American literature, with emphases on Asian American writers, transpacific narratives and comparative racialisation. His academic writing has been published (or is forthcoming) in *Studies in American Fiction*, *American Literary Realism*, *Early American Literature* and *Leviathan: A Journal of Melville Studies*.

INTRODUCTION

EDWARD SUGDEN

'I can't tell what's my name, or who I am!' said Rip van Winkle, having slept through the revolutionary rupture of 1776 (Irving 1820: 85).

'I was conscious for a time of nothing but existence,' said Edgar Huntly, after waking up in a cave without a subjectivity to give definition to the all-encompassing darkness around him (Brown [1799] 1988: 152).

'I become a transparent eye-ball; I am nothing,' said Ralph Waldo Emerson, rapt and wraith-like in the midst of nature (Emerson 1836: 13).

'I am no man, no woman, nothing,' said Laurence – or is it Laurent? – in Julia Ward Howe's *The Hermaphrodite*, surveying the simple fact of their existence (Howe 2004: 22).

This, here, is the narrative of my life, said Frederick Douglass, using a surname that was not his own, appending the legal and ontological non-being of 'an American slave' to it, next to a portrait in which his torso dissolves almost into invisibility (Douglass 1845).

'I am a citizen of somewhere else,' said Nathaniel Hawthorne after being ingloriously chucked out of his Custom House gig and into the writing of *The Scarlet Letter* (Hawthorne 1851: 51).

'Call me Ishmael,' said someone who may or may not be named Ishmael, in a year that is never directly stated (Melville [1851] 2001: 3).

'I'm Nobody! Who are you?' said Emily Dickinson, polemically advising against being 'Somebody' on a piece of now speculatively dated paper (Dickinson [1861] 1999: 116).

'*Who* are we? *Where* are we?' said Thoreau, in a moment of visionary dissolution, as he stood on top of Ktaadn demanding 'contact', crying out, on the page, from beyond the grave (Thoreau [1864] 2004: 71).

'And now tell me,' said Cassandra, in the midst of an identity crisis in *The Morgesons*, 'what am I?' (Stoddard [1862] 1984: 226).

'I insist upon knowing where I am,' said Julian West, disoriented time-traveller, not knowing where or when he was, upon waking in the year 2000 in Edward Bellamy's *Looking Backward* (Bellamy 1889: 27).

For a century in which biopower concretised selfhood around the fused axioms of state, body, race, gender and sex, changing simple and arbitrary elements of biology into fate (Castiglia 2008; Schuller 2018); in which the political shibboleths of individual rights and citizenship took hold, leading to the birth of new modes of government and the dominance of what Immanuel Wallerstein termed the age of 'liberal centrism' (Wallerstein 2011; see also Armitage 2007); in which the free market encouraged increasingly selfish and mean-spirited egotism and bestowed upon the world a secularised form of vocational calling in which one's alienated labour gave definition to the creative expression of individual bodies (Anthony 2009); in which people were, to use Anthony Giddens's term, 'disembedded' from heterogeneous local positions into supra-local identity categories like the nation-state (Giddens 1990); in which the central epoch-defining documents, in the United States at least, came with assertive names like 'Self Reliance' and 'Ain't I A Woman?';[1] in which the world became mapped from pole to pole as trade, travel and war completed their endless circuits; and the United States itself grew from coast to coast, unbelievably fulfilling the most feverish dreams of national destiny present at the moment of its emergence; in which an era became historically conscious as an era, as the *nineteenth century*, a period of progress, acceleration, enlightenment (Koselleck 2004); all of the above statements of non-, problematic, riven or uncertain selfhood detached from space and time are, well, strange, and ostensibly very much out of step with the age they are in.

That, in nineteenth-century American literature, statements like these – formed from an unsettling refrain of 'I am' followed by negation, uncertainty, ambivalence, plotted across unstable and relativistic axes of self, space, time and history – repeat insistently suggests that something else might be going on. The scene of breakdown, of falling backwards onto a self that, it appears, is either not there or so definitionally amorphous as to amount to something similar, too recurs, to the extent that it becomes generic, a stock gesture hardwired into many different modes. In all the above, the speakers seem alternately to revel in and be terrified by their glorious and beguiling impossibility, to nurture and lament their categorical indistinctiveness, and to propose and then withdraw often provisional and semi-articulate frameworks through which they might one day become comprehensible to themselves and their various audiences, dotted across time. These invocations implicitly come with the insistence that the modes through which they – and indeed we now – might describe their identities – rooted in the fusion of biopower and liberalism – nation, race, gender, sex, ethnicity, region, period – are perhaps less binding than they might at first sight appear, open to swellings of speculation, counterfactual diversions into other realms of identification, and even chance-like and utopian spots of consciousness that might promise access to different histories.

Did nineteenth-century Americans really know who they were? (Or perhaps more precisely: did they know themselves in terms that we would recognise?) It does not seem that way. And, if not, can literary critics and historians truly know them in the twenty-first century? The answer is, I think, yes, but the terms by which we know them might appear counterintuitive, unnatural, provisional and only semi-articulate. *Crossings* is a collective attempt to define some of these terms. As a whole, it seeks to nourish the definitional uncertainty of the nineteenth century, proposing new dimensions, directions and axes for making the era comprehensible in a way that takes these moments of identity panic as a starting point. In so doing, it develops a political language of self-identification that only partially intersects with the axioms of biopolitical liberal modernity. It reads the past structurally and systemically in a way that dwells on seeming incommensurability and, accordingly, moulds historical trajectories against the grain. It dwells on the oddities of the era, the strange meetings, the bizarre coincidences, the occult beliefs, the antique detritus, not as oddities but as possibly historically representative occurrences, even if these occurrences did not become historical as such. In short, it fleshes out the world that surrounds these testimonies of non-, partial or differently constituted being and seeks to account for them. It does so in ways that are simultaneously attentive to the terminology and forms of being of a bygone era and curious about what, if any, afterlives these alternative modes of existence, individual, historical and systemic, might have now and, indeed, the contemporary conditions by which they might suddenly and urgently be relevant and comprehensible.

The chapters use the rubric of 'crossing' to do so. Crossing is a way of self-reflectively reading, building upon and further opening out shifts in critical paradigms over the past fifteen years in terms of geography, history and identity; and as a still fruitful methodology for capturing and defining what otherwise might remain indistinct or uncharted in the nineteenth century (even if crossing, post-transnationalism, might be met with a non-surprised shrug of the shoulders). With each chapter beginning with a crossing or what the subtitle terms a 'juncture', the collection positions itself at the meeting points between places, people, systems and periods with a view of making visible, explaining and accentuating unlikely occurrences. The volume uses quite literal and local examples of crossing as the basis for exploring modes of being in the world that might be more appropriate for describing the era. This is a book that takes the surprising and quite often, nigh on inexplicable collision between social forces and individuals as its often literal starting points. The chapters draw on the unlikelihood of such encounters while seeking to discover an archaeology for them. They identify the categorical modes that such meetings elide and propose more apt ones. The collective aim is to suggest that it is *because* nineteenth-century Americans did not know who, what, when or where they were that the field of nineteenth-century American literary studies can imagine and define itself.

In this, the collection bears the impress of the fact that the constitutive elements of the field – 'nineteenth-century' and 'American' – have over the past fifteen years undergone a similar and parallel crisis of identity, energetically expansive but perhaps self-cancelling, capacious and widening, but vertiginously so, as the historical objects of its study. A combination of the transnational turn, the temporal turn, multilingual study, minoritarian critique and new materialism have extended the understanding of the historical period, the geographical terrain and the forms of identity within them to the extent that the field is now partially detached from its ostensible adjectival and noun referents (for useful summative and self-reflective collections on these turns, and indeed for books that, quite simply, inspired this volume, see Blum 2016; Luciano and Wilson 2014; Castiglia and Gillman's forthcoming at the time of writing collection *Neither the Time Nor the Place* will also prove useful). Yet, increasingly these changes have energised works of speculative historical worldmaking rather than disaggregation, as scholars have explored the positive modes by which individuals lived beyond – touched by, but not totally so – the edicts of liberalism and biopower, experiencing as they did so generously open states of political being, whether to do with nationhood, freedom, sexuality, citizenship, or indeed the category of the 'human' itself (Berger 2020; Coronado 2013; Coviello 2013; Ellis 2018; Hyde 2018; Kazanjian 2016; Rusert 2017; Taylor 2013). Building on both trends, when read together the work of the volume as a whole is partially negative: to explore what its objects of enquiry are not; and to extract the objects of study from frameworks that they insist ought not to form the conditions of their legibility. But, in conversation with these new critical, socio-political and historical terminologies, more pressing is a work of conceptual crafting, as each essay seeks to capture what their subject is on their own terms and to build a historical and theoretical world that might render their historical experience legible.

The nineteenth-century crisis of identity is best thought of as a crisis of foundation – as Americans worked out what it was to be American when the meanings of that word were historically charged with potentiality, when the relationship of the nation to the world and its era was still aligning, when liberalism was moving from being emergent to ideologically dominant. The current one might, instead, be a parallel one of dissolution. The structural decline of the United States, from 9/11, the Iraq War, the 2008 financial crisis and the

Trump presidency, as well as the rise of new forms of autocratic non-US capitalism, particularly concentrated in Russia and China, has made visible – by virtue of a structural similarity between the two ends of a historical parabola, the rise and fall of the American empire, the decay of centrist liberalism – similarly unsettled modes of identification and placement. Of course, on top of this, pressures internal to scholarly study, based around employment, student numbers, and political meddling, neo-utilitarian reductionists, and marketisation of higher education have only added to this sense of field crisis. For all this, if the crisis allows scholars to view parallel scenes of callowness and incompletion in a more uneven nineteenth century, then – if our own sense of structural and vocational displacement is also a mode of scholarly vision – at the very least, we might make the past resonate with our own time in ways that are historically more accurate.

Several central theoretical nodes are prominent in this volume. Many of the essays consider aberrant selfhoods and marginal bodies: ones that exist outside of normative modes of categorisation, which challenge taxonomic formulations that seek to delimit their selfhoods and, on occasion, refute their material foundation. Readings of time, history and space recur as particularly resonant modes that register the often surprising collisions that make up the volume and which we can now use to reperiodise the century accordingly. The essays all, to some extent at least, bear the influence of the work of transnationalism, insofar as none accept the nation-state as the preeminent unit for socio-political formulations of collectives and all are interested in the liminal points where seemingly separate and incommensurate individuals and systems clash. Taken together they paint nineteenth-century America as a provisional construction, bursting and exceeding the constraints of identity, geography and history. In this sense, crossing might not only be the dominant activity of the era but one structurally necessitated by it, even if this activity has now been obscured by transformations that occurred subsequent to the era.

The first section, 'Elsewheres', charts a series of spaces that exceed the limitations of embodiment and cartography. They plot out a world in which nineteenth-century Americans barely knew of their location in the world and strained against increasingly dominant geographical and material models that would circumscribe them. The spaces that emerge leave the earth and the body behind to journey into immaterial realms of fantasy and space. Dreams, visions and the cosmos mingle in this section. The chapters look at spaces that are off the map: either states of mind that escape the material world and enter into something more evanescent and spiritual, or realms that exceed the limiting imperatives of national cartography.

In Chapter 1, 'Material/Immaterial: Frederick Douglass and the "Moral Chemistry of the Universe", 1855', Cody Marrs releases Douglass from the hold of materialist print culture through exploring his commitment to the imagination, his theories of mind and his spiritual vision. Douglass is, Marrs suggests, a writer who frequently makes journeys from the world of textual circulation into realms that material contexts cannot account for. The self-consciousness that Douglass strives for in his autobiographies fundamentally emerges out of the incessant, undetermined encounter between mind and the body's worldly entanglements. To read Douglass as merely a creature of print culture – which is to say, through his role as media impresario – is to delimit the stretch of his imagination. Ultimately, this is a chapter which calls into question the dominance of accounts of material circulation in the antebellum era, that desire to place literature's meanings against the conditions of its production and where and when it was read. Douglass shows that it is not just print as such that merits attention, nor is it the material grounds for writing, but, rather, the immaterial forces that imbue literature with meaning and provide it with a moral scope and metaphysical vision. Familiar scenes, such as Douglass's early and ecstatic meeting with the printed word, connote in new ways, as the ideal intersects with the real in them.

In Chapter 2, 'Earth/Atmosphere: The Leonid Meteor Shower, 1833', Gordon Fraser leaves the earth behind to journey into the cosmos to articulate a postnational vision of identity for nineteenth-century American literary studies. While this extends the scale through which we might frame the United States, the presence of the stars on the flag reveals that such a scale has always been written into the idea of America. Fraser examines various responses to the Leonid meteor shower of 1833, a flash of shooting stars witnessed by diverse observers: Prussian scientist Alexander von Humboldt, Kiowa historian Dohäsan, future abolitionist Frederick Douglass and an anonymous enslaver from Combahee, South Carolina, whose account of it would be memorialised in astronomy textbooks for a half century. Thousands of shooting stars made observers fear that the world might be ending, calling into question fundamental assumptions about the nation, the natural world and the order of the universe. While the stars on the flag had long provided an axis with which Americans configured their national identity, the effects of the meteor shower were substantially more disruptive. This moment in the atmosphere, where cosmic debris crossed into a terrestrial orbit, enabled Prussian, Kiowa and Black thinkers to challenge US nationalist ideologies and forced US nationalists to question their cosmic certainty about the national future. Yet, in the present, it might be that looking towards the stars with these other citizens allows us to generate paradigms that invoke more emancipatory visions of the nation-state.

In Chapter 3, 'Body/Spirit: Walt Whitman's Hicksite Quaker Poetics, 1855', Rachel Heffner-Burns argues that Walt Whitman's engagement with Quaker religious doctrine forces us to cast him as a poet of disembodiment rather than embodiment. Her work suggests that the spiritual always frames Whitman's depictions of bodies, particularly those of white working-class men, images which formed the basis for his democratic vision for the United States. The key figure here for Whitman was Elias Hicks, a preacher who in 1855 delivered a sermon that prioritised the believer's capacity to experience the divine light of God speaking from within herself. Whitman was drawn to the egalitarian power and to the sensuous aesthetics of this version of spirituality. In his 'Song of Occupations', he transformed this belief into a political programme for the empowerment of the working class. While dominant capitalist ideology values workers for the productive capacity of their bodies alone, Whitman emphasised how labour generated a spiritual consciousness that allows them to participate in an incorporeal spiritual American community. In this sense, we have to reconfigure not only how we think of Whitman's depictions of work and bodies but also the nature of capitalism's political potentialities in the nineteenth century. Whitman's vision of labour is not one of alienation or exploitation but of a transcendent connection with a secular form of inner light; and, indeed, there is a suggestion that the biopolitical focus on the body might divert our attention away from spiritual 'bodies' that had an equally important role in the productive economy of the nineteenth century.

The second section, 'Excess Identities', tracks an archive of those whose excessive selfhoods are not reducible to modernity's identity categories. These are not selves that can be subsumed into racial, national, ethnic, gender or sexual categories – or at least, if they are, they are only subsumed partially. The subjects of this section are messy and beguiling, exceeding the limits of their ostensible categorical containers. They point towards an unfamiliar nineteenth-century America in which the modes by which we think of individuals applied only provisionally, or not at all. This section is concerned with examples of identities that fail to coalesce into any of the dominant modes that operated in nineteenth-century America, whether nation, race, gender or sexuality. Instead, each describes an excessive sense of self that eschews the limitations of the flattened identity categories that characterise modernity.

In Chapter 4, 'Latinx/Confederate: Loreta Janeta Velazquez as a Cross-Dressing Soldier, 1861', Leigh Johnson studies the narrative of a Latinx Confederate solider who does not fit into our conceptions of either the national or gendered body at the time of the Civil War. In their story, Velasquez marshals cross-dressing as means of dramatising the conflict between their seemingly contradictory identification as simultaneously Latinx and Confederate. Not only does the narrative challenge what we understand as an American in the nineteenth century, but also the non-national and emergent forces of social identification with which it experiments. The same experiments interact in a coterminous way with the narrative's configuration of gender, which shares in a similar state of flux. Even then, cross-dressing and swapping political sides introduce forms of identity that go even beyond the more obvious form of her unsettling of gender. In this way, many of the categories by which we might make sense of the narrative – gender, nationhood, ethnicity, pro-or-antislavery, Latinx or American in particular – simply fail to connote in the way that we think they ought to.

In Chapter 5, 'Philippines/United States: David Fagen Defects to the Filipino Army, 1899', Spencer Tricker demonstrates how transnationalism does not necessarily resolve into a utopian politics. Instead, race, nation and empire enter into a relationship of almost irresolvable contradictions that nonetheless generates a dynamic of further racialisation. The chapter tracks the literary appropriation of David Fagen, a Black soldier in the Philippine-American War (1899–1903), to illustrate that although Afro-Philippine crossings were commoditised for white readerly consumption at the end of the long nineteenth century, they retained a subversive capacity to expose the dubious and fragile expediency of what W. E. B. Du Bois famously designates as the global colour line. Through analysing stories by Rowland Thomas about Fagen, Tricker shows how the circulation of this figure allows us to recognise the Philippine-American War as an oft-forgotten yet pivotal site for theorising the mutually constitutive racialisation of Black and Asian people. This is a peculiarly literary drama insofar as it takes place through instabilities in plot arcs, literary typologies and stock racial characters. What looks familiar in the sense of literary types and generic archetypes often, when placed against the racial balancing act that was the Philippine-American War, operates differently than we might expect. As a result, the chapter as a whole challenges some of the pluralist tenets that have underpinned thinking about cosmopolitan figures and representations.

In Chapter 6, 'White/Not-White: Robert Montgomery Bird's Racial Transformations, 1839', Hannah Lauren Murray demonstrates how race was a changing social characteristic rather than a fixed biological category in antebellum America. Her exploration centres on, in particular, the category of the 'non-white' that takes place through various forms of amorphous, if at times overdetermined, modes of racial performance. She does so through exploring the titular character of Robert Montgomery Bird's *The Adventures of Robin Day*. In this novel, Day racially crosses showing how whiteness, far from being a solid and impermeable form of identity, could slide into a more liminal, gradated whiteness. Robin's temporary loss of his whiteness emphasises pressing anxieties about white precariousness and marginalisation that extend through to the contemporary. Whiteness ceases to be an abstract universal in Murray's analysis – or, at least, ceases to be *just* that. The analysis shows how even dominant categories of identity in the early United States were provisional, fluid and ever open to reformulation through contact with changing social milieus.

In Chapter 7, 'Ecology/Radical Politics: Thoreau's Science of Civil Disobedience, 1849', Michael Jonik rereads the work of Henry David Thoreau in order to capture the essence of his radicalism. This chapter engages Thoreau to explore how, in the light of new materialist and posthumanist understandings of agency as distributed and inclusive of non-human actants, we understand 'individual' political resistance. For Jonik, Thoreau is not a libertarian individualist, but quite the opposite. In his radical work, Thoreau proposes a new category of 'transindividual' subjectivity, construed with/in one's broad eco-social relations. The chapter asks how we might expand the sense of individual 'conscience' staked out in 'Civil Disobedience' into what could be called an earth-conscience of civil disobedience, resonant with the 'intelligence with the earth' Thoreau calls for in *Walden*. This 'earth-conscience' is a life-labour of finding novel modes of interactivity, both of navigating a world that is indeterminate and volatile, plural and wild, and of undertaking civil disobedience as the action and performance of right: of disrupting and revolutionising relations. Any form of action in Thoreau's world is therefore necessarily collectivist, even if predicated on this different non-liberal form of individual conscience. In proposing this, Jonik recodes our understanding of what Emerson and Thoreau would have meant by 'self' reliance. Following Thoreau, the chapter makes us ask how acts of civil disobedience can reconfigure the material relations that subtend and make possible the essentials of our lives – our food, our clothing, our fuel – and how we can trace the allegiances of our dollars or conduct life histories of commodities or material-flow analyses to find out from where the objects that surround us come, in what eco-social networks they are imbricated, and where they are ultimately going.

The third section, 'Chance Encounters', spies on meetings between individuals, objects and forms whose coming together is surprising. In these encounters, individuals who have no business being together enter into conversation and, accordingly, seemingly incommensurate worlds collide. Narrating these moments forces us to disturb some of the structuring teleologies of nineteenth-century America so that we might account for how these coincidences and oddities came into being. The interest in these chance encounters, therefore, implicitly invites further speculation on history – its shape, how individuals moved around in it and, indeed, how they come to be remembered, stored in our own present.

In Chapter 8, 'Mexico/Britain: A History of Julia Pastrana's Teeth, 1860–2013', Marissa López uncovers why it is that a cast of Julia Pastrana's upper and lower jaws can be found in the Odontological Collection at the Hunterian Museum at the Royal College of Surgeons in London. Pastrana was an Indigenous Mexican woman born in Sinaloa in 1834 who suffered from gingivial hyperplasia (enlarged gums) and generalised hypertrichosis (hairiness) and travelled the world as part of her husband Theodor Lent's freak show. Both during her lifetime and after her death, she was something of a global sensation: she gained the attention of Charles Darwin among others, her mummified remains travelled the world until the 1970s, and a play was written about her in 2013. This chapter begins with a simple question: why *are* Pastrana's teeth in London? Answering this question involves building on Pastrana's peregrinations in life and death to recreate a surprising triangulation between Mexico, the United States and Britain that still functions today. For Pastrana reverberates through space and time to trace circuits that run like a live wire through alternative, transatlantic histories that are still with us. The essay reveals that we can generate a direct line from relative US disinterest in Pastrana to contemporary immigration crises in the US that reveals the British fascination with Pastrana offers an affective measure of racial hypocrisy in the US from the nineteenth century to the present. Moreover, the crossings and legacies of Pastrana necessitate a more capacious vision of what constitutes the 'human' if we are to capture something of the lived reality of her existence.

In Chapter 9, 'Matanzas, Cuba/Keswick, England: Maria Gowen Brooks Visits Robert Southey, 1831', Erin C. Singer tracks the poet Maria Gowen Brooks's trip to England in 1831 to meet Robert Southey. This surprising meeting reveals a previously hidden network of print-cultural links and the ways in which gender intersected with this material world of texts. It begins in the years after the death of Brooks's husband (thirty years her senior), when Brooks, fresh from a sojourn on her brother's plantation in Cuba, returned to New England. She brought with her a poetry manuscript entitled *Zophïel*, which was to be her magnum opus, and a new persona: 'Maria del Occidente'. After reading Poe's reviews of her work, Robert Southey, the then poet laureate, invited her to England with the promise of publication. This trip brings together a strange geography – encompassing Cuba, New England and London – with an odd literary alignment between Poe, Southey and Gowen. Even more beguilingly, it creates a personage – Maria del Occidente – that is far from reducible to this unfamiliar geographical and sociocultural formation. In this sense, Brooks/Del Occidente's circuit not only goes beyond forms of national belonging, but also the now more naturalised models for transnational identity. The register for this excessiveness of identity is particularly visible for literary scholars, as Brooks writes in hybrid epic, poetess and high Romantic tradition, with a variety of different languages featuring and shaping her poetic practice.

In Chapter 10, 'England/New England: A British Quaker and a Fugitive from Slavery Encounter Each Other on a Train, 1850', Bridget Bennett narrates a meeting between the Leeds-based abolitionist and merchant Wilson Armistead and a fugitive from slavery, Thomas Jones, on a train passing through New England. During this journey, Jones told Armistead of his remarkable history and, most likely, passed on to him his pamphlet, *The Experience of Thomas Jones, Who Was a Slave for Forty-Three Years* (1850). Multiple crossings coalesce in a fleeting encounter between strangers on a train. They include the passage from slavery to freedom; journeys across the Atlantic; a conviviality allowing for trans-racial sympathies and conversation; and finally the complex transformation of African American testimony into print culture. The story that unfolds involves questions of agency and recovery. It exemplifies the kinds of issues raised in a post-crossings critical age. It requires us to reflect upon textuality, including the practices of nineteenth-century print culture; to probe where and what are our archives; to ask how we expand our conversations and research methodologies to recover neglected and important figures like Armistead and Jones; and finally, to acknowledge the impact of chance as a substantive energy in history.

The fourth section, 'Impossible Systems', focuses on systemic incommensurability, the way in which seemingly mutually self-contradictory political structures temporarily align and interact in nineteenth-century America. These are chapters that explore the coexistence of modes of organising the world that seem, on the surface at least, very much at odds with one another. In placing themselves at the meeting points between these systems they seek to account for their counterintuitive coming together. Uniting this section is an interest in historical and political repulsion at a structural level. The essays demonstrate how contradictory socio-political systems and historical timeframes were not only co-present in nineteenth-century America but also, often, mutually constitutive. Thus capitalism and slavery, the classical and the modern, millenarianism and secular liberalism, and democracy and the state exist side by side.

In Chapter 11, 'Slave Labour/Wage Labour: Reading Bartleby's Refusals, 1850', Tomos Hughes explores the imbrication of capitalist freedom and racialised slavery in the midcentury to argue that these ostensibly opposed systems were once thought of as equivalent and equal possibilities. He does so through a reading of 'Bartleby, the Scrivener' that is positioned against the political economy of George Fitzhugh and the Fugitive Slave Act of 1850: 'Bartleby' responds in particular to the Compromise's seeming deterritorialisation of slavery (encapsulated by a reinvigorated Fugitive Slave Law). Set in the hybrid space of 'the Mississippi of Broadway', Melville's story depicts a wage worker who, by withdrawing his labour, becomes a slave. Tracing the narrator's crossings between pro-slavery ideology and the pro-labour language of wage slavery, he argues that Melville reimagines an important rhetorical figure in mid-nineteenth-century Atlantic thought, the wage slave, as an impossibly concrete character. Rather than allegorise a political subject, Bartleby's contradictory silence allows Melville to approach the material crossover between the simultaneous expansion of slavery and the wage form using a language other than the pejorative (and often reactionary, anti-Black) discourse of wage slavery. More broadly, the essay flips nineteenth-century history on its head to recapture a moment when it seemed that the trajectory of history was less a liberal one that journeyed from slavery to freedom, than one that journeyed from capitalism to a universalised form of post-capitalist bondage.

In Chapter 12, 'Antiquity/Modernity: An Issue of *Puck* Magazine, 1889', Mark Storey explores the coming together of the classical world, Gilded Age print culture and the remnants of antebellum slavery into a self-conflagrating historical space. The 17 July 1889 issue of *Puck* magazine brings together two cultural artefacts that exist uneasily together: a cartoon that satirised the newly elected Republican party with a caption that read 'Master and Slave', and a half-page sketch by Charles Chesnutt entitled 'A Roman Antique' in which a white narrator encounters a homeless Black man who claims to have been Julius Caesar's manservant. Storey explores the historical time that might make this strange coalescence comprehensible: the discrete date of 17 July 1889 is simply not enough. Instead he generates a historical model, discovered through the embedded trope of Spartacus, that involves the coterminous overlap of Gilded Age New York, ancient Rome, the antebellum South and the revolutionary Caribbean of the 1790s. The picture of historical time that emerges is synchronic, existing flatly across the present, but involves a form of synchronicity that necessarily contains both active and inactive fossil traces of past historical constellations. Antiquity and modernity thus collapse into one another in an apocalyptic now.

In Chapter 13, 'Democracy/State: James Fenimore Cooper on the Frontier, 1826/1757', Cécile Roudeau recovers the oxymoronic alignment between democracy and the state in early America in a way that goes against the idea that to be free and individual is to be opposed to the government. In *The Last of the Mohicans*, Cooper returned to 1757, a key moment in the Seven Years' War, to experiment with democratic practices of state government once thriving but no longer available as futurities in post-revolutionary America. Roudeau explores the role of the state in controlling the circulation of financial and representational value. To become usable again in Cooper's present, the crossing between 'democracy' and 'the state' was displaced from politics to literary fiction, or rather, experimented with at the crossroads between the two. This essay considers these conceptual and disciplinary crossings and argues for a historicisation of both, not to relegate them safely to Cooper's early nineteenth century but to reinvigorate their critical potency today. Reading *Mohicans* against the grain of the liberal critique of democracy and the state that has dominated much US literary scholarship since the postwar years forces us to unlearn what we think we know about democratic power. To allow this past to fictionally happen we need to disable the post-1945 hydraulic model of 'more democracy, less state; less state, more democracy'. Doing so uncovers in Cooper's fiction the messy beginnings and 'truncated possibilities' of a past that until recently could not have *yet* happened and recursively activates the democratic as possibility within state formation.

In Chapter 14, 'Ulster, 1785/Pennsylvania, 1817/Ulster, 1845: James McHenry's Palimpsest of Anglo Settler Colonialism', Jared Hickman uses the career of the first Irish American novelist, James McHenry, to reflect on a history of Anglo settler colonialism that joins the nineteenth-century United States to seventeenth-century Ulster in a feedback loop. McHenry's corpus of historical romances, evenly split between US and Irish settings, features the Ulster Scot as an agent of civilisation over and against a figure of the Indigene, whether Catholic Irish or non-Christian Amerindian. McHenry's return to Ulster in 1842 as US consul offers further occasion to think about this historical compounding of Anglo settler colonialism: the fifth-generation Scots settler of Irish Ulster, after having (re)enacted his settlerism in Native America, *re*-settles Irish Ulster by assuming a diplomatic position in Londonderry that presupposes the settler sovereignty of the United States and United Kingdom. Hickman shows how McHenry's work can serve the theorisation of Second and Fourth Worlds – that is, the settler societies of Ireland, the United States, Canada, Australia and elsewhere, whose existence is predicated on the elimination of the Indigenous societies that unsettlingly preexist them and defiantly persist. The overall historical argument is that settler colonialism is, on this basis, a form of political theology that, by virtue of persistent Indigenous genocide, naturalises itself through the eternal and disinterested categories of secular liberalism. At the heart of the capitalist project, as an erased or present but invisible presence, is a more ancient form of millenarianism that is made particularly visible through the manifold absurdities and peregrinations of McHenry's religiously inflected work.

The end of this introduction might call for a final grand statement of purpose. However, instead I want to take a moment to thank all the contributors for all of their own crossings in the making of this collection. The vast majority of work on this project was completed against the backdrop of a global pandemic that placed unprecedented pressures on academic labour time and much more besides. I am immensely grateful to them for having taken the time to contribute. While our interactions have been virtual, it has been a great pleasure to stay in touch with people through this volume. The collection contains multiple institutional crossings of its own: between different Anglophone and non-Anglophone university systems, between different career stages, between different disciplinary specialities and subfields. These crossings and connections have provided a lifeline to a world beyond my computer and I hope, soon, we will all meet again to talk about this book.

Works Cited

Anthony, David (2009), *Paper Money Men: Commerce, Manhood, and the Sensational Public Sphere in Antebellum America*, Columbus: The Ohio State Press.

Armitage, David (2007), *The Declaration of Independence: A Global History*, Cambridge, MA: Harvard University Press.

Bellamy, Edward (1889), *Looking Backward 2000–1887*, Boston and New York: Houghton, Mifflin and Company.

Berger, Jason (2020), *Xenocitizens: Illiberal Ontologies in Nineteenth-Century America*, New York: Fordham University Press.

Blum, Hester, ed. (2016), *Turns of Event: Nineteenth-Century American Literary Studies in Motion*, Philadelphia: University of Pennsylvania Press.

Brown, Charles Brockden [1799] (1988), *Edgar Huntly or, Memoirs of a Sleep Walker*, London: Penguin.

Castiglia, Christopher (2008), *Interior States: Institutional Consciousness and the Inner Life of Democracy in the Antebellum United States*, Durham, NC: Duke University Press.

Coronado, Raúl (2013), *A World Not to Come: A History of Latino Writing and Print Culture*, Cambridge, MA: Harvard University Press.

Coviello, Peter (2013), *Tomorrow's Parties: Sex and the Untimely in Nineteenth-Century America*, New York: New York University Press.

Dickinson, Emily (1999), *The Poems of Emily Dickinson, a Reading Edition*, ed. R. W. Franklin, Cambridge, MA: Harvard University Press.

Douglass, Frederick (1845), *Narrative of the Life of Frederick Douglass, an American Slave*, Boston: Anti-Slavery Office.

Ellis, Cristin (2018), *Antebellum Posthuman: Race and Materiality in the Mid-Nineteenth Century*, New York: Fordham University Press.

Emerson, Ralph Waldo (1836), *Nature*, Boston: James Monroe and Company.

Giddens, Anthony (1990), *The Consequences of Modernity*, Cambridge: Polity Press.

Hawthorne, Nathaniel (1851), *The Scarlet Letter, a Romance*, Boston: Ticknor, Reed, and Fields.

Howe, Julia Ward (2004), *The Hermaphrodite*, Lincoln: University of Nebraska Press.

Hyde, Carrie (2018), *Civic Longing: The Speculative Origins of US Citizenship*, Cambridge, MA: Harvard University Press.

Irving, Washington (1820), *The Sketch Book of Geoffrey Crayon, Gent.*, London: John Miller.

Kazanjian, David (2016), *The Brink of Freedom: Improvising Life in the Nineteenth-Century Atlantic World*, Durham, NC: Duke University Press.

Koselleck, Reinhardt (2004), *Futures Past: On the Semantics of Historical Time*, trans. Keith Tribe, New York: Columbia University Press.

Luciano, Dana, and Ivy G. Wilson, eds (2014), *Unsettled States: Nineteenth-Century American Literary Studies*, New York: New York University Press.

Melville, Herman [1851] (2001), *Moby-Dick, or The Whale*, ed. Harrison Hayford, Hershel Parker and G. Thomas Tanselle, Evanston: Northwestern University Press.

Rusert, Britt (2017), *Fugitive Science: Empiricism and Freedom in Early African American Culture*, New York: New York University Press.

Schuller, Kyla (2018), *The Biopolitics of Feeling: Race, Sex, and Science in the Nineteenth Century*, Durham, NC: Duke University Press.

Stoddard, Elizabeth [1862] (1984), *The Morgesons & Other Writings, Published and Unpublished*, ed. Lawrence Buell and Sandra A. Zagarell, Philadelphia: University of Pennsylvania Press.

Taylor, Matthew A. (2013), *Universes without Us: Posthuman Cosmologies in American Literature*, Minneapolis: University of Minnesota Press.

Thoreau, Henry David [1864] (2004), *The Maine Woods*, ed. Joseph J. Moldenhauer, Princeton: Princeton University Press.

Wallerstein, Immanuel (2011), *The Modern World System IV: Centrist Liberalism Triumphant, 1789–1914*, Berkeley: University of California Press.

NOTES

1. Thanks to Xine Yao for noting that this was not Sojourner Truth's original title for the speech, but rather one appended to it in Frances Gage's likely inaccurate version. For more information see https://www.thesojournertruthproject.com/.

PART I

ELSEWHERES

I

MATERIAL/IMMATERIAL: FREDERICK DOUGLASS AND THE 'MORAL CHEMISTRY OF THE UNIVERSE', 1855

CODY MARRS

Throughout the last decade or so, scholars have revealed nineteenth-century American literature to be deeply embedded in 'matter' of one form or another. This scholarship goes by different names and uses different methods, but it tends to foreground the interpretive importance of literature's material dimensions, which encompass everything from paper and print production to animals, the environment and the economy. Such work differs notably from earlier analyses of literature's 'contexts', which the New Americanists tended to construe in a cultural sense to encompass a text's broader discursive milieu.[1] Whether it focuses on objects, energy or empiricism itself, today's post-New Americanist scholarship places a more literal and pronounced emphasis on matter qua matter and the ways in which it conditions nineteenth-century writing.

This materialist scholarship has illuminated several aspects of nineteenth-century American literature that had been either underemphasised or overlooked. It has demonstrated that many of the era's writers saw themselves as archivists and historians, actively seeking to record the world just as it slips away. It has also shown that many writers engaged with vitalism, physics and other methods of empirical inquiry; anticipated posthumanist insights into identity and the environment; and understood literature in terms of very specific genres, formats and media. I have learned a great deal from this work, but I think some caution is warranted. It is important to keep in mind that when it comes to literature, materiality and immateriality are inevitably entangled, and a great deal of what makes American literature what it is – what makes it distinctive and important – has to do with its immaterial qualities. It is certainly possible that, as Jonathan Senchyne aptly puts it, 'many writers and readers . . . found meaning quite literally in the materiality of texts, in paper as well as on it' (Senchyne 2020: ix). But it is difficult to square that account of literature's power with most writers' actual motives and ambitions, or with the reception of works such as *Moby-Dick*, *Uncle Tom's Cabin* and *Common Sense*, which eclipse their material histories in spectacular ways. I also suspect it is difficult for many scholars to square that view of literature with their experiences in the classroom, or with their own experiences as readers.

The following pages explore this issue, and argue for the relevance of the immaterial, by way of Frederick Douglass. On the one hand, Frederick Douglass was undoubtedly a creature of print culture – a prolific writer, editor and reprinter who navigated various media with aplomb.[2] Yet his writings also burst with the immaterial, repeatedly drawing attention to that which exceeds the bounds of print or paper. To read Douglass is to encounter wishes and dreams as well as spirits and 'moral battles'. Nations, Douglass said, have 'souls', and even the cosmos has a 'moral chemistry' (Douglass [1855] 1999: 314; Douglass [1885] 1995: 415). Of the Civil War, he remarked, it 'will not consent to be viewed simply as a physical contest . . . . It was not even a war of geography or . . . of race . . . . It was a war of ideas, a battle of principles' (Douglass [1878] 1999: 631). This fervent interest in the immaterial forces that structure the world bubbles up in almost everything he wrote, providing his speeches, essays and autobiographies with a sharp moral vision and wide metaphysical scope.[3] That interest is reflected, too, in the books that lined the shelves of his library – books about moral philosophy and theology; John Ruskin's studies of atmospheric art; works by Friedrich Schiller, Johann Gottlieb Fichte and Ludwig Feuerbach; and still other books about spirit pictures, religious sentiment and the bond between nature and the soul.

What are we to do with this other, less concrete, less corporeal side of Douglass's life and writing? How do we interpret the unarchived? Or – perhaps more vexing – the unarchivable? It's tempting to view one of the sides as dominant, to see Douglass either as a thoroughgoing materialist who prioritised history, print and politics, or as a kind of abolitionist preacher who practised a nascent version of liberation theology. But I would suggest we take a cue from Douglass himself, who tended to view the world in terms of 'compositeness', and approach these dimensions as co-extensive and mutually enfolded. Douglass was less of a materialist or a spiritualist than a dialectical thinker who, in writing, life and politics, prioritised immanent struggle and paired reversal.[4] Thus, we might want to conceive of the material and the immaterial as Douglass did: as jointly bound and almost catalytically connected. Perhaps this is what Douglass meant when he said, 'Here, as elsewhere, there are centripetal and centrifugal forces forever at work. Those of the physical world are not more active, certain and effective, than those of the moral world' (Douglass [1883] 1992: 130). Without collisions between bodies and ideas, between principles and actions, there would be no change and no progress. I take that as a lesson for the field itself. As students and scholars of nineteenth-century American literature, we must be attuned to the myriad ways in which the material and the immaterial collide, and in doing so, construct worlds both real and imagined.

MATERIALITY AND IMMATERIALITY IN DOUGLASS'S READING

Douglass's ideas about these issues grew out of his reading. Many of the books that Douglass owned inquire into the vast, kaleidoscopic array of immaterial forces that animate history and nature alike, shaping events as well as our perception of them. His collection included works by Jonathan Dymond (1829) on the relation between political rights and moral principles, and Herbert Spencer on the role of belief in forming consciousness. As Spencer puts it, 'Dig down as deep as we may, we can never get to anything beyond beliefs; seeing that the deepest thing we reach becomes a belief at the moment of its disclosure . . . . Belief is the fact which, to our intellects, is antecedent to, and inclusive of, all other facts. It is the form in which every fact must present itself to us, and therefore underlies every fact' (1855: 15). Douglass also owned nearly all of William Ellery Channing's works, and he would have noted Channing's efforts to merge Unitarian theology with abolitionist philosophy. For Channing, the evil of slavery lies in its power to 'destroy the . . . consciousness and spirit of a Man. The slave, regarded and treated as property, bought and sold like a brute . . . How must his spirit be crushed!' Slavery, Channing says, is chiefly felt from 'within', echoing Douglass's framing of slavery as a spiritual and psychic condition as well as a material relation. That is why, as Douglass posits during the Civil War, there is 'no such thing as immediate emancipation': 'The slave', he says, 'will be bound in the invisible chains of slavery long after his iron chains are broken' and 'the master will carry into the new relation of liberty much of the insolence, caprice and pretention exercised by him while the admitted lord of the lash' (1884: 501).

There's also notable overlap in the way that Douglass reads the Constitution in the 1850s and the way that William Paley reads Scripture in the 1780s, elevating the spirit over the letter and taking silence as hermeneutically significant. As Paley writes in *The Principles of Moral and Political Philosophy* (1785), 'Slavery was a part of the civil constitution of most countries when Christianity appeared; yet no passage is to be found in the Christian Scriptures by which it is condemned,' yet it does not 'follow, from the silence of Scripture concerning them, that all the civil institutions which then prevailed were right', or 'that the bad should not be exchanged for better' (Paley 1851: 49).[5] For both Paley and Douglass, liberty documents need not spell out – in material form – everything they intend precisely because of the emancipatory spirit that imbues them.

Douglass's reading was itself both material and immaterial. His books were the result of print networks and technologies – all that we tend to group under the unwieldy headings 'History of the Book' and 'History of Print' – but reading is also one of the most unpredictable, immaterial experiences we can have. To read is to have your ideas tested or sharpened, beliefs deflated or recharged and feelings aroused, often in ways that affect our level of focus as well as the pace at which our eyes move across the page. And that experience, in turn, is imprinted on our memory, becomes part of the ever-evolving, inchoate project we call the self. Reading, in other words, is yet another encounter between the material and the immaterial that generates change – as well as writing and revision.

After all, Douglass's literacy was gained through struggle. Everything he read and wrote came from both material and immaterial resistance. After overhearing Hugh Auld declare that reading 'would forever unfit him to be a slave' because he 'would at once become unmanageable, and of no value to his master', Douglass endeavoured to master the art of reading by any means necessary – hiding books, learning rhetoric in secret and tricking white 'urchins' to teach him letters. Out of that struggle for literacy came 'new train[s] of thought . . . [and] revelation[s]': a multiplicity of ideas, perspectives and possibilities that not only enabled him to deepen his understanding of the world but also empowered him to remake it (Douglass [1845] 1994: 37, 41).

Spirit and Matter in *My Bondage and My Freedom*

The link between the material and the immaterial is vividly depicted in *My Bondage and My Freedom*. Here Douglass tends to present transformations, large and small, as events sparked by the continuous, open-ended encounter between corporeal and incorporeal experiences – a wrestling match that revives his 'Baltimore dreams' and rekindles 'the smoldering embers of liberty', or a chance encounter with a book that enables him to give tongue to 'thoughts, which had frequently flashed through my soul, and died away for want of utterance' (Douglass [1855] 2020: 172). As Robert S. Levine has convincingly demonstrated, 'identity is never stable in Douglass; it is tied to the contingencies of the historical moment and to the problematics (and challenges) of the autobiographer's art': to understand his writings, we must account for 'the centrality of revision and seriality to his . . . imagination' (Levine 2015: 27). Celeste-Marie Bernier similarly observes that Douglass was a 'compulsive revisionist' who 'retold, revisualized, and restaged multiple . . . narrative vignettes of selfhood throughout his lifetime' (Bernier 2012: 292). That revisionary impulse is intimately bound up with Douglass's philosophical inquiry into the nature of the world, his abiding interest in the causal forces and patterned structures that frame human experience. Although the binary form of *My Bondage and My Freedom* seems to imply linear growth, change erupts across both sections. Douglass repeatedly has to learn what slavery is, so unnatural is this imposed condition; and when he learns to read, his initial elation shades slowly but surely into a deepened sorrow.

These mixed states not only illuminate just how fluid and processual the self can be, they also indicate *how* change occurs. Nowhere is this more evident than in Part 2, when Douglass escapes from slavery and arrives in New York only to discover that freedom is quite different from anything he'd imagined:

> *A sense of my loneliness and helplessness crept over me, and covered me with something bordering on despair. In the midst of thousands of my fellow-men,* and yet a perfect stranger! . . . I was without home, without friends, without work, without money, and without any definite knowledge of which way to go, or where to look for succor. Some apology can easily be made for the few slaves who have, after making good their escape, turned back to slavery, preferring the actual rule of their masters, to the life of loneliness, apprehension, hunger, and anxiety, which meets them on their first arrival in a free state . . . . *It takes stout nerves to stand up, in such circumstances. A man, homeless, shelterless, breadless, friendless, and moneyless, is not in a condition to assume a very proud or joyous tone; and in just this condition was I, while wandering about the streets of New York city and lodging, at least one night, among the barrels on one of its wharves. I was not only free from slavery, but I was free from home, as well.* (Douglass [1855] 2020: 231)

Is one truly free if one is simply free to starve? Through his personal experiences, Douglass landed on a vital truth: freedom does not merely entail being removed from someone or something else – what political philosophers dub 'negative liberty' (Berlin 2004). Real freedom, living as one sees fit and making meaningful choices, requires certain material and institutional conditions (see Marrs 2020: 145–6). But Douglass is also making a broader point here: that freedom and unfreedom alike inhere in mental states as much as they do in material relations. That is why the word 'free' morphs across the passage, modifying itself to different situations which slip between corporeal and incorporeal states – hunger, loneliness, unbelonging. To put perhaps too fine a point on it: freedom as a discrete, abstract ideal does not exist. It can only be lived in the body and in the mind, and its quality or fervency has to do with how those dimensions come together, making the ideal match the reality (or not).

I am also taking a cue here from Nick Bromell (2011), who notes that Douglass tends to use such passages to distance himself from William Lloyd Garrison and his former friend's penchant for treating liberty and slavery as diametrically opposed states. Douglass, Bromell writes, 'strove to fuse or balance opposites in dynamic tension with each other', because he realises that 'his thinking occurs in a realm where the winds of history constantly bend ideas to their always-changing meanings' (Bromell 2011: 710). Perhaps that 'realm', wherein history 'bends' ideas, is the realm of the material – in which case, Douglass's views on identity might be much closer to Fichte's than we tend to assume. In *The Foundations of Natural Right*, a book that Douglass owned (and probably read in the 1850s with Ottilie Assing), Fichte contends that self-consciousness does not emerge exclusively in the mind or in one's worldly entanglements, but in the incessant, undetermined encounter between the two.[6] We of course have, as Fichte puts it, an 'intellectual intuition' of our independent existence, but that's very different from *identity*, which forms and continually reforms through social and material interactions. One of the corollaries of Fichte's philosophy is the way it presents unqualified, universal freedom as necessary for the species' growth and evolution. In Fichte's words,

> We ourselves have not yet attained to a consciousness of our freedom and self-activity, for then we should necessarily desire to see around us similar, that is, free beings. We are slaves ourselves; and look around us but for slaves. Rousseau says 'A man often considers himself the lord of others, who is yet more a slave than they.' He might with still greater justice have said 'He who considers himself the lord of others is himself a slave.' . . . He only is *free*, who would make all around him free likewise; and [really] does [so]. (Fichte 1848: 193)

Yet the Fichtean undertones of *My Bondage and My Freedom* are only a small part of the book's ardent, recurring interest in immateriality. There's Douglass's insistence that 'the slaveholder, as well as the slave, is the victim of the slave system'; his linguistic scepticism ('language', he says, 'has no power to convey a just sense of [bondage's] awful criminality'); his coupling of memory with hearing ('I write from sound,' states Douglass); and his repeated suggestion that enslavement has psychic dimensions, whether during the planned holiday excess that provides 'safety-valves', or Covey's psychological torture, which is directed primarily at the soul (Douglass [1855] 2020: 144). Or there's the entire chapter, 'Religious Nature Awakened', in which Douglass reflects on the sources of spiritual hope and recalls his tutelage under Uncle Lawson, the illiterate man who taught him about scripture's liberatory and levelling spirit.

Douglass's investment in incorporeal experience also plays a role in his falling out with the Garrisonians. Not only did Douglass increasingly view the 'spirit' of the founding documents as hermeneutically decisive, he also resented the Garrisonians' efforts to restrict his philosophy to mere matter:

> During the first three or four months, my speeches were almost exclusively made up of narrations of my own personal experience as a slave. 'Let us

have the facts,' said the people. So also said Friend George Foster . . .
'Give us the facts,' said Collins, 'we will take care of the philosophy.' Just
here arose some embarrassment. It was impossible for me to repeat the
same old story month after month, and to keep up my interest in it . . . .
[I]t was an old story to me; and to go through with it night after night,
was a task altogether too mechanical for my nature . . . . I was now reading and thinking. New views of the subject were presented to my mind.
It did not entirely satisfy me to narrate wrongs; I felt like denouncing
them. I could not always curb my moral indignation for the perpetrators
of slaveholding villainy, long enough for a circumstantial statement of the
facts which I felt almost everybody must know. Besides, I was growing,
and needed room. (Douglass [1855] 2020: 244)

The problem is not that Douglass doesn't want to deal with facts or discuss his
life story. The problem is that facts and philosophy are intertwined. As 'new
views' present themselves to his mind, old experiences get recast; and those
adjusted memories, in turn, shape and refine his emerging ideas. Douglass's
desire to combine facts with philosophy is also a desire to denounce as well
as narrate, an effort to assail slavery from a broader, moral perspective that
fuses his bound past with his boundless, ever-growing mind. As he writes in the
introduction, 'I have never placed my opposition to slavery on a basis so narrow as my own enslavement, but rather upon the indestructible and unchange-
able laws of human nature, every one of which is perpetually and flagrantly
violated by the slave system' (Douglass [1855] 2020: 212). Above all else, *My
Bondage and My Freedom* is Douglass's attempt to get from here to there, from
his own enslavement to the invariable laws of human nature – in short, from
material experience to immaterial truth.

That 'composite' perspective also extends beyond Douglass's second autobiography, anchoring many of his other writings and providing us with a repar-
ative method that reckons simultaneously with the materiality of history and
the immateriality of experience. Douglass's writings brim with visions, ideas
and emotions that are only incompletely recorded by his writing, so much of
which bears witness to experiences that are as inexpressive and evanescent as
they are significant.

The same is true, to one degree or another, of most literature in this era. It is
hard to think of a poem, novel or short story that does not extend beyond the
bounds of its text to convey something – a feeling or idea, a dream or conceit –
that leaps beyond print and paper. To account for this complexity requires attending to the material and immaterial aspects of writing together, construing them
as part of the same dialectical formation we call 'literature'. This inexorable link
between materiality and immateriality has consequences for students and scholars
alike, prompting us to account for what often lies just outside of one's analytical

purview – the aesthetic dimensions of archives, for example, or the material histories of spiritual movements. As Douglass's writings suggest, attending to such confluences is both necessary and potentially illuminating, making way for changes large and small.

WORKS CITED

Berlin, Isaiah (2004), *Liberty*, New York: Oxford University Press.

Bernier, Celeste-Marie (2012), *Characters of Blood: Black Heroism in the Transatlantic Imagination*, Charlottesville: University of Virginia Press.

Blight, David W. (2018), *Frederick Douglass: Prophet of Freedom*, New York: Simon and Schuster.

Bromell, Nicholas (2011), 'A "Voice from the Enslaved": The Origins of Frederick Douglass's Political Philosophy', *American Literary History* 23(4).

Brooks, Johns (2021), 'Sandy's Root, Douglass's *Métis*: "Black Art" and the Craft of Resistance in the Slave Narratives of Frederick Douglass', *J19: The Journal of Nineteenth-Century Americanists* 9(1) (Spring): 185–205.

Cassuto, Leonard (1996), 'Frederick Douglass and the Work of Freedom: Hegel's Master-Slave Dialectic in the Fugitive Slave Narrative', *Prospects* 21: 229–59.

Channing, William Ellery (1884), 'Slavery', in *The Complete Works of William Ellery Channing*, New York and London: Routledge & Sons.

DeLombard, Jeannine Marie (2007), *Slavery on Trial: Law, Abolitionism, and Print Culture*, Philadelphia: University of Pennsylvania.

Diedrich, Maria (2000), *Love across Color Lines: Ottilie Assing and Frederick Douglass*, New York: Hill and Wang.

Dinius, Marcy J. (2012), *The Camera and the Press: American Visual and Print Culture in the Age of the Daguerreotype*, Philadelphia: University of Pennsylvania Press.

Douglass, Frederick [1883] (1992), '"It Moves," or the Philosophy of Reform', *The Frederick Douglass Papers, Series One: Speeches, Debates, and Interviews*, vol. 5, eds John W. Blassingame and John R. McKivigan (New Haven: Yale University Press).

— [1845] (1994), *Narrative of Frederick Douglass* in *Autobiographies*, ed. Henry Louis Gates Jr, New York: Library of America.

— [1878] (1995), 'There Was a Right Side in the Late War', in *The Life and Writings of Frederick Douglass, IV: Reconstruction*, ed. Philip Foner, New York: International Publishers.

— [1885] (1995), 'The Return of the Democratic Party', in *The Life and Writings of Frederick Douglass, IV: Reconstruction*, ed. Philip Foner, New York: International Publishers.

— [1855] (1999), 'The Anti-Slavery Movement', in *Frederick Douglass: Selected Speeches and Writings*, eds Philip Foner and Yuval Taylor, Chicago: Lawrence Hill, 1999.

— [1855] (2020), *My Bondage and My Freedom*, eds Nick Bromell and R. Blake Gilpin, New York: Norton, 2020.

Dymond, Jonathan (1829), *Essays on the Principles of Morality, and on the Private and Political Rights and Obligations of Mankind*, 2 vols, London: Hamilton, Adams & Co.

Fichte, Johann Gottlied (1848), *The Foundations of Natural Right*, in *The Popular Works of Johann Gottlieb Fichte*, trans. William Smith, London: John Chapman.

Foucault, Michel (1995), *Discipline and Punish: The Birth of the Prison*, trans. Alan Sheridan, New York: Vintage.

Geertz, Clifford (1973), *The Interpretation of Cultures*, New York: Basic Books.

Hack, Daniel (2012), 'The Canon in front of Them: African American Deployments of "The Charge of the Light Brigade"', in *Early African American Print Culture*, eds Lara Langer Cohen and Jordan Alexander Stein, Philadelphia: University of Pennsylvania Press.

Kohn, Margaret (2005), 'Frederick Douglass's Master-Slave Dialectic', *Journal of Politics* 67(2): 497–514.

Laski, Gregory (2019), 'Reconstructing Revenge: Race and Justice after the Civil War', *American Literature* 91(4): 751–81.

Lee, Maurice (2012), *Uncertain Chances: Science, Skepticism, and Belief in Nineteenth-Century American Literature*, Oxford: Oxford University Press.

Levine, Robert S., John Stauffer and John R. McKivigan (2015), 'Introduction' to *The Heroic Slave: A Cultural and Critical Edition*, New Haven: Yale University Press.

Marrs, Cody (2020), *Not Even Past: The Stories We Keep Telling About the Civil War*, Baltimore: Johns Hopkins University Press.

Paley, William (1851), *The Works of William Paley*, London and Edinburgh: T. Nelson and Sons.

Senchyne, Jonathan (2020), *The Intimacy of Paper in Early and Nineteenth-Century American Literature*, Amherst: University of Massachusetts Press.

Spencer, Herbert (1855), *The Principles of Psychology*, London: Longman, Brown, Green, and Longmans.

Stauffer, John (2005), 'Frederick Douglass and the Aesthetics of Freedom', *Raritan* 25(1): 114–36.

NOTES

1. This earlier understanding of 'context' can be traced back to two major influences: Clifford Geertz's anthropological interpretation of culture as a 'system of inherited conceptions expressed in symbolic forms' and Michel Foucault's reframing of power as a dispersed and decentred regime. See Geertz (1973) and Foucault (1995).

2. Scholars have demonstrated that Douglass was not only immersed in print culture but also deeply influenced by it. See Jeannine Marie DeLombard (2007), Marcy J. Dinius (2012: 192–232), David W. Blight (2018), Daniel Hack (2012) and Robert S. Levine, John Stauffer and John R. McKivigan (2015).

3. This side of Douglass has been thoroughly and thoughtfully examined by several scholars. Robert S. Levine (2015), for example, has shown how Douglass's ideas about identity – which he tended to view as fluid and contingent – shaped his autobiographies. John Stauffer (2005) has explored the aesthetic and philosophical resonances of *My Bondage and My Freedom*, emphasising Douglass's use of freedom as both an artistic and political ideal; Nicholas Bromell (2011) has disclosed Douglass's sustained interest in democratic theory and political philosophy; Maurice Lee (2012) has examined Douglass's ideas about chance and probability;

Gregory Laski (2019) has analysed Douglass's evolving understanding of justice; and John Brooks (2021) has documented Douglass's use of African cosmologies.

4. On Douglass's use of dialectics, see Margaret Kohn (2005) and Leonard Cassuto (1996).

5. We do not know whether or not Douglass owned or borrowed a copy of Paley's book, but this quote circulated widely in nineteenth-century abolitionist and Christian circles. He also encountered this quote in Dymond's *Essays*.

6. On Douglass's relationship with Assing, see Maria Diedrich (2000).

2

EARTH/ATMOSPHERE: THE LEONID
METEOR SHOWER, 1833

GORDON FRASER

Since 1777, the union of the United States had been represented by an arrangement of stars. In that year, the wartime Continental Congress ordered that the US flag display 'thirteen stars, white in a blue field, representing a new constellation' (United States Continental Congress 1907: 464). Indeed, many in the late eighteenth century regarded the new nation through the metaphor of a 'constellation'. One of the original six frigates built for the United States Navy was called the USS *Constellation*, and an early set of coins bore the Latin inscription '*Nova Constellatio*' (Footner 2002; McCarthy 2017). The metaphor was apt. As historian Jill Lepore has pointed out, the United States that emerged from the American revolution cannot be understood as a nation-state, a cultural group whose members imagine themselves into relation with each other and form a government. Rather, it was what she calls a state-nation: a political and legal confederacy whose leaders attempted to form a single national culture from disparate parts (Lepore 2019). Independent bodies (stars or states) were brought together by the fiction of perspective, enabling some observers to see in separate political communities a mythic national body. Reflecting on how the United States of America was and is a constellation – a myth, a contingent arrangement united by the position of observers – reveals at once the problem of treating it as an object of study. Look closely at the United States, and you will see that it is neither as united nor as bounded as it first appears.

And scholars have looked closely, indeed. The myth of the US nation-state has been decisively demythologised. At least since the so-called 'transnational turn in

American Studies' – which can be dated to the end of the Cold War era, although the period would not receive its present name until 2004 – scholars and critics in the field have challenged national frameworks: temporal, historical, geographical and definitional (Fishkin 2005: 17–57).[1] This effort to demythologise the nation has ushered in an age of permanent revolution, an era that Hester Blum describes in *Turns of Event* as enabling not only the transnational, but also the hemispheric, postnational, spatial, temporal, post-secular, aesthetic and affective 'turns'. For Blum, these deviations from past practices have been a boon, a 'constitutive strength' of a field on the move (Blum 2016: 2–3).[2] And yet as illiberal political movements from Brazil to the United Kingdom to Hungary to the United States have met with electoral success, many scholars have turned with new attention to the guiding constellations of liberal patriotism.[3] Christopher Castiglia, for instance, has proclaimed in an echo of Granville Hicks that 'I like America'. 'America', in Castiglia's formulation, functions as an empty signifier that allows 'citizens to define, support, and organise themselves locally under the rubric of the nation' (Castiglia 2017: 43). The United States of America – that constellated illusion of perspective – functions as an organising principle around which emancipatory movements might coalesce. As Lepore tersely explains: 'When serious historians abandon the study of the nation, when scholars stop trying to write a common history for a people, nationalism doesn't die. Instead, it eats liberalism' (Lepore 2019). Scholars such as Lepore and Castiglia have called for a renewed consideration of the United States not because it has represented an emancipatory past, but because in its mythic potential it might represent an emancipatory future. They have called for a consideration of the US nation that recognises it as an illusory formation, but that nonetheless enables individuals, including scholars, to love it.

But what might it mean to recognise the United States of America as a constellation, an illusion of perspective, and yet to treat it as an organising principle for scholarly inquiry – or even for love? And what might it mean to be clear-eyed about the crimes perpetrated in the name of the United States of America, and yet to declare – with Hicks and Castiglia – that 'I like America' for its possible future, if not its often catastrophic and inhumane past? In the pages to follow, I will offer a provisional answer. And my answer begins, appropriately, with the stars. Stars were central to the contingently adopted liberal patriotism that characterised the labours of dissident nineteenth-century authors such as Frederick Douglass or even Harriet Jacobs, both of whom I will consider briefly below. I will suggest that the plasticity of the constellation metaphor has enabled people across time to radically rewrite the national project. Constellations are fictions of perspective, illusions onto which people project collective meaning. But fictions are not lies. They are instead shared inventions through which individuals narrativise their relation to the world, to the universe and to each other.

WHEN THE STARS FELL

In his second autobiography, *My Bondage and My Freedom* (1855), Frederick Douglass adds an astronomical detail omitted from the version of his life story published a decade earlier. In this latter account Douglass explains that, in 1833, he witnessed the 'gorgeous spectacle' of the Leonid meteor shower, the November display of shooting stars seen that year by observers throughout North America. Meteor showers such as the Leonids are caused by the earth's passage through a stream of debris left behind in the trail of a comet: in this case, the comet Temple-Tuttle. As the earth's atmosphere collides with this trail, the debris vaporises – producing the flashes conventionally known as shooting stars. There were thousands of such falling stars that November in 1833. They blanketed the sky and appeared to observers to radiate outward from the constellation Leo (Douglass 1855: 186 and Jenniskens 2006: 99).

Douglass recalls this moment – watching the 'sublime scene' at dawn – as a time of spiritual doubt, but also one that augured catastrophic wars. He writes,

> of that strange phenomenon, when the heavens seemed about to part with its starry train. I witnessed this gorgeous spectacle, and was awestruck. The air seemed filled with bright, descending messengers from the sky. It was about daybreak when I saw this sublime scene. I was not without the suggestion, at the moment, that it might be the harbinger of the coming of the Son of Man; and, in my then state of mind, I was prepared to hail him as my friend and deliverer. I had read, that the 'stars shall fall from heaven;' and they were now falling . . . and I was beginning to look away to heaven for rest denied me on earth. (Douglass 1855: 186)

Douglass sees in the disturbance of the heavens a sign of his own spiritual doubt and despair. Seeking in his then limited reading a corollary to what he sees in the natural world, he reaches for an explanation from Christian scripture: 'And the stars of heaven shall fall, and the powers that are in heaven shall be shaken' (Mark 13: 25). In Douglass's narrative, this memory ostensibly serves as a marker of time. He knows that he left for the village of St Michael's in 1833 because the meteor shower appeared most spectacularly in that year.

But Douglass's reference to the Leonid meteor shower does more than locate him in time. As Anna Mae Duane and Robert S. Levine have separately observed, Douglass's *My Bondage and My Freedom* – published ten years after his *Narrative* (1845) – can be read as an elaborate response to the fractious politics of the 1850s: the emergence of race science as a powerful, mainstream discourse, the increasing interconnection of Black activists, and the increasing radicalism of the abolitionist movement (Duane 2010: 461–88 and Levine 2016: 163). The

Douglass who recalls in 1855 the falling stars of two decades before is reminding his biblically literate readership that such sights augur apocalyptic conflict, a time when 'nation shall rise against nation, and kingdom against kingdom' (Mark 13: 8). Indeed, Douglass and others often spoke of celestial appearances as a means of highlighting the precarity of the US national project. He would go on to note in 1860 that news of the revolutionary abolitionist John Brown and his raid on the federal armory at Harper's Ferry, Virginia, 'flashed across the oceans and continents like a splendid meteor' (Douglass 1999: 412). And Douglass was far from the only abolitionist to remind white Americans that their nation, represented by a constellation of stars, was as impermanent as the turbulent heavens. In *Blake; or the Huts of America* (1859, 1861–2), Martin Delany's novel of Black emancipation, the revolutionary protagonist Henry Blake 'stood motionless in wonder looking into the heavens' from the deck of a riverboat, witnessing celestial movement that held 'more than ordinary importance' for his revolutionary project (Delany 2017: 125; Rusert 2013: 820). And in the pages of the *Liberator*, editor William Lloyd Garrison published a parody of the US national anthem that mocked the American constellation: 'Oh, say do you hear, at the dawn's early light | The shrieks of those bondmen, whose blood is now streaming | from the merciless lash, while our banner in sight | With its stars mocking freedom, is fitfully gleaming?' (Atlee [1844] 1988: 156–7). Douglass recognised – just as many other antebellum writers recognised – that inexplicably falling stars could easily symbolise a threat to the constellated republic.

Numerous, strange celestial appearances during the antebellum period fuelled the suspicion that the United States might not long survive. The Black revolutionary Nat Turner began his August 1831 rebellion in Southampton County, Virginia, shortly after seeing the sun turn a shade of green, likely caused by the eruption of a far-off volcano (Allmendinger 2014: 312, n. 55). This event was closely followed by the Leonid meteor shower in 1833, a particularly dramatic appearance of the Northern Lights in 1837, and the so-called 'Great Comet' of February 1843, the brightest visible comet of the nineteenth century. William Miller, who founded the apocalyptic Christian sect that predicted that the end of the world would come about in 1843, did not specifically point to these celestial phenomena as auguring the end times, but many of his followers nonetheless did (Aveni 2016: 22). Even the authors of fiction joined in the predictions of cosmic doom. In a short story entitled 'The Conversation of Eiros and Charmion', Edgar Allan Poe depicted a comet striking the earth, igniting the atmosphere and killing all human life (Poe 1839: 321–3).

Abolitionists, radicals and revolutionaries throughout the antebellum period capitalised on the close association of the United States with the stars. '[C]an you not think the . . . strange appearances about this time in the heavens might prompt others, as well as myself, to this undertaking,' the Black radical Nat Turner asked an interlocutor shortly after he had been captured and imprisoned (Gray [1831] 1999: 45). In other words, Turner suggested that he was not the only enslaved person who might look to the sky and see in its strange transformations a prophecy of national doom. If the stability of the United States was made visible in the radiant permanence of the stars – what Daniel Webster called 'the American constellation' – then disruptions in the stars prefigured disruptions on earth. And, indeed, many were hoping to see such disruptions (Webster [1826] 1828: 245). As Douglass explained in a 5 July 1852 address, the 'Star-Spangled Banner and American Christianity' were 'co-extensive' with slavery. 'Where these go', he said, 'may also go the merciless slave-hunter' (Douglass [1852] 1999: 199). American stars were the symbol of slavery and empire, but such stars were not as permanent as they appeared. Indeed, they could fall from the heavens and vaporise, and their fall could fulfil biblical prophecies of civil war, revolution and the return of Jesus Christ.

Yet the emancipatory potential of the American constellation changed decisively with the US Civil War. Suddenly, abolitionist writers did not find themselves hoping to see stars fall from the sky. The US flag no longer featured 'stars mocking freedom' (Atlee [1844] 1988: 156–7). Rather, the 1777 constellation, which had symbolised the unity of former colonies in the face of the British empire, became instead the symbol of a very different struggle for justice. It became the symbol of a constellated, composite nation.

Soldiers You Have Made It

The author and educator Harriet Jacobs stood before a Colored Infantry Regiment in Union-occupied Alexandria, Virginia, on 1 August 1863, and she delivered an address marking the emancipation of enslaved people in the British West Indies. But her address also marked the presentation of an American flag, which was to be given to the Union hospital in Alexandria. 'Three years ago,' Jacobs explained to the gathered soldiers,

> this flag had no significance for you, we could not cherish it as our emblem of freedom. You then had no part in the bloody struggle for your country, your patriotism was spurned; but to-day you are in arms for the freedom of your race and the defence [sic] of your country – to-day this flag is significant to you. Soldiers you have made it the symbol of freedom for the slave, unfurl it, stand by it and fight for it, until the breeze upon which it floats shall be so pure that a slave cannot breathe its air. ('Flag Presentation', 1864: 1)[4]

Jacobs was generous when she said that, in prior years, the flag had 'no significance'. Indeed, it had great significance – as a symbol of slavery, dispossession and empire. The flag, she had written in 1853, 'should be [called] stripes and scars' because it represented a nation of enslavers (Yellin 2004: 123 and Perry 2008: 597). And yet here Jacobs appropriates and reinterprets the mythic symbology of the American constellation. The 'scars' that flew above 'the merciless slave-hunter' as he scoured the countryside are reimagined by Jacobs in 1863 as a 'symbol of freedom' for the enslaved (Douglass [1852] 1999: 199).

Jacobs would not be the last to reinterpret the American constellation, to remake an eighteenth-century symbol of revolution into a nineteenth-century symbol of emancipation. 'Notwithstanding the dark picture I have this day presented of the state of the nation,' Douglass had explained in his July 1852 oration, 'I do not despair of this country' (Douglass [1852] 1999: 204). And he didn't. When war broke out, Douglass described a 'revolution' in northern sentiment, explaining: 'Every pulsation of our heart is with the legitimate American Government, in its determination to suppress and put down this slave-holding rebellion. The *Stars and Stripes* are now symbols of liberty' (Douglass [1861] 1999: 445). Douglass's about-face was, like that of Jacobs, symbolic. The flag that had flown above the slave hunter now flew above an army arrayed against the slave power, and so he seized upon the potential force of this symbol and deployed it for his own purposes.

In part, this was because constellations are contingent arrangements, visible only from a particular time and place.[5] The problem for the wartime Continental Congress in 1777 had been that of uniting disparate colonies. The problem for the emancipationist project would be that of uniting people across the divisions of race and legal status. In pursuing this goal, Douglass took up whatever symbols were available. And the constellation was a useful and powerful symbol. In a later address, Douglass explained that the future of the United States would be that of a 'composite nation', a nation not only of white and Black people, but of people of Chinese, Japanese, Irish, German, Polynesian and other descents. The United States was already 'the most conspicuous example of composite nationality in the world', Douglass explained. He went on: 'We shall spread the network of our science and civilisation over all who seek their shelter whether from Asia, Africa, or the Isles of the sea. We shall mold them all, each after his kind, into Americans' (Douglass [1869] 2018: 302–3). This was the virtue of the constellated, composite nation. Symbolised by a contingent arrangement, it could be endlessly renewed, expanded and transformed to describe the composite present. Soldiers made the US constellation a symbol of freedom, but so could Indigenous peoples, slaves, immigrants and the poor.

The Indifferent Stars

When the earth passed through a stream of debris left behind by the comet Temple-Tuttle in November 1833, individuals throughout what we call the United States of America reacted differently. Frederick Douglass recalled the

Gospel of Mark and wondered if the falling stars might prompt wars between nations and peoples, foretelling the return of Jesus Christ (Douglass 1855: 186). In Combahee, South Carolina, a white enslaver heard people reacting to the shooting stars and believed he was going to be attacked. He took up his sword and ran outside ('Letter from Combahee, S.C.', 1833: [3]). In Port Tobacco, Maryland, a young, enslaved girl named Jane Clark was walking to fetch water when she saw the meteor shower, and she recalled later to an amanuensis that she 'ran along trying to catch the stars as they fell' (Bernstein, 2018). Captain Gideon Parker, commanding the ship *Junior* in the Gulf of Mexico, attempted to estimate the number of shooting stars, but lost count. And a woman milking cows on her farm in upstate New York came to believe that the meteors fell all the way to the earth, leaving on the ground a lumpen paste that looked like 'boiled starch' (Littmann 1999: 13). What did it all mean?

Nothing and anything. The heavens were, and are, indifferent to human desires and narratives, and vaporising particles from a comet are only noteworthy from a particular viewpoint at a particular time. Falling stars, like constellations, are a matter of perspective. And yet from their perspectivally limited observations of the heavens, human beings ultimately *do* produce narratives, stories and meaning. The meanings that we project onto an indifferent universe are not mistaken or false, but they are fictional. And fictions have a tremendous power in unifying or dividing people, in producing functional political communities or dismembering them.

Today, I suggest, we need renewed fictions. The end of the Cold War inaugurated a fundamental transformation in the field of American Studies. A discipline that in the 1950s featured what one scholar of that generation called 'quasi-official State Department connections' had by the 1980s and early 1990s come to regard itself as complicit in the project of American empire (Marx 1999: 43 and 48).[6] As the field made its 'transnational turn', its practitioners came to regard themselves first and foremost as critics of various US hegemonies: military, economic, political, cultural and linguistic, among others. As Amy Kaplan wrote in her preface to *Cultures of United States Imperialism* (1993), that volume aimed to take up subjects that had been 'relegated to the unnarrated background' of American cultural studies: the 'multiple histories of continental and overseas expansion, conquest, conflict, and resistance which have shaped the cultures of the United States and the cultures of those it has dominated within and beyond its geopolitical boundaries' (Kaplan 1993: 4). In short, American Studies would reveal what American imperialists had long sought to conceal: the nation's role in the work of empire.

But while American empire has persisted, political conditions have changed. The period immediately following the end of the Cold War was the apotheosis of a neoliberal order that acted through misdirection, conflating human freedom with market liberalisation and communicating through racial dog whistles. This order has given way to an oligarchic populism guided by leaders who straightforwardly avow their hatreds. As a result, Americanists find themselves at yet another moment of transformation. A fundamental question about the future of the United States has been clarified: Shall it be a composite nation, a constellation of peoples from Africa, Asia, Europe, Oceana, Australia and the Americas, as Frederick Douglass urged? Shall it be a unifying fiction around which we might organise new forms of human freedom and imagine new possibilities? Or shall it, instead, come to represent the 'merciless' use of US power against the poor, the desperate and the weak? This is a question not merely, or even primarily, for scholars. But it is a question scholars will play a role in answering.

A great deal is at stake in how we answer. For better and often for worse, nations remain what Douglass called the 'grandest aggregations of organised human power' (Douglass [1869] 2018: 280). Nation-states produce the laws, armies, police forces, bureaucracies, prisons and schools that shape the lives of individuals. And to define a nation is to exert power through it. Americanists in the early decades of the twenty-first century have been dedicated to a long-term project of unsettling the exceptionalist mythology of the United States. As Janice Radway explained in her presidential address to the American Studies Association, our aim has been to 'complicate and fracture the very idea of an "American" nation, culture, and subject' (Radway [1998] 1999: 17). And yet this work of fracturing breaks apart the imagined community to which people might pledge themselves. I am proposing here that we in the field of American Studies consider the work of remaking the composite America by examining its imagined and yet unrealised potential. We should, in essence, study a dream from the past – the dream of a constellated, composite nationality.

In 1998, the same year as Radway's presidential address, Leo Marx described a conversation he had four decades earlier with Richard Hoggart, the British scholar of literature and cultural studies. Hoggart was confused by the American Studies movement, particularly after having met a young practitioner. It was not, Hoggart suggested, methodologically distinctive. Marx recalled the British academic's litany of complaints: 'Combining the study of history and literature? We've been doing that for generations, said Hoggart. Studying the culture as a whole? Nothing very new about that either, said Hoggart. After many attempts, in a fit of exasperation, Hoggart's eager but frustrated American interlocutor exclaimed: "But you don't understand, I *believe* in America".' Like Christopher Castiglia or Granville Hicks or even, sometimes, Harriet Jacobs, the Americanists who emerged in the period after the Second World War shared a commitment to 'American nationhood' as a premise and a promise (Marx 1999: 47).

But their liberal patriotism was hardly unique. Others had believed in America, or liked it, or made meaning from it.

Douglass and Jacobs understood that the American constellation was both everything and nothing. As an illusion of perspective, it had no substance at all. And yet, as a thing without substance, it provided the empty field onto which individual people could project dreams of solidarity and interdependence. Nationality based not upon descent but upon shared enterprise was a new endeavour in 1777, when the Continental Congress decided to describe the union of former colonies as a 'constellation' and to represent that union with stars. In the intervening years, the proliferation of stars in the American constellation has represented the geographic expansion of an imperial power. It has represented the domain of slave hunters and oligarchs. And yet this constellation has *also* represented the efforts of those soldiers who, as Harriet Jacobs said, 'made it the symbol of freedom for the slave' ('Flag Presentation', 1864: 1). It has represented a nation that Granville Hicks could declare that he liked, and that Frederick Douglass could describe as 'the most conspicuous example of composite nationality in the world' (Castiglia 2017: 43 and Douglass [1869] 2018: 285). The discovery that national myths are in fact myths can foster disillusionment, but it should not. It should, instead, prompt us to recover from the past those unrealised dreams projected onto a fiction in the sky. It should prompt us to carry those dreams forward by telling new stories about the United States – that illusion of perspective, that constellation of imagined stars, that potential composite of peoples.

WORKS CITED

Allmendinger, David F. (2014), *Nat Turner and the Rising in Southampton County*, Baltimore: Johns Hopkins University Press.

Atlee, E. A. [1844] (1988), 'New Version of the National Song', *Liberator*, 13 September 1844, reprinted in Vicki Lynn Eaklor, *American Antislavery Songs: A Collection and Analysis*, New York, Westport and London: Greenwood Press, pp. 156–7.

Aveni, Anthony (2016), *Apocalyptic Anxiety: Religion, Science, and America's Obsession with the End of the World*, Boulder: University Press of Colorado.

Benjamin, Walter (2006), 'On the Concept of History', in Howard Eiland and Michael W. Jennings (eds), *Walter Benjamin: Selected Writings, Vol. 4, 1938–1940*, Cambridge, MA, and London: Belknap Press, pp. 389–400.

Benjamin, Walter, and Theodor Adorno (1992), *Sprache und Geschichte: Philosophische Essays*, Ditzingen: Reclaim.

Bernstein, Robin (2018), 'Jane Clark, A Newly Available Slave Narrative', *Commonplace* 18(1), <http://commonplace.online/article/jane-clark/> (accessed 2 April 2020).

Blum, Hester (2016), *Turns of Event: Nineteenth-Century American Literary Studies in Motion*, Philadelphia: University of Pennsylvania Press, 2016.

Castiglia, Christopher (2017), *The Practices of Hope: Literary Criticism in Disenchanted Times*, New York: New York University Press.

Delany, Martin [1859, 1861–2] (2017), *Blake; or, The Huts of America*, ed. Jerome McGann, Boston: Harvard University Press.

Douglass, Frederick (1855), *My Bondage and My Freedom*, New York and Auburn: Miller, Orton, & Mulligan.

— [1852] (1999), 'What to a Slave is the Fourth of July', in Philip S. Foner (ed.), *Frederick Douglass: Selected Speeches and Writings*, Chicago: Lawrence Hill, pp. 188–206.

— [1860] (1999), 'The Presidential Campaign of 1860, speech at celebration of West India Emancipation, August 1, 1860', in Philip Foner and Yuval Taylor (eds), *Frederick Douglass: Selected Speeches and Writings*, Chicago: Lawrence Hill, pp. 401–12.

— [1861] (1999), 'Sudden Revolution in Northern Sentiment', in Philip Foner and Yuval Taylor (eds), *Frederick Douglass: Selected Speeches and Writings*, Chicago: Chicago Review Press, p. 445.

— [1869] (2018), 'Our Composite Nationality', in John R. McKivigan, Julie Husband and Heather L. Kaufman (eds), *The Speeches of Frederick Douglass: A Critical Edition*, New Haven and London: Yale University Press, 278–303.

Duane, Anna Mae (2010), '"Like a Motherless Child": Racial Education at the New York African Free School and in *My Bondage and My Freedom*', *American Literature* 82(3): 461–88.

Fishkin, Shelley Fisher (2005), 'Crossroads of Cultures: The Transnational Turn in American Studies: Presidential Address to the American Studies Association, November 12, 2004', *American Quarterly* 57(1): 17–57.

'Flag Presentation at L'Ouverture Hospital, Alexandria, Va' (1864), *Anglo-African Magazine*, 3 September: 1.

Footner, Geoffrey M. (2002), *USS Constellation: From Frigate to Sloop of War*, Annapolis: Naval Institute Press.

Gray, Thomas Ruffin [1831] (1999), *The Confessions of Nat Turner*, ed. Kenneth S. Greenberg, Boston: Bedford.

Jenniskens, Peter (2006), *Meteor Showers and Their Parent Comets*, New York and Cambridge: Cambridge University Press.

Kaplan, Amy (1993), '"Left alone with America": The Absence of Empire in the Study of American Culture', in Donald Pease and Amy Kaplan (eds), *Cultures of United States Imperialism*, Durham, NC and London: Duke University Press, pp. 3–21.

Lepore, Jill (2019), *This America: The Case for the Nation*, Kindle Edition, New York: Norton.

'Letter from Combahee, S.C.' (1833), *Independent Inquirer* [Brattleboro, Vermont], 30 November, [3].

Levine, Robert S. (2016), *The Lives of Frederick Douglass*, Cambridge, MA: Harvard University Press.

Littmann, Mark (1999), *The Heavens on Fire: The Great Leonid Meteor Storms*, New York and Cambridge: Cambridge University Press.

Matthiessen, F. O. [1941] (1968), *American Renaissance: Art and Expression in the Age of Emerson and Whitman*, London and New York: Oxford University Press.

Marx, Leo (1999), 'Reflections on American Studies, Minnesota, and the 1950s', *American Studies* 40(2): 39–51.

McCarthy, David (2017), 'Nova Constellatio: Identifying the First US Coin', *The Numismatist* (August), <https://www.money.org/nova-constellatio> (accessed 10 September 2019).

Perry, Lewis (2008), 'Harriet Jacobs and the "Dear Old Flag"', *African American Review* 42(3–4): 595–605.

Poe, Edgar Allan (1839), 'The Conversation of Eiros and Charmion', *Burton's Gentleman's Magazine* [Philadelphia] 5(6): 321–3.

Radway, Janice (1999), 'What's in a Name? Presidential Address to the American Studies Association, 20 November, 1998', in *American Quarterly* 51(1): 1–32.

Rusert, Britt (2013), 'Delany's Comet: Fugitive Science and the Speculative Imaginary of Emancipation', *American Quarterly* 65(4): 799–829.

— (2017), *Fugitive Science: Empiricism and Freedom in Early African American Culture*, New York: New York University Press.

Simpson, James (2019), *Permanent Revolution: The Reformation and the Illiberal Roots of Liberalism*, Cambridge, MA: Harvard University Press.

United States Continental Congress (1907), *Journal of the Continental Congress, 1777, Volume 8*, Washington: US Government Printing Office.

Webster, Daniel (1828), 'Extracts from the Eulogy Pronounced in Faneuil Hall, Boston, Mass., August 2, 1826', in Samuel Clark (ed.), *The American Orator*, Gardiner, ME: Intelligencer, pp. 220–45.

Yellin, Jean Fagan (2004), *Harriet Jacobs: A Life*, New York: Basic Civitas.

Notes

1. Fishkin's address to the American Studies Association, in which she named the 'transnational turn', was dedicated to Gloria Anzaldúa, whose *Borderlands/La Frontera: The New Mestiza* (1987) emblematised the transnationalism Fishkin described.

2. The phrase 'permanent revolution' has roots in Marxist philosophy, but it has also been used to describe the birth of liberalism. See Simpson 2019: 29. Blum is careful to distinguish between scholarly 'turns' and 'revolutions' because the former do not return scholars to points of origin. Rather, 'turns' are 'extrapolations or deviations' from earlier forms.

3. The study of such liberal patriotism was formerly a central project of American Studies scholarship. F. O. Matthiessen, for instance, read in the work of Walt Whitman an identification of a central problem for the future of the United States – the conflict between individualism and national-scale mutuality, or patriotism. Whitman suggested that the problem could one day be resolved. See F. O. Matthiessen [1941] 1968: 591, n. 8.

4. For a discussion of this incident, see Perry 2008: 595–605.

5. The German philosopher Walter Benjamin struck on this when he suggested that the historian who abandons narrow 'historicism' (*Der Historismus*) – in essence, who stops narrating a chain of causation – is able to think instead in terms of constellations formed by the present and the distant past. Benjamin writes of such a historian: 'He grasps the constellation into which his own era has entered, along

with a very specific earlier one' (*Er erfasst die Konstellation, in die seine eigene Epoche mit einer ganz bestimmten früheren getreten ist*). See Benjamin 2006: 397 and Benjamin and Adorno 1992: 153.

6. As Leo Marx explains, the field began with the work of left-liberal scholars committed to the principles of the New Deal, but its institutional mission was advanced in the 1950s by institutional leaders guided in their funding decisions by an 'excessive, chauvinistic emphasis on ideas and things American'.

3

BODY/SPIRIT: WALT WHITMAN'S HICKSITE QUAKER POETICS, 1855

RACHEL HEFFNER-BURNS

In 1888, Walt Whitman penned a brief sketch of the life of the venerated Quaker orator, Elias Hicks, for inclusion in his publication of *November Boughs* (1888). Hicks was, for Whitman, an influential figure, not only for the insight he offered when he preached, but for the charismatic manner with which he did so. In *Boughs*, Whitman recounts how, at ten years of age, he attended a gathering of the Society of Friends at the Morrison Hotel in Brooklyn, New York, to hear Hicks speak. Whitman remembered that the 'handsome ballroom' of the Morrison was 'large, cheerful, [and] gay-color'd', with 'glass chandeliers bearing myriads of sparkling pendants, plenty of settees and chairs, and a sort of velvet divan running around the side walls' in which sat 'the principal dignitaries of the town' (Whitman [1888] 1982, 'Notes': 1233). The people in attendance made quite an impression on young Walter for, as divisive a figure as Elias Hicks was, a broad spectrum of New York City's eclectic population had turned out to hear him speak. Outside of the public figures in attendance, Hicks's audience consisted of Brooklyn youth; sophisticated, wealthy women; and a group of naval officers. Most significantly, Walter noticed 'on a slightly elevated platform . . . a dozen or more Friends, most of them elderly, grim, and with their broad-brimmed hats on their heads. Three or four women, too, in their characteristic Quaker Costumes and bonnets. All still as the grave' (1233).

But as is customary in the Meetings of assembled Friends, the listeners then waited in silence. Finally, Elias Hicks rose to speak. He was a 'tall, straight figure, neither stout nor very thin, dress'd in drab cloth, [and with a] clean-shaved face' (1233). Young Walter was impressed by Hicks's immediate command of the room. For a long dramatic moment, Hicks's 'black eyes that blazed like meteors' surveyed the crowd in absolute stillness (Whitman [1888] 1982, 'Father Taylor': 1145). Then, 'the words come from his lips, very emphatically and slowly pronounc'd, in a resonant, grave, melodious voice, "*What is the chief end of man?* I was told in my early youth, *it was to glorify God, and seek and enjoy him forever*"' (Whitman [1888] 1982, 'Notes': 1233).[1] Elias Hicks then offered the assembled New Yorkers a message that revealed his 'pleading, tender, nearly agonizing conviction and magnetic stream of natural eloquence, before which all minds and natures, all emotions, high or low, gentle or simple, yielded entirely without exception' (1234).

Recounting this story half a century later, Whitman recollects with perfect clarity the delivery and tenor of Hicks's speech, but he cannot recall the specifics of the message itself except for its opening call to the Meeting. For Whitman, experiencing Hicks's oratorical power in person was akin to witnessing 'the rhetoric and art, the mere words, (which usually play such a big part) [as they] seem'd altogether to disappear, and the live feeling advanced upon you and seiz'd you with a power before unknown. Everybody felt this marvelous and awful influence' (Whitman [1888] 1982, 'Father Taylor': 1144-5).[2] In this description, we glimpse what it must have felt like for young Walter to witness Hicks be overcome by the light of God within him and to give public voice to the spiritual message that experience yielded.

Whitman was drawn to this particular Hicksite Quaker religious practice, of giving voice to one's 'Inner Light,'[3] for its facilitation of a believer's encounter with God. In defining this practice as pivotal for all Quakers' spiritual health, Hicks affirmed that all individual believers possessed the capacity to experience revelation for themselves: they need not rely on the Bible, or ordained clergy, to connect them to the divine. But while Whitman saw great value and power in the mysticism of Hicks's democratic theology, he did not ascribe to the explicitly religious dimensions of Hicks's Quaker tradition, especially his devout commitment to worshipping God and Jesus Christ. Thus, when adapting this practice for poetic form in *Leaves of Grass*, Whitman consciously abandoned the Inner Light's theistic dimension, or its bridge between the spirit of God and the Quaker who gives voice to it in Meeting. Instead, the poet emphasised what he perceived to be the practice's mystical and ecstatic qualities, and thus, the manner with which believers experienced spiritual revelation as a result of it. In *Leaves*, Whitman composes an egalitarian poetry of the body in which he renders Hicks's Inner Light as the basis for his celebration of his readers' divine inner selves and their bodily experiences of revelation.

In 'A Song for Occupations', in particular, Whitman turns his eye to his readers' lived experience of work and their participation in the greater American marketplace. In the same manner with which Hicks spoke out on behalf of dis-enfranchised working-class Friends, Whitman attempts to right a political and cultural wrong by addressing the way that American industry has dehumanised white working-class families, by consuming but not rewarding their labour. To do this, the poet writes himself into his literary work, where he then illustrates the call of the Inward Light and its intrinsic connection to spiritual and bodily epiphany. First as poet-speaker, Whitman attempts to transcend the material boundaries of his published work and to meet his readers in the flesh; failing in this effort, he then invites his readers to immerse themselves within the world of the poem as he does. In 'A Song for Occupations', the poet uses the Inner Light as a model for reclaiming and redeeming his readers' labouring bodies, and marking as sacred and meaningful the work they undertake and the products or services they put out into the world.

*

Whitman's perception of Hicks as a radical reformer is based, in part, on the fundamental role the orator played in the first Schism of American Quakerism that occurred in Philadelphia Yearly Meeting 1827. The widening political and theological rift that led to this traumatic split for American Quakers resulted from conflicts between evangelical or Orthodox Friends and reformers like Elias Hicks. Orthodox Friends occupied the majority of governing positions within the larger regional Meetings, and often lived in urban, wealthy areas. These Friends favoured a strong central governing body for their 'peculiar' religious institution; they also increasingly came to rely exclusively on strict biblical interpretation and narrowly defined religious creeds for their defini-tion of what the Society of Friends embodied and would tolerate morally for its members.

By contrast, Quaker reformers like Elias Hicks and his followers frequently came from lower-income backgrounds and often from rural communities, and they valued local autonomy over the centralising authority that their evangeli-cal opponents preferred. And in sharp disagreement with their more orthodox brethren, Hicksite Quakers absolutely eschewed the Orthodox Friends' empha-sis on cementing the Bible and other written creeds as the ultimate textual authorities from which the Society of Friends should operate. Quaker reform-ers stressed, as Larry Ingle puts this, 'the mystical and inward rather than the formal and outward, and insisted on the right of individual interpretation of doctrine' just as the founder of Quakerism, George Fox, had done (Ingle 1986: xiv). Whitman was attracted to Hicksite Quakerism both for its emphasis on the 'mystical and inward' elements of Quaker religious practice and the man-ner in which this same practice empowered Friends from white, working-class communities, the people with whom Whitman most identified.

Whitman correctly describes this 'Separation' within the Philadelphia Yearly Meeting as a '[vulgar] division' that had been building for quite some time (Whitman [1888] 1982, 'Notes': 1240). Significantly, the Schism of 1827 had its roots not only in theological conflicts, but in the political and cultural divisions within American Quakerism as well. As Howard H. Brinton has demonstrated, the more educated, cosmopolitan Quakers living in urban centres like Philadelphia held considerably more sway within the Society of Friends than their rural, often less educated, counterparts. This imbalance in cultural power persisted despite the Friends of rural communities being more numerous in population than their corresponding urban equivalents. So while Hicksite reformers gained a more concrete following in the lead up to the split by building support from those Friends who wanted to retain a focus on the mystical, inward experience of the Quaker faith, their evangelical opponents, 'whose temperament and positions naturally caused them to fear disorder and unrest', were ready to embrace 'the newly emerging industrial world' and shed their more mystical spiritual past in doing so (Ingle 1986: xiv). Years later, Whitman recognised the ways that both rural and urban working-class people were being left behind in this 'newly emerging industrial world'. Despite forming the backbone of the growing American economy, white working-class families – Whitman's primary concern in this poem – did not see a substantive increase in their economic well-being or political agency as a result of their labour. Instead, the dehumanising effects of the marketplace seemed to sever them from their work (and by extension from their professional selves), sending the material benefits of their labour to business owners and captains of industry instead. Whitman sought to rectify this injustice by empowering his white working-class readers, forcing them to recognise the spiritual value of their work, and by extension, the beauty and power of their labouring bodies.

*

In his *November Boughs* essay on Hicks, Whitman describes a kinship with the Quaker orator that went beyond his appreciation for Hicksite theology and religious practice and the political inclinations of both. In fact, Whitman depicts Hicks's upbringing in cultural terms that he could readily apply to his own childhood. Hicks was born on Long Island to parents, both Friends, 'of that class working with their own hands [. . . who were] mark'd by neither riches nor actual poverty'; as a youth, he 'had small education from letters, but largely learn'd from Nature's schooling' (Whitman [1888] 1982, 'Notes': 1223). This 'Nature's schooling' resulted from Hicks's interactions not only with the natural, rugged landscape of Long Island, but with the men who tilled her fields and navigated her waters. In a touching description of the Long Island terrain and her 'strong, wild, peculiar' inhabitants, Whitman enthusiastically aligns his own educational background with the same influences that forged Hicks's intellectual development.[4] Whitman felt compelled to write to and for the working class because his youth was also crucially shaped by his friendships with the 'crude, but good-hearted people' he encountered on Long Island (Allen 1955: 16). That 'his companions were outdoor men, especially uneducated herdsmen, farmers, pilots, fishermen' demonstrates that Whitman's fascination with the rugged heroes of the American landscape began far before he was envisioning poetry that would celebrate these very same trades (16).

Whitman especially lauded Hicks for his embrace of a more egalitarian form of Meeting and his celebration of all Quaker believers' access to God's inward law and light. According to Whitman, Hicks taught that 'the ideals of character, of justice, of religious action, whenever the highest is at stake, are to be conform'd to no out-side doctrine of creeds, Bibles, legislative enactments, conventionalities, or even decorums, but are to follow the inward Deity-planted law of the emotional soul' (Whitman [1888] 1982: 'Notes', 1235). It was this premise of Hicksite Quakerism and the power of the political move towards egalitarianism that it engenders that caused Whitman to embrace his religious inheritance with such fervour. Whitman declared Hicks to be a fountain of 'all naked theology, all religion, all worship, all the truth to which you are possibly eligible – namely in yourself and your inherent relations' (1221). For while 'others talk of Bibles, saints, churches, exhortations, vicarious atonements – the canons outside of yourself and apart from man', Whitman intoned, Hicks spoke 'to the religion inside of man's very own nature', and due to this, he 'is the most *democratic* of the religionists – the prophets' (1221).

Hicks once described the importance of a believer heeding the voice of his or her 'light within' in his journal when he wrote that the 'cross of Christ' is:

> The perfect law of God, written on the tablet of the heart, and in the heart of every rational creature, in such indelible characters that all the power of mortals cannot erase nor obliterate it. Neither is there any power or means given or dispens'd to the children of men, but this inward law and light, by which the true and saving knowledge of God can be obtain'd. And by this inward law and light, all will be either justified or condemn'd, and all made to know God for themselves . . . By which it is evident that nothing but this inward light and law, as it is heeded and obey'd, ever did, or ever can, make a true and real Christian and child of God. (Hicks 2009: 450–1)

For Hicks, embracing and living by God's 'inward law and light' was one of the only acts by which Friends could become true Christians. Whitman grasped that Hicks's defiant theological stance was rooted in his emphasis on Friends experiencing the presence of God for themselves, when speaking their own messages or witnessing those of fellow Quakers. He then adapted the Inner

Light's facilitation of this experience of revelation for his own political project in poems like 'A Song for Occupations'.

*

Many critics have described the lasting impact that both Quakerism and Hicks made on Whitman's writing. This conversation evolved from an early discussion of Whitman's Quaker character to the manner in which Hicksite Quakerism framed Whitman's perspective on American democracy and the political power of poetry to influence it. In a note composed for a book of reminiscences following Whitman's passing, for example, William Sloane Kennedy describes Whitman's Quaker traits as being particularly evident in Whitman's 'personal habit and temperament' rather than in his verse (Kennedy 1893: 213–14). By contrast, F. O. Matthiessen explored the emotional tenet of what he termed the 'Quaker strain' in Whitman's verse (Matthiessen 1941: 269, 536). Similarly, David Reynolds established how Hicksite Quakerism's 'ecstasy and intuition' appealed to Whitman and noted how Hicks's eloquent oratorical style influenced Whitman's sense of rhythm and form (Reynolds 1995: 38–9). Lawrence Templin also contributed to Whitman-Quaker studies by shedding light on the paradox of individualism and community that run throughout both Whitman's verse and Hicks's theological writings (Templin 1970). Finally, Glenn Cummings has argued that we must trace what he terms the 'Hicksite aesthetic' in Whitman's work, especially in the poet's emphasis on simplicity, candour and an emotional appeal that transcends the power of language (Cummings 1998: 76–8). More recently, scholars have argued that Whitman's Quaker inheritance whetted his political appetite and shaped how he approached issues of public concern within his writing. Susan Dean has asserted that Whitman took from his Quaker heritage a political, activist instinct and Mitchell Santine Gould has explored how Whitman could at once be 'the voice of the fundamental human right to sexual self-determination and the voice of Long Island Quakerism' (Gould 2007: 17).

I recognise the Hicksite Quaker roots of Whitman's political instincts as Dean and Gould do. I also agree with Cummings that Whitman portrays the inward light as a mystical experience that goes beyond what can be expressed within the written or spoken word. In my readings of the Hicksite Quaker strain in poems like 'A Song for Occupations', it is Whitman's emphasis on extending the ecstasy of his religious inheritance to the body which matters most. Only by grappling with how Whitman uses bodily experience and embodiment in poems like this one can we come to terms with how the poet employed his religious inheritance for a particular social-justice-oriented effect: to urge his working-class readers to view their labour as sacred in and of itself, and in doing so, to encourage them to take greater ownership over their own lives.

In this effort, Whitman actively counters Karl Marx's position that, as an exploitative system, capitalism fully strips objects of their material histories and alienates workers from their labour. Instead, Whitman asserts, the products and services we create through our occupational efforts retain the traces of humanity with which they were first imbued when we made them. Adapting the democratic theological premise of the Hicksite Quaker Inner Light for his own political purpose, Whitman proposes that labour is itself a sacred act because it is we, as human beings, who put our divinely rendered bodies, spirits and minds into our work, an endeavour through which we may experience spiritual and bodily revelation in return. Similarly, Whitman asserts, it is his working-class readers who are most in need of recognising this fact.

*

In the untitled 1855 poem that would later become 'A Song for Occupations', Whitman implores his readers to recognise the intimacy of their shared connection. Calling his readers 'lovers' and urging them ever closer to his poetic persona, Whitman advocates that his readers ultimately do away with reading printed works altogether. Made restless by the 'unfinished business' of his lack of physical connection with his audience, the poem's speaker openly fears that the printed page has created a gulf between them that cannot be bridged. He questions, 'how is it with you?' for 'I was chilled with the cold types and cylinder and wet paper between us./I pass so poorly with paper and types .... I must pass with the contact of bodies and souls' (Whitman [1855] 1982, 'A Song': 89). The urgency of this opening question displays the familiarity Whitman's poetic persona presumes to occupy in his relationship with readers. This warm intimacy is immediately cooled, however, by our thrust into the machinery that is printing Whitman's books. Here we witness and feel the stamp of the cold types, the roll of the cylinder that moves each sheet through the machine, and we can almost smell the wet paper, fresh from being marked. For Whitman's poetic persona – who is here embodied by the chill offset by the deeply impersonal nature of the printing marketplace – such absence of warmth is deeply unsettling. For a poet who wants to yield the best he possesses to his readers, and for them to yield the same to him in return, the transactional nature of the printed page cannot help but present an irresolvable difficulty. As Andrew Lawson has noted, this section of the poem appears to lend itself to the reading that 'Whitman's experience of wage labor and mechanization is of an alienating abstraction of values that were formerly tactile and located in an immediate social context,' thus affirming Marx's depiction of this exploitative process (Lawson 2006: 21).[5]

Instead, though, Whitman's insistence on drawing attention to this distance between poet and reader creates a striking parallel for his subsequent explorations of 'occupation' within this poem. While the work of various types of industry may be cold, formal and disconnected from human touch, in reality, from Whitman's perspective, these products hold nothing without the value such human touch imbues them with, and the brilliance, charisma and ingenuity with which they were created and produced in the first place. When Whitman declares, 'I must pass with the contact of bodies and souls,' we witness his ever-insistent desire to wed the physical realm to the spiritual one. Here this statement is made in the specific context of the industrial world (Whitman [1855] 1982, 'A Song': 89). Whitman's emphasis on the embodiment of work – both physically and spiritually – produces a particular foundation for his ability to connect with his reader's daily lives. He has passed through the disorienting chill of the commodifying process of industry, yet he is unbroken by it.

It is worth again referencing Whitman's youth on Long Island and the manner with which he connected his exposure to the natural elements and his friendships with the 'strong, wild, peculiar race' of men who lived there with Hicks's biographical background (Whitman [1888] 1982: 'Notes', 1224). Young Walter chose to spend his free time experiencing the day-to-day life of what many working-class men of the Brooklyn and Long Island communities did to put bread on the table for their families. For these men, this work was never-ending, hazardous at times, and filled with struggle and uncertainty. It was shaped as much by nature itself as it was by the American populace at large. But for young Walter, whose 'childlike wonder' and 'boyish relish of sensory stimulation' remained paramount even as a young adult, these men were living a fascinating, meaningful life (Allen 1955: 16). This is not to say that Whitman was ignorant to the struggles of these outdoor companions as he accompanied them on their adventures or that he did not truly have affection for them, but rather, that Whitman's perception of what this work meant was, in part, a spiritual one. The poet thrilled to experiences that heightened his physical senses and aroused his curiosity, especially with regard to those occupations that were tied to navigation of the outside world and in professions dependent on physical exertions. 'A Song for Occupations' presents Whitman's effort to catalogue the efforts of the American working man and woman as a means of celebrating their daily lives, and thereby to inspire and empower them. The theological example Hicks first set – through his insistence on first-hand spiritual experience and his political work on behalf of rural, uneducated Quakers – provided Whitman with a framework for this type of politically charged verse. The echo of Hicksite Quakerism can thus be seen within this poem's exploration of the meaning of labour and the way that labour production shapes the realities of American workers.

By the 1892 edition of *Leaves*, however, Whitman had pushed beyond physically grounding this poem in the intimacy of the poet/reader relationship to declaring boldly the object of his praise to be:

A SONG for occupations!
In the labor of engines and trades and the labor of fields I find the
    developments,
And find the eternal meanings.
(Whitman [1892] 1982: 'A Song', 355)

Here the poetic speaker moves straight to the task at hand: he means to celebrate the 'eternal meanings' he has discovered in the daily occupational experiences of his readers. Whitman's primary aim in this section of verse is to lay the groundwork for how readers are to perceive his role as a political lyricist. Whitman astutely defines himself as both an outsider to the experience of the American labour market – independently secure in his own sociocultural role as poet despite economic pressures – and as an equal to his readers, having endured the same daily struggles that they have as workers. He writes: 'Neither a servant nor a master am I,/I take no sooner a large price than a small price . . . . I will have my own whoever enjoys me,/I will be even with you, and you shall be even with me' (355). In the same manner as Hicks before him, then, Whitman insists on his poetic narrative being taken on equal footing with his readers' experience of the world.

Whitman sparks a necessary confrontation between his readers' embrace of his ambitious poetic vision and their own sense of self-worth. The poem's speaker provocatively asks his readers why they have failed to recognise their own social and cultural power as producers and consumers within the American economic landscape: 'Why what have you thought of yourself?/Is it you then that thought yourself less?/Is it you that thought the President greater than you?/Or the rich better off than you?/or the educated wiser than you?' (356). Here Whitman contrasts his readers' lack of confidence with the self-possession displayed by the American elite. By juxtaposing the common worker's identity and circumstances with those of the wealthy, educated class of citizens who wield the greatest amount of commercial and social power, Whitman dares to suggest his working-class readers may have internalised their political and cultural marginalisation within American life as indicative of their actual value as human beings. Each subsequent section of 'A Song for Occupations' works to undo this fraught and damaging perception of identity in order to offer Whitman's working-class audience a means of re-envisioning their place within American society.

Echoing Hicks's emphasis on empowering his Quaker brothers and sisters to recognise the light of God within them as the key to their moral character and salvation, the second section opens with Whitman's call for his readers to recognise that they hold the key to their own spiritual rejuvenation and their increased political and cultural participation in American democratic life. He writes: 'Souls of men and women! it is not you I call unseen, unheard,/untouchable and untouching,/It is not you I go argue pro and con about, and to settle whether/you are alive or no,/I own publicly who you are, if nobody else owns' (356). Here Whitman strategically calls to account not his readers' souls, but rather that untouchable and living part of themselves that remains 'unseen, unheard'. Though Whitman's adaptation of the Hicksite Inward Light remains tied to a secular humanist or transcendentalist view of the universe in which human beings are each empowered by a divinity deriving from their own experience of the world, the method by which he defines this essential but ethereal part of the self remains tied to the paradigm Hicks first constructed. Whitman writes, 'I bring what you much need yet always have,/Not money, amours, dress, eating, erudition, but as good,/I send no agent or medium, offer no representative of value,/but offer the value itself' (357). In much the same way, Hicks also preached that he offered only his own account of God's light speaking through him, a message which could not or should not be taken by listeners first hand, without their own experience of the light within. Hicks declared:

> For all that books and men can do, be they ever so great and good in themselves, is nothing more than I have been endeavoring to do – they can do no more than to rally you to the standard of light in your own souls. I have done this, and here is the end of my chain; here is the end of all my power, and I cannot go any further. I cannot help you on your way, only to recommend you to the right means, which is the light in your own souls, and here I must leave you. And that has been the case with all the ministers that the Lord has sent unto the earth – even his beloved Son. (Hicks 1828: 26)

Here Whitman adapts this paradigm for his readers. However, he moves to ground the nature of this divine self as embodied within the corporeal human form, as separate from but ultimately connected to our sensory experience of the world.

Moreover, Hicks, like Whitman, explicitly disavowed inheriting spiritual wisdom from previously written sacred texts or historical accounts. He preached: 'Shall we endeavor to be instructed in darkness? For many look to men and books, and turn away from this divine instructer [. . .] No book is light – no man is light, as it regards us. God only is light and he is in us and not without us' (25). In this passage, Hicks offers a radical theological interpretation of Quaker doctrine. He reiterates his familiar stance about the necessity for a believer's first-hand exposure to experiencing God's light within themselves, but he also defines God's very existence in terms of the deity's capacity to dwell in the light and thus within humankind. Whitman grapples with this Hicksite definition of the Light Within in the final stanza of the second section. He writes:

> There is something that comes to one now and perpetually,
> It is not what is printed, preach'd, discussed, it eludes discussion
> and print,
> It is not to be put in a book, it is not in this book,
> It is for you whoever you are, it is no farther from you than your
> hearing and sight are from you,
> It is hinted by nearest, commonest, readiest, it is ever provoked
> by them. (Whitman [1892] 1982: 357)

Here Whitman describes that part of his poetic identity which cannot be adequately captured by human speech or printed texts. Whitman also notes that this ethereal, divine part of the self is not only unique to each individual's experience of the world, but that it is 'no farther from you than your hearing and sight are from you'; in fact, '[i]t is hinted by nearest, commonest, readiest, it is ever provoked by them' (357). In this section of verse, Whitman aligns his identity as a poet with his reader's sense of self, not just through their spiritual perception of the cosmos, but also as tied to their physical experience of it. By insisting that this sacred part of human nature is felt most readily, or is provoked most frequently by one's senses, Whitman offers a unique means of reconciling the ineffable, indescribable part of the human experience with the grounded reality of daily life. In doing this within 'A Song for Occupations', Whitman creates a dynamic platform for arguing how one's physical and mental labours to create, produce and consume within the American marketplace do not ultimately dehumanise those who participate in it, but rather, demonstrate how their efforts empower them to contribute meaningfully to the world around them.

In the third section, Whitman connects his readers' daily toil in the American marketplace with the power of spiritual and intellectual creation. This metaphor is most provocatively rendered when Whitman redefines the sacred power of religious texts: 'We consider bibles and religions divine – I do not say they are not divine,/I say they have all grown out of you, and may grow out of you still'; for '[it] is not they who give the life, it is you who give the life', and '[l]eaves are not more shed from the trees, or trees from the/earth, than they are shed out of you' (359). Whitman's definition of the power of human touch – here intellectually made manifest through people's efforts to endeavour to understand the spiritual world – is consistent. It is his readers' efforts to create – to 'grow' cultural artefacts – which imbues them with their power, however, not the texts or products themselves which possess the ability to govern human lives.

In the fourth section, this dichotomy is made even more explicit. Whitman argues that it is our physical participation in the production and consumption of labour which connects with and informs our spiritual experience of the world.

All music is what awakes from you when you are reminded by the
    instruments,
It is not the violins and the cornets, it is not the oboe nor the
beating drums, nor the score of the baritone singer singing
his sweet romanza, nor that of the men's chorus, nor that
of the women's chorus,

It is nearer and farther than they. (359)

Our spiritual enlightenment, and our potential as political and cultural actors, is informed by how our identities are forged from these same experiences. It is for this reason that in section 5, the climax of 'A Song for Occupations', Whitman focuses on immersing his readers within the physical sensations of working-class American labourers as his means of celebrating and empowering the daily lives of his working-class readers.

In the first catalogue of this section, Whitman begins his excavation of the sensory experience of working in American mines. Drawing attention to the tension between the search for known minerals and the risk of injury and death to mineworkers, Whitman asserts that coal miners face 'all that is down there'. They see 'lamps in the darkness' and hear 'echoes, songs, what meditations, what vast native thoughts looking through smutch'd faces' (360). Whitman attempts to have his readers sense the darkness and the lamps that light the pathway down into the depths of the mountains and back out towards clean air and freedom, and to experience briefly the sense of claustrophobic pressure miners face on a daily basis as they begin their commute downward. The 'echoes' and 'songs' we hear as readers both reveal the haunting nature of working below ground and the camaraderie that results from shared labour in close quarters. Ending on 'what meditations, what vast native thoughts' these miners must develop behind their 'smutch'd faces', Whitman offers a nod towards the unknowable refrain of what it must be like to complete such gruelling, risky work deep underground, scouting for the rich materials necessary for America's survival, but without getting to partake in any of the monetary rewards that result from your efforts.

Then Whitman expands his vision of mining work outwards to how these mined materials contribute to America's burgeoning infrastructure as a democratic republic. He describes the '[i]ron-works, forge-fires in the mountains or by river-banks, men/around feeling the melt with huge crowbars, lumps of ore,/ [and] the due combining of ore, limestone, coal.' They labour at the 'blast-furnace and the puddling-furnace' and yield the 'bars of pig-iron, [and] the strong clean-shaped T-rail for rail-roads' (360). By drawing his readers' attention away from the miners' echoes in the darkness and upwards to the heat of the forging fires and the heaviness of the labourers' equipment, Whitman connects mineworkers' efforts with the physical toil of steelworkers and railroad build-ers, all of whom shape the developing navigation of the American landscape. Immersing his readers, however briefly, within the daily experiences of these workers sheds light on the pivotal role they play in America's development.

The other point of immersion worth exploring here stems from the agri-cultural end of the span of occupations. Whitman utilises imagery from work completed by farmers, butchers and millers to give readers a sense of how their food arrives on our tables. In doing so, he helps us see the myriad hands that tend and shape the meat and grow and harvest the grains we consume each day. And yet, Whitman's desire to honour American workers would have suc-ceeded even more readily if he had grounded this section of text more firmly within these workers' lived experiences of completing this labour, rather than shifting our focus to the movement of the various products they create and the tools they employ. As readers, we recognise that these products embody the passion and commitment these labourers have committed to their trades; Whitman has already illuminated how these creations and productions are imbued with spiritual and symbolic meaning as well as economic and social power. Whitman's attempt to honour the American worker falls short of his lofty objective in this section of the poem when we lose complete sight of the workers themselves.

These portraits are narrowly drawn. The working-class audience Whitman addresses and constructs here is, by almost any definition, exclusively white and male. Indeed, Whitman's ambition for this poem never moves beyond this initial framework in which he juxtaposes the manner in which his working-class readers *should* view their occupational efforts with their disillusionment, sense of powerlessness and lack of perceived agency. Whitman does not address his critique of the marketplace in terms of currency or actual capital; in fact, he never proposes a specific plan of action to remedy the unjust conditions under which his readers labour and live. Alan Trachtenberg has argued that Whitman does not 'ask how labor, property, and society might otherwise look . . . [or] imagine the overthrow of the system of occupations or the social relations of labor'; instead, he merely 'subsumes the system by singing . . . it to an ideal version, a convertible America the poet's work might bring about' (Trachten-berg 1994: 131). Yet, I would argue that Whitman's effort here is not in vain. Instead, Whitman's choice to 'sing' about the ongoing struggles of his working-class readers reveals a means of concretely addressing them. Section 5 of 'A Song for Occupations' concludes:

> The hourly routine of your own or any man's life, the shop,
>   yard, store, or factory,
> These shows all near you by day and night – workman!
> whoever you are, your daily life!

In that and them the heft of the heaviest – in that and them far
more than you estimated, (and far less also,)
In them realities for you and me, in them poems for you
and me,
In them, not yourself – you and your soul enclose all things,
regardless of estimation,
In them the development good – in them all themes, hints,
possibilities.
(Whitman [1892] 1982: 362)

These shows of workmanship – the hourly routines of the shop, yard, store and factory – not only define the daily lives of the men (and women) who participate in them, but they are far more critical to the life of the nation than Whitman's readers are likely to have previously considered. By shifting the poem's focus away from these reductive market-driven societal roles and towards the daily realities of American workers, Whitman demonstrates to his readers that their work does not limit but rather empowers them, as they participate in the larger American community by contributing necessary and meaningful labour to its creation and upkeep. Though these workers are frequently scorned or marginalised politically or culturally within American society at large, Whitman urges them to know that their realities are poetic in the utmost sense. By adapting a Hicksite religious practice both as a political foundation and as the literary means of drawing his readers into their experience of this poetic world, Whitman argues that his working-class readers perform not only physical or intellectual labour, but spiritual work. 'In them' or your working realities, he writes, 'you and your soul enclose all things' including 'all themes, hints, [and] possibilities' (362). In this way, Whitman has publicly celebrated the daily struggles of men and women who are all too often dehumanised by a cold and impersonal marketplace and a capitalist economic system which threatens to alienate them from the roots of their labour.

Works Cited

Allen, Gay Wilson (1955), *The Solitary Singer*, New York: Grove Press.

Benjamin, Walter (1969), 'The Work of Art in the Age of Mechanical Reproduction', in Hannah Arendt (ed.), *Illuminations*, New York: Schocken Books.

Brinton, Howard H. (1993), *Friends for 350 Years*, Wallingford, PA: Pendle Hill Publications.

Cummings, Glenn N. (1998), 'Placing the Impalpable: Walt Whitman and Elias Hicks', *Modern Language Studies* 28(2): 69–86.

Dean, Susan (1999), 'Seeds of Quakerism at the Roots of Leaves of Grass', *Walt Whitman Quarterly Review* 16(3): 191–201.

Erkkila, Betsy (2007), 'Whitman, Marx, and the American 1848', in Susan Belasco et al. (eds), *Leaves of Grass: The Sesquicentennial Essays*, Lincoln: University of Nebraska Press, pp. 35–61.

Gould, Mitchell Santine (2007), 'Walt Whitman's Quaker Paradox', *Quaker History* 96(1): 1–23.

Elias Hicks (1828), 'Sermon I. Delivered by Elias Hicks at Horsham, Montgomery County, Pennsylvania, December 16, 1826', *Quaker, Or a Series of Sermons*, 4, pp. 9–31.

— (2009), *The Journal of Elias Hicks*, ed. Paul Buckley, San Francisco: Inner Light Books.

Ingle, Larry H (1986), *Quakers in Conflict: The Hicksite Reformation*, Knoxville: University of Tennessee Press.

Kennedy, William Sloane (1893), 'Quaker Traits of Walt Whitman', in Horace Traubel, Richard Maurice Bucke and Thomas B. Harned (eds), *In Remembrance of Walt Whitman*, Philadelphia: David McKay.

Killingsworth, M. Jimmie (1989), *Whitman's Poetry of the Body: Sexuality, Politics, and the Text*, Chapel Hill: University of North Carolina Press.

Lawson, Andrew (2006), *Walt Whitman and the Class Struggle*, Iowa City: University of Iowa Press.

Matthiessen, F. O. (1941), *American Renaissance: Art and Expression in the Age of Emerson and Whitman*, New York: Oxford University Press.

Moon, Michael (1993), *Disseminating Whitman: Revision and Corporeality in Leaves of Grass*, Cambridge, MA: Harvard University Press.

Reynolds, David S. (1995), *Walt Whitman's America: A Cultural Biography*, New York: Knopf.

Templin, Lawrence (1970), 'The Quaker Influence on Walt Whitman', *American Literature* 42(2): 65–80.

Trachtenberg, Alan (1994), 'The Politics of Labor and the Poet's Work: A Reading of "A Song for Occupations"', in Ed Folsom (ed.), *Walt Whitman: The Centennial Essays*, Iowa City: University of Iowa Press, pp. 119–33.

Traubel, Horace (1915), *With Walt Whitman in Camden, Vol. 2*, ed. Mitchell Kennerley, *Walt Whitman Archive*, <https://whitmanarchive.org/criticism/disciples/traubel/WWWiC/2/whole.html> (accessed 29 October 2021).

Whitman, Walt [1855, 1892] (1982), 'A Song for Occupations', in Justin Kaplan (ed.), *Walt Whitman: Poetry and Prose*, New York: Library of America, pp. 89–99, 355–62.

— [1888] (1982), 'Elias Hicks, Notes (Such as They Are)', in Justin Kaplan (ed.), *Walt Whitman: Poetry and Prose*, New York: Library of America, pp. 1221–44.

— [1888] (1982), 'Father Taylor (and Oratory)', in Justin Kaplan (ed.), *Walt Whitman: Poetry and Prose*, New York: Library of America, pp. 1143–6.

NOTES

1. Hicks opens this message by quoting from the famous opening lines of the Westminster Shorter Catechism, a traditional Christian doctrine which places particular emphasis on creedal authority. This emphasis aligns closely with how orthodox Quakers embraced religious doctrine at the expense of a believer's direct experience of revelation. This is why Hicks's inclusion of the phrase 'I was told in my early youth' is so pivotal here. Because Hicks and his followers did *not* subscribe to this theological perspective, his use of the opening lines from this catechism appear to serve as a place from which to pivot to his actual message.

2. This is the language Whitman utilises to describe the preaching of Father Taylor, another Protestant figure whom he admired and whose oratorical style he compares to that of Elias Hicks. He notes that both men 'had the same inner, apparently inexhaustible, fund of latent volcanic passion – the same tenderness, blended with a curious remorseless firmness, as of some surgeon operating on a belov'd patient. Hearing such men sends to the winds all the books, and formulas, and polish'd speaking, and rules of oratory' (1145).

3. This theological concept and its corresponding religious practice has been called by a number of names within the Society of Friends, including the Inward Light, the Inner Light and the Light Within.

4. Whitman once asserted: 'I knew the habitats of Hicks so well – my grand-parents knew him personally so well – the shore up there, Jericho, the whole tone of the life of the time and place – all is so familiar to me: I have got to look upon myself as sort of chosen to do a job as the Hicksite historian. I have seemed, to myself at least, to be particularly equipped for doing just this thing and doing it as it should be done – have felt that no one else living is exactly so well appointed for it' (qtd in Traubel 1915: 18).

5. Betsy Erkkila offers a fascinating account of where Whitman's and Marx's ideas 'appear to converge' in some of their early writings. In particular, Erkkila draws attention to how Whitman and Marx use diametrically opposed language to describe similar issues. Despite this, she writes, against 'the dehumanizing force of capitalism, [both] Marx and Whitman called for the liberation of man in the fullness of his physical and social being' (Erkkila 2007: 44). One of the places where Whitman does this most explicitly, I would argue, is within 'A Song for Occupations'.

PART II

EXCESS IDENTITIES

4

LATINX/CONFEDERATE: LORETA JANETA VELAZQUEZ AS A CROSS-DRESSING SOLDIER, 1861

LEIGH JOHNSON

Loreta Janeta Velazquez (*The Woman in Battle*, 1876) is a Latinx confederate who does not 'fit' our narratives of the national body at the time of the Civil War. A woman whose family had moved from Mexico to Cuba after the US-Mexico war, Velazquez assumed the identity Lieutenant Henry Buford and participated as a Confederate soldier in the Civil War. She was married multiple times, spied and smuggled for the Confederacy, and eventually moved to the western United States. Her effort (or lack of effort) to mould herself into an American, and our efforts to read her fairly, reflect the cultural anxieties of our historical moment in which racial and gender identifications are fluid, fraught and fragile. This essay argues that the multiple crossings (gender, political, national, linguistic and social) embedded in Velazquez's memoir complicate understanding of American national identity in the nineteenth century as the text challenges the reader to see the author through a more complex process of identity formation than usually available in nineteenth-century texts. Through self-centred excess, Velazquez performs multiple identity markers and reflects upon them as she connects with and teases her reader. The narrative challenges what it meant to be an American in the nineteenth century. The emergent forms of social and national identification that the narrative experiments with share a similar state of flux to the narrative's configuration of gender. In this way, many of the categories by which scholars might make sense of the narrative – gender, nationhood, ethnicity in particular – simply fail to connote in the way that one thinks they ought.

Velazquez narrates her family history of landed power and privilege in Mexico and subsequent political and economic dispossession at the hands of the United States after the war with Mexico, which leads her family back to Cuba with a strong distaste for Americans. However, her family sends her to school in New Orleans for the advantages that would convey on her in the future. There she elopes with her best friend's boyfriend, and finds herself estranged from her family. Her father's disapproval is particularly hard to bear and travels with her through her later exploits: 'When I met him for the first time after my marriage, he turned his cheek to me, saying, "You Can never impress a kiss upon my lips after a union with my country's enemy," – from which I concluded that it was not so much my marriage without his consent, as my alliance with an American soldier that imbittered him' (Velazquez [1876] 2003: 50). She convinces her young husband to join the Confederate forces, as it helps her reconcile her marriage with her father's disapproval. If she and her husband take up arms against the Americans, then she can imagine that revenge has been served for the land dispossession her family faced.

During the war, after the deaths of her three children, she dresses as Lt Henry Buford to fight for the Confederacy. She fancies that her appearance will be a welcome surprise for her husband at the front. Yet her decision to cross-dress seems inevitable, because long before she marries a soldier and shocks his sympathies with her desire to be a man – in the barroom and on the battlefield – she reveals to the reader, 'I was especially haunted with the idea of being a man [. . .] it was frequently my habit, after all in the house had retired to bed at night, to dress myself in my cousin's clothes, and to promenade by the hour before the mirror, practicing the gait of a man, and admiring the figure I made in masculine raiment' (42). Even before she hatches her plan to become a solider and fight alongside her husband, she has already drawn the reader into her performance of masculinity. By expressing her desires early in the narrative, she explains that she has never fitted into the American mould insofar as gender binaries are upheld. Her awareness of how rigid gender roles limit her choices in life is clear from the beginning of the narrative.

Later, as Buford, she seduces young women and participates in the battles at Balls Bluff and Bull Run. She continues her memoir with multiple marriages – each more absurd than the last. After her first husband dies, she becomes engaged to Captain De Caulp, who does not recognise her in her masculine garb, and even shows Velazquez a picture of herself as a widow as he waxes on about how much he loves her and has impressed her with his military service (329). She reveals herself to him dressed as Buford, and they agree to marry quietly in the hospital as soon as she can procure women's clothes for the wedding. Later, caught out again as a woman, she occupies her time spying in the North and the South, leading to more absurd situations in which she encounters various generals and bounty hunters looking for her.

After the war, she undertakes a voyage to Cuba and an eventual sojourn through the US Southwest in search of a place to call home. The entire text, with multiple fraught identities and quick changes of loyalty, is the fascinating portrayal of a woman who did not fit the American cloth, so she changed her clothes to suit her identity at the moment. The only identity she seems remotely reluctant to part with in her changes is her Catholicism, but because her first husband is Protestant, she reconciles herself to becoming a Methodist (49). Throughout the text, she shape-shifts depending on how she needs those around her to see her. She performs masculinity, hyper-femininity, multiple ethnicities, competing national loyalties and varying social classes. In fact, she performs self-centred excess, winking at the reader as she lets them in on her secrets.

Velazquez engages with the audience at every juncture of the narrative, especially when marking a particular performance. She is acting out the narrative for the audience's approval, and the polyvocality of the narrative suggests that she is conscious of pleasing many audiences at once. Velazquez negotiates with the audience so much that it seems like there is an excess of effort to form a bond with the reader. It is as if she hopes someone will understand her impulses, as varied and fluid as they are.

In an effort to define Velazquez's self-centred excessive performativity, I turn to Judith Butler's comments on gender performance: 'The possibilities of gender transformation are to be found precisely in the arbitrary relations between such acts, in the possibility of a failure to repeat, a de-formity, or a parodic repetition that exposes the phantasmatic effect of abiding identity as a politically tenuous construction' (Butler 2005: 503). Every time Velazquez's moustache threatens to fall off or she is shown a picture of herself as a woman while she is dressed as a man, she enacts the possibly of a failure to repeat the gender performance she engages, but her turn to the reader in these situations is what marks them as self-centred. She shows that she is performing, but for the reader, pinning down just what exactly her performance depends on is difficult because there are so many elements to parse. Butler takes into account gender, but within this text Velazquez performs linguistic identity, ethnic identity and national loyalty, among other identities. Any one of these can also be seen as an excess of her performance in which Velazquez creates a 'phantasmatic effect' of identity in a politically tenuous environment. With the aspersions and doubt that greeted her narrative, it is even more obvious that the intimate relationship she shares with readers is fraught with the potential for misunderstanding and derision.

Scholarly Reception

While contemporary critics have relished Velazquez's narrative as an important and stimulating recovered text, debate and controversy over the text swirled at both its original publication and recent recovery. One of the most significant aspects to the recovery of this text is the position it holds in the concept of the Latinx nineteenth century. While early American women's writing, including stories of cross-dressed soldiers and travellers, experienced a tremendous recovery by scholars in the 1970s and 1980s, interest in recovering Latinx writings from early American literature has faced several obstacles, including tension over geographic borders, English-language preference in American literature, and a need for archival support. The foremost scholars of Velazquez's work, Jesse Alemán (2003), Elizabeth Young (1999) and Richard Hall (2002), find much to comment on with regard to her place in nineteenth-century American literature. All take her account seriously as a literary work.

In the context of this volume, I build gratefully upon their work to examine her text as a construction of excesses. Within her memoir exists an excess of identity that then creates the excesses of categorisation that intensify readers' scrutiny of her and their desire to pin her in to a manageable body in a static place and time. Yet, her every narrative and performative move resists categorisation along those rigid lines.

While some early readers of her book, notoriously Confederate General Jubal Early, found the work scandalous and titillating, dismissing it out of hand as falsely constructed, scholars have excused some of the excesses. Alemán remarks, 'Velazquez's very existence, as with the narrative attributed to her, rests somewhere in between history and story, where even a seemingly inauthentic author can nonetheless produce an authentic cultural text that embodies and enacts the prevailing beliefs and anxieties of its historical context' (Alemán 2003: xix). Recovered stories mark the silences of history that were repressed and discounted at the time they happened. While William Davis (2016) spends a determined, if unconvincing, 376 pages arguing against the veracity of the narrative, calling Velazquez a prostitute and camp follower of the Mormon Rebellion (9–10) and pointing to minor details of the narrative as anachronous, Richard Hall's research concludes: 'What errors she does make probably are attributable to faulty memory and careless mistakes made in haste rather than to deliberate fabrication' (Hall 2002: 230). Hall points out some of the inaccuracies of the narrative, such as her relationships with De Caulp, because records at the National Archives put him elsewhere, but Hall also supports the tale of her spying in Canada and being honoured in Kentucky by citing a photograph that looks like Velazquez (233). And while Elizabeth Young acknowledges that the production and reception of *The Woman in Battle* contained tension between fact and fiction, she asserts, 'What emerges in the absence of authenticity is the presence of the literary' (Young 1999: 160). The scholarly emphasis on the literariness of the narrative is particularly appropriate for my analysis of the text because a triangulation between the text, reader and author and the transactions among them forms the basis for seeing and responding to the excesses of the narrative.

Velazquez's work is important because she embodies so many different categories of identity and she grapples with each of them throughout the text. She was not the only woman to participate in the war by cross-dressing and passing as a man. Francis Louisa Clayton and Sarah Edmonds Seelye both served in the Union Army, and Seelye received a pension for her participation in the war. Most well-documented female soldiers fought for the Union. Nor is Velazquez the only Cuban to have participated in the US Civil War. Frederick Fernandez Cavada and his brother Adolfo both fought for the Union, whereas Ambrosio José Gonzalez was a Confederate soldier (Tucker 2002: 5–6). She was not even the only Cuban woman to participate in the war, as Lola Sanchez acted as a spy for the Confederacy after her hacienda was raided (7).

Each of these stories is fascinating yet different from that of Velazquez, because each of the previously mentioned participants maintained a fixed loyalty and positionality during the war and afterwards. On the contrary, Velazquez undeniably sees her identity as a series of performances, never more clearly than when she interacts with women, such as those in Paris, Tennessee. In competition with her colonel and captain for the attentions of the ladies, she revels in her private joke: 'They did not understand the situation as I did, they were, of course, unable to see exactly where the laugh came in. Could they have but known who I really was, they would, undoubtedly, have been intensely amused, and would have enjoyed the whole performance immensely' (Velazquez [1876] 2003: 156). She is conscious of performing each identity and committed to changing the trappings of that identity to suit the needs of the moment. Here, as often occurs, she is not content to simply perform, but she does so excessively. She gives up the competition, but not until she has satisfied herself, and those around her, that she could have been the most extra (in the colloquial sense) man there.

This pleasure in her action is on spectacular display in the scene where Velazquez evades the federal officer sent to capture her. She identifies him, and they sit together on the train. Debating which accent to affect, she opts for an Irish brogue over a Spanish lilt, fearing that someone would have put into her file that she was Spanish. The agent shows her a picture of herself, enquiring if she has seen the woman. Velazquez queries, 'She is very handsome. [. . .] Is she your wife?' (416). This flusters the agent with the emasculating insinuation that his wife has left him, and he struggles to regain his dignity, ranting against 'she devils' and 'Copperheads' (416). At the height of irony, the agent offers to carry Velazquez's bag for her on disembarking. Contained within the bag is 'eighty-two thousand dollars belonging to the Confederate government, and a variety of other matters' (417). Regaining her satchel, she gives the password to the Customs agent and crosses into Canada with the smuggling and spying successful. Relating the story to her Canadian friend, Velazquez is pleased with her friend's reaction: that she seems 'to be tolerable able to take care' of herself (417). And this perhaps is the point of the performance – to secure her independence from others' expectations. Velazquez invites the reader to participate in her performance, detailing how she selects her accent, narrating moments where she thinks one thing, but says another to the agent, and describing the winking getaway she pulls off.

EXCESSIVE PERFORMANCES AS NARRATIVE DESIGN

The layered identities Velazquez brings to her work account for some of the ways scholars have chosen to focus on individual aspects at the expense of others. When grappling with this story, entry points abound, and deciding which to pursue is challenging. Should it be genre? Racial and ethnic identity? Class? Gender? Confederate sympathies? Or the antithesis to all of these? The scholarly debates about her work suggest a rich and rewarding reading experience. Anzaldúa's parsing of different reading relationships is useful for understanding how Velazquez's text might strike readers. For instance, 'when one reads something that one is familiar with, one attaches to that familiarity and the rest of the text, what remains hidden, is not perceived' (Anzaldúa 1998: 272). Anzaldúa uses this to explain why straight readers enjoy gay literature, partly as negative identity formation and partly from a sense of curiosity that can hyper-focus on sex instead of 'the full complexity of our lives' (272). Identifying an empathetic reader means the text yields different meanings. Anzaldúa concludes her observation by differentiating between sets of reading skills (conventionally narrow vs flexibly trained) that would enable someone to read a 'strange' text (272). Here, then, the scholarly debates make sense. Aside from obvious sexuality and gender fluidity, Velazquez's focus on the audience and her enactments for them mark *The Woman in Battle* as a queer text, embodying the jouissance of narrative performance that the story can provoke in a reader attuned to the broad strokes of the nuances of her displays.

Her continued shape-shifting is central to the text. Encounters with ladies, generals, country folk and government officials demand different performances. Yet, even though Velazquez is comfortable with each of her performances, she never settles into a place where she can feel comfortable being herself. By the end of the narrative, she is still looking for a place to land. Coleman Hutchison describes this affect as that of a restless text, suggesting that Velazquez remaps the American Civil War via disruptions in immigration, slavery, capital and competing nationalisms (Hutchison 2007: 425). Within the narrative, Velazquez engages multiple international dimensions such as those between England and France, the Canadian border that she crosses, Irish emigrants and other soldiers, and Confederates moving to Latin America. She often embodies these other ethnicities, taking on an Irish brogue or French affectation to hide her 'true' identity. The linguistic accent play is almost as common as her costuming.

The text moves rapidly between and among locations in the Americas. Hutchison concludes that the text does not privilege one location, as Velazquez is always on the move (435). For instance, while she spends little time in Cuba, there is a scholarly focus on her Cuban-ness. The danger in this condensed focus, perhaps, is that Velazquez's narrative is so performative (and so long) that it would be easy to zoom in on a particular aspect that serves to obscure broader themes. In other words, it is easy to get sidetracked and lost in the details of this expansive narrative, but scholars would do well to keep a broader look at the scope of the action and events.

Velazquez details several mishaps in her first spying career in New Orleans which result in her skulking away from the city, getting mixed up in skirmishes in Richmond, and resuming her male attire. As she comes to terms with the likely long duration of the war, she notes that she does not intend to tell the history of the war, preferring to entertain the reader with her exploits, noting that her 'experiences [. . .] gain their chief interest from the fact that they were different in a marked degree from those of any other participant in the war on either side' (Velazquez [1875] 2003: 275). She marks her story for its difference from other narratives of the time. Unlike other memoirists, she is not interested in preserving the Lost Cause narrative or the realistic horrors of the war. Instead, she uses the narrative to extol her own performances, those that succeed and those that do not. In this way, Velazquez consciously constructs the identities she deploys in the text and invites the reader to enter into the perspectives she offers.

Using this performative joy to read the text allows for play within the categories scholars have identified and debated. For instance, Young underscores the elements of play by describing the episodic structure akin to a picaresque novel or adventure story like those by Mark Twain and Horatio Alger. However, as women writers were excluded from these forms by social dictate, Young remarks that women can only enter this genre through masquerade (Young 1999: 160). Velazquez quickly puts on the trappings of male identity, going so far as to learn to walk like a man and affixing a moustache to her face, which then leads to comical fears that it will fall off over dinner (Velazquez [1876] 2003: 77). Her desire to have an adventure and write her own story of heroism propel the narrative, and the costuming changes support the contention that Velazquez has embraced a masquerade. In this way, she is able to embrace and enact narrative genres that would otherwise be inaccessible to her.

If the gender-bending is joyful and humorous burlesque, sexual identity complicates and potentially anachronises some of her performance. While Young reads Velazquez's cross-dressing 'as a metaphorical point of exchange for intersections between individual bodies and the national body politic' (Young 1999: 152) and points out that the nation is divided by region and race and the individual by sex and sexuality, Velazquez is undeniably queering the performance of gender and sexuality. Perhaps the most compelling chapter in this regard is chapter 16, 'An Unfortunate Love Affair', in which Velazquez begins as a woman, changes into her male attire, finds her slave, poses with women, reads a love letter from a Confederate officer who knows her as a man and as a woman (but does not know they are the same person) and assesses the conventions of society with regard to which gender may make the first move in love affairs. Young explains part of this complexity by explaining how cross-dressing 'moves from the controlled performance of both masculinity and femininity into a more blurred narrative of gender indeterminacy and same-sex eroticism' (162). Young reads the work as part of a protolesbian Confederacy in which Velazquez, through her disgust at the women around her, expels sisterhood from the protolesbian plot (174). However, the blurring of the ways that Velazquez troubles gender binaries indicates a queerness to the text that readers and scholars have had trouble expressing due to the narrative's braggadocio and rhetorical shifts. Shifting to understanding the self-centred excessive performance of the narrative opens up more avenues for analysis.

Velazquez disparages the women she seduces as well as the men she fights next to, making the only personage to meet her high standards of sexual and gender propriety her own self. The ramifications of her judgements allow her to grant herself immunity from all of the transgressions she identifies in others, from overly flirtatious women at quilting parties to crass and vulgar men in the barroom. Each place that she deems the people out of line are times in which she has turned inward to show herself as resisting these very same impulses. In this way, the text might be read as one that questions the demarcations of gender as such.

After all, if Velazquez can cross between genders and gain insight into each, and if both are equally hypocritical in their expectations of behaviour and propriety, then what logically requires the presence of gender other than social norms being upheld through performance? Young observes, 'The hostility to women in Velazquez's text is, at least in part, a result of nineteenth century social constraints that might make "the ladies", confined to a round of domestic duties, seem less appealing companions than male adventurers' (Young 1999: 175). Yet, Velazquez finds some pleasure in being around women while in her male garb that is not altogether designed to poke fun at the women who fall in love with her; she also revels in her ability to perform domestic tasks, while dressed as a man, that upend the expected gender binaries and social customs. When she does these things, such as quilting, conversing and dining, with a sensitivity she attributes to her own womanly behaviour, she is subverting gender roles for her audience's entertainment, and perhaps more subversively, engendering discomfort with these binary identities in the first place. Additionally, by embedding this domestic competition into the adventurous tale, Velazquez subverts domestic fiction that women dominated at the time.

She seems to suggest that she could write that just as well as anyone, but that she has chosen to bend the adventure genre to her purposes.

However titillating the semi-seduction narrative is, Young regards the text as containing a compulsory heterosexuality 'so lackluster' that its visibility calls it into question (169). Velazquez judges the young women who fall in love with Buford, but she recounts her own elopement at the expense of her friend's love interest, as a harbinger to the relationships she enters into later in the narrative. The loyalties Velazquez claims, to the Confederacy and to herself, stem from similar entitlement. Her relationships are often calculated through an interconnected web of self-serving extrapolation, whether they are personal or political. For example, after her father disapproves of her husband, believing that Velazquez has gone to bed with his enemy, she embraces the Confederacy, contra the American identity that has disenfranchised her family. Fighting the Americans gives her a way to imagine herself back in her family's good graces, despite the fact that she has also betrayed their expectations for her marriage and educational future. Her shifting, double-agent behaviour portends the consistent 'the enemy of my enemy is my friend' calculations that seem to govern most of her strategic decisions about money, career and travel.

IMPLICATIONS FOR TEACHING

Certainly the American literature nineteenth-century survey course is a space long dominated by slavery, captivity, temperance, civil disobedience and Manifest Destiny; in order make this literature clearly relevant to undergraduates, it can be urgent to show how recovery from the national wounds demands looking at all the nuances of resistance and complacence that haunt a text. Where narratives reveal the ways that history bears upon the present are useful tools for discussion and examination. In many ways, despite her Confederate identity, Velazquez has come into her own in today's climate, which is beginning to understand gender as fluid and transformable. My students are very willing to accept her gender performance as an element of transgender identity; however, they are more titillated at her experiences with flirting with women. The memoir details her transformation into a man via clothing, a haircut, lessons on drinking and language, and she seems sad to realise the limits of her transformation are only outwardly performative. Within the context of performance, Velazquez recognises that every element of her disguise is performative, to be observed, studied, practised and perfected.

Velazquez's narrative offers a counterpoint to nineteenth-century Mexican American author María Amparo Ruiz de Burton's *Who Would Have Thought It?* and *The Squatter and the Don*. These texts hold a certain allure for scholars with their place as the first novels by a Mexican American author written in English and with their well-drawn depictions of the class structure and political shenanigans of Americans, women's sexual awakening and the standards of beauty and race in the nineteenth century. Furthermore, the texts fit comfortable paradigms of dealing with gender, religion, national division and racial performance – getting a little risqué, but ultimately upholding the available avenues of literary value and theoretical textual approaches.

Another way in which Ruiz de Burton's texts affirm scholarly paradigms is by eliding the pro-Confederate discourse that circulated in some minority communities and texts. Yet, many scholars have revealed the complexities of *Who Would Have Thought It?* to great effect, especially with regard to calling into question the subaltern status of the narrative voice; as José Aranda points out, 'She wrote and negotiated her world with a defined and sophisticated alternative history, but she was clearly a daughter of the Enlightenment and a colonialist' (Aranda 2016: 147). So, if Ruiz de Burton's text is alternative, but not all that resistant to dominant political thought of the East Coast elite, it can only offer so much in the way of fodder for discussing the unstable binaries within the text – even though it is, of course, rich ground for discussing the nineteenth-century elite Mexican American experience.

At the twenty-fifth anniversary of the Recovering the US Hispanic Literary Heritage conference, Jesse Alemán challenged scholars and teachers to rethink the Ruiz de Burton dependency, commenting: 'because as long as we uphold her elite life and novels as representative of Mexican American modernity, the longer it'll take us to recover all the other lives and stories that, while perhaps not as ornate or well-written as la doña's, nevertheless remind us of who we were and what we've become' (Alemán 2017). While not denying that Ruiz de Burton has a fascinating history and literary presence, I would suggest that Velazquez's book is harder to reconcile into neat, digestible units of study.

Yet, in exciting ways, nineteenth-century Latinx memoir can speak to a present-day political climate that has only begun to publicly address the problem with fetishising of Confederate statues and memorials. Velazquez's performance asks what kind of nation fawns over a past that has no future. She answers that by moving away from the Confederate past on her own terms. It is important to discuss and acknowledge that when scholars discuss recovered texts by Latinx authors as resistant, the question rightly becomes: resistant to what? However, by answering this question as resistant to Anglo narratives of conquest, and allowing the recovered text to claim moral high ground, what happens when the Latinx writer embodies the wrong side in that historical conflict? Ruiz de Burton offers a voice that does not glorify the Confederacy, even though some scholars have identified a pro-Southern vein running through her writing; but Velazquez offers 'no apologies' for her part in the war (Velazquez [1876] 2003: 606); coming off a trip through Texas, she sees all that her family had lost at the hands of the US plunder of Mexico, even as she has already moved on to another chapter heading in her story. Ultimately, Velazquez rejects

American-ness on Anglo terms. She centres herself in the story she tells, even if that means alienating everyone.

Conclusion

After these complicated and provocative crossings are read, and then read back again from the opposite lens, the narrative is left to wander away to the borders of the nation, unbound from the binaries that structured the narrative. It's significant that Velazquez mentions becoming a mother, but because her children die before she assumes masculine dress, she still is able to reproduce herself in multiple guises via the narrative. When she only spends a few sentences on motherhood, she deflects the expected domestic end to women's stories. Sager captures this idea of unboundedness well: 'It appears as if the civil wars that rage within Velazquez stem, in part, from her rebellion against any possibility of dependency. She constantly moves between identity markers in search of a position that provides her with the best possibility of control over her own destiny' (Sager 2010: 35). Our difficulties in pinning her into a particular identity or place, then, are part of the frustration and the joy of the narrative's crossings. Her restlessness, as Hutchison (2007) calls it, is too inextricably part of the text and forces the audience to sit with the ambiguity of her performance long after she has abandoned male garb, the southern states and vestiges of capital and wealth.

Velazquez remains loyal to the Confederacy for a good chunk of the narrative, which poses problems for presenting the text as transgressive. If, as Young persuasively claims, Velazquez is both anti-woman and antifeminist, what are the ramifications for reading the text in a protolesbian vein, or in an anti-racist vein? By looking at the text as a whole, Young concludes, '*The Woman in Battle* debases the value of Confederate iconography by literalizing its terms, turning Confederate masculinity into femininity, femininity into fakery, and sexual prowess into vulnerability to assault' (Young 1999: 193).

Velazquez's centring of the text on her own experience is transformational. While reading her excesses as performative and outside the bounds is helpful in getting a handle on the vast landscape of the memoir, a paradigm shift renders this text central to hearing the muted voices of the nineteenth century. Velazquez, embracing excessive performance of identity and despite being pushed to the margins her whole life, successfully queers the dominant narrative to make herself the centre.

Works Cited

Alemán, Jesse (2003), 'Authenticity, Autobiography, and Identity: *The Woman in Battle* as a Civil War Narrative', in Loreta Janeta Velazquez, *The Woman in Battle: The Civil War Narrative of Loreta Janeta Velazquez, Cuban Woman and Confederate Soldier*, pp. ix–xli.

— (2017), 'Recovering from Ruiz de Burton', Twenty-Fifth Anniversary Conference, Recovering the US Hispanic Literary Heritage, Houston, TX.

Anzaldúa, Gloria (1998), 'To(o) Queer the Writer – Loca, escritora y chicana', in Carla Trujillo (ed.), *Living Chicana Theory*, Berkeley: Third Woman Press, pp. 263–76.

Aranda, José (2016), 'When Archives Collide: Recovering Modernity in Early Mexican American Literature', in Rodrigo Lazo and Jesse Alemán (eds), *The Latino Nineteenth Century*, New York: New York University Press, pp. 146–67.

Butler, Judith (2005), 'From *Gender Trouble: Feminism and the Subversion of Identity*', in Wendy K. Kolmar and Frances Bartkowski (eds), *Feminist Theory: A Reader*, 2nd ed., New York: McGraw Hill, pp. 496–503.

Davis, William C. (2016), *Inventing Loreta Velazquez: Confederate Solider Impersonator, Media Celebrity, and Con Artist*, Carbondale: Southern Illinois University Press.

Hall, Richard (2002), 'Loreta Janeta Velazquez: Confederate Soldier and Spy', in Philip Thomas Tucker (ed.), *Cubans in the Confederacy: José Augustin Quintero, Ambrosio José Gonzales, and Loreta Janeta Velazquez*, Jefferson, NC: McFarland, pp. 225–41.

Hutchinson, Coleman (2007), 'On the Move Again: Tracking the Exploits, Adventures, and Travels of Madam Loreta Janeta Velazquez', *Comparative American Studies* 5(4): 423–40.

Sager, Robin C. (2010), 'The Multiple Metaphoric Civil Wars of Loreta Janeta Velazquez's *The Woman in Battle*', *Southern Quarterly* 48(1): 27–45.

Tucker, Phillip Thomas, ed. (2002), *Cubans in the Confederacy: José Augustin Quintero, Ambrosio José Gonzales, and Loreta Janeta Velazquez*, Jefferson, NC: McFarland.

Velazquez, Loreta Janeta [1876] (2003), *The Woman in Battle: The Civil War Narrative of Loreta Janeta Velazquez, Cuban Woman and Confederate Soldier*, Madison: University of Wisconsin Press.

Young, Elizabeth (1999), *Disarming the Nation: Women's Writing and the American Civil War*, Chicago: University of Chicago Press.

5

PHILIPPINES/UNITED STATES: DAVID FAGEN DEFECTS TO THE FILIPINO ARMY, 1899

SPENCER TRICKER

In April 1905, a story entitled 'Fagan' appeared in *Collier's Weekly*. Prominently advertised on the front cover, the piece had won first prize in a short story competition, besting the work of established authors like Edith Wharton and John Luther Long. In the process, it brought the unheralded writer Rowland Thomas a whopping $5,000 (approximately $145,000, at a 3 per cent inflation rate, in today's currency), as well as the remarkable, if now forgotten, sobriquet 'the American Kipling' (Thomas 1909a). 'Fagan' was based on the life of a real historical figure: David Fagen, an African American soldier who defected from the United States Army during the Philippine-American War (1899–1902).[1] Originally from Tampa, Florida, and witness to Southern Jim Crow segregation and racist violence, Fagen became a formidable guerrilla leader of Filipino troops whose name, according to recent biographer Michael Morey, became 'virtually a household word in America, particularly among African Americans' (Morey 2019: 3).

If the real Fagen posed a significant problem to the US military, his fictional counterpart in Thomas's prize-winning tale is that of an infantilised, tragicomic figure – a gentle 'black giant', mishandled by his Northern white superiors (Fagen's actual commanding officer, Lt James A. Moss, was, in fact, from Louisiana) who lacks any political consciousness (Thomas 1905: 21). The narrator describes him as a 'good-natured, childlike' being, while white officers from the South wistfully designate him 'a n***** like we had before the war' (Thomas 1905: 20, 17). A caricature of primitivity, Thomas's protagonist soon attains widespread notoriety among the American soldiers as 'Wild Fagan' because he swings his rifle as a club rather than firing it (17). Right from the start, then, Thomas paints his subject in the recognisable hues of local colour fiction and, more specifically, the plantation-school tradition popularised by writers like Thomas Nelson Page and Joel Chandler Harris. The use of eye dialect in 'Fagan' strengthens this generic link, while the overall narrative – rather unusually, given Thomas's New England roots – tends to blame misguided Northern intervention for the failures of Reconstruction.

While these stylistic attributes register how 'Fagan' replicates typical magazine fare of the period, the story's representation of contemporary white anxiety regarding race and national identity – namely, the issue of whether Black troops could be relied on to fight brown people in the Philippines – stands out for the way Thomas works to depoliticise Fagan's defection by individualising his relationship to the people of the Philippines. Rather than displaying Fagan as an adept military leader directing and collaborating with Filipino forces, Thomas focuses attention on a fabricated romantic relationship between Fagan and a young Filipina named Patricia, whom Thomas portrays as a malicious Oriental stereotype. This Afro-Asian couple presents readers with two entwined versions of primitivity central to the burgeoning US imperial imaginary of the period. The first, represented through Fagan, is that of the infantile, Uncle-Tom-like Black slave of the plantation-school tradition whose roots extend well into the antebellum period. The second, represented in Patricia, is that of the cunning Malay pirate – less prominent in the US cultural imaginary, but one which emerges more clearly through the figure of the *insurrecto* (the name given by US troops to Filipino freedom fighters) who so vexed American forces after 1898. The first image enshrouds the perceived threat of Black corporeality – figured in Fagan's physical prowess – with a comforting mantle of docility and childlike good humour. The second image, while threatening in its evocation of violence, is mitigated through a vision of the Other as physically diminutive and feminised. Combined, however, these two differently racialised aspects of primitivity pair physical power and violent intent in a manner that poses a potent threat to US imperialism and the white supremacist foundations upon which it rests. To defuse the radical potential of such a combination, Thomas turns to a third image of the primitive: the obscurely perceived tribal native.

At the end of the story, having mercifully spared the life of a young US lieutenant, Fagan flees into the mountains of Luzon with his Filipina bride. Thomas describes their ascent as a movement into deeper primitivity. Leaving 'the snug little brown house' they had previously occupied, Fagan and Patricia set 'out on the High Trail, the unknown of the people of the plains, a broad highway to things with hoofs and claws and wings, and to men little less wild than these, the men of the hills' (Thomas 1905: 22). In this milieu, they ultimately succumb to an indistinct but malevolent 'spirit of the forest' (22). In the final scene, Fagan dozes beneath a tree, soon to be destroyed by a wild enemy he cannot see. The moral of Thomas's tale is that the road from civilisation, as represented in Fagan's rejection of national identity as a US soldier and subsequent embrace of racial identification with Patricia, can only lead to degeneration and death.

To articulate the domestic stakes of this imperial message for Black Americans at the turn of the twentieth century, I would like to turn briefly to a very different sort of mountain journey. This vertiginous quest appears at the beginning of one of the era's most important and well-known works of literature: W. E. B. Du Bois's *The Souls of Black Folk* (1903). As with 'Fagan', *Souls* is deeply concerned with Blackness and the South, even as it understands the 'Black Belt' as a local manifestation of a colour line that 'belts the world' (Du Bois 1906). In an extended metaphor at the end of the first chapter, Du Bois figures racial uplift and the quest for education and higher knowledge as a 'mountain path to Canaan' (Du Bois [1903] (1986): 367). Reflecting on this ascent, he remarks:

> It was weary work . . . to the tired climbers, the horizon was ever dark, the mists were often cold, the Canaan was always dim and far away. If, however, the vistas disclosed as yet no goal, no resting-place, little but flattery and criticism, the journey at least gave leisure for reflection and self-examination; it changed the child of Emancipation to the youth with dawning self-consciousness, self-realization, self-respect. In those somber forests of his striving his own soul rose before him, and he saw himself – darkly as through a veil; and yet he saw in himself some faint revelation of his power, of his mission . . . For the first time he sought to analyze the burden he bore upon his back, that dead-weight of social degradation partially masked behind a half-named Negro problem. (Du Bois [1903] (1986): 368)

Whereas the fictionalised Fagan of Thomas's tale ascends beyond the pale of White American modernity compelled by primitive urges that lead to his death, the Black protagonists of Du Bois's mountain metaphor climb to transcend 'the veil' of racial prejudice, reckon with the split subjectivity of 'double consciousness' and surmount centuries of oppression (364). For Du Bois's 'climbers' – a precursor to his notion of the 'talented tenth' – the ascent has been a process of spiritual growth and political understanding, rather than degeneration into childhood and self-destruction.

What can these disparate scenes tell us about how 'the problem of the Negro' was being renegotiated, through literary culture, from the end of Reconstruction through the early rise of US imperialism overseas? If, as Du Bois famously diagnoses, 'the problem of the twentieth century is the problem of the color line', then the cause of US imperialism in the Philippines proffered an easy, if dubious solution to Black men considering enlistment: if they would 'hold the line' of the nation-state against its foreign enemies, the colour line might begin to fade, domestically (372). What proves troublesome, given the prevailing tendency in transnational American Studies to understand movement across borders as subversive, anti-nationalist and counter-hegemonic, is the fact that despite Du Bois's call for solidarity among the 'darker races of mankind', many Black American soldiers of the period were willing to accept this tradeoff. Rather than indicating a simple disjuncture between the individual and his intended public, this discordant social reality actually refracts Du Bois's own investment in the ideology of racial uplift, analysed by Kevin Gaines (1996) as a contested, but largely elitist platform with limited power to critique white supremacy, and complicates the anti-imperialist standpoint with which he is often associated. For, as Vince Schleitwiler has lately observed, 'At the twentieth century's dawn, uplift encompassed both the range of projects to improve the social conditions of African Americans *and* the guiding rationale for US colonialism in the Philippines' (Schleitwiler 2017: 11).

I examine this paradox in the following pages, beginning with the unusual circumstances of the *Collier's* short story prize and how the opinions of its three judges – two from the publishing world, the other an imperialist politician – bear witness to how dominant literary taste – institutionalised in North-eastern magazine culture – continued to venerate the plantation-school tradition of reactionary white supremacist nostalgia, even as the exigencies of US foreign policy began to necessitate a more inclusive understanding of American identity. This section illustrates the continuing importance of studying the American South in relation to the US imperial project overseas. Next, I provide a short survey of the real David Fagen's life and the responses to his defection and guerrilla career in contemporary periodical culture and especially the Black press. Finally, I discuss some of the key revisions Thomas made to 'Fagan' for inclusion in his 1909 collection *The Little Gods*. Here I suggest that the figure of the Igorot headhunter, a stereotype of the mountain-dwelling Indigenous people of the Philippine cordillera, who becomes a graphic spectacle in the revised version, prompts Thomas's expedient redrawing of the global colour line. This act constitutes the real significance of Fagen's defection for American literature and culture: namely, its unmooring of race from an aesthetic anchorage. Having appraised the real ambivalence of African Americans towards Fagen and his defection during the early twentieth century, I end by resisting the methodological urge – attractive though it may be – to celebrate Fagen's defection as a luminous instance of Afro-Asian solidarity contra US imperial subjecthood. Instead, I suggest that the most subversive political consequence of Fagen's transpacific crossing in the Philippines is less the act of defection itself – an act which, again, was not broadly condoned by the Black American community or seen as a viable, alternative mode of being – but by its frustration, through the rupture of dominant aesthetics, of white supremacist attempts to manipulate the colour line towards global imperialist ends.

'Fagan' and the Collier's Short Story Prize

Thomas's fictionalised version of 'Fagan' came to prominence through the improbable circumstance of winning a major prize contest, the judges of which included not only prominent magazine editors, but also a US Senator known for his imperialist agenda. The *Collier's* contest was announced on the first of February 1904. Limited to submissions by Americans, the contest would award prizes of $5,000, $2,000 and $1,000 to its first, second and third-place submissions respectively ('$5,000 for a Short Story' 1904: 19). On the eleventh of February 1905, the magazine announced the results of the competition, followed by 'The Opinions of the Judges'. Remarkably, none of the contest's judges actually rated 'Fagan' as their top choice. Magazine editors Walter Hines Page and William Allen White rated the story third among their selections, while US Senator Henry Cabot Lodge did not place it in his top three. Nevertheless, 'Fagan' was the most consistently high-ranked entry on a shortlist of nine stories (whittled down from 12,000 total submissions). Among the judges' comments, a few points are worth noting: 1) that Page was the most complimentary, highlighting its 'self-restraint', lack of 'literary adornment' and 'simply constructed . . . straight narrative of a man's life' ('Opinions' 1905: 13); 2) White's criticism that 'Fagan' was too much a 'biography', when, in his opinion, 'the best short story . . . is one that handles an incident – a cross-section of life' (14); and 3) Lodge's terse dissent, which did not even mention 'Fagan' and lamented his fellow judges' failure to award first prize to 'The Best Man', a realist work by Edith Wharton that, curiously, concerns a principled politician who refuses to be blackmailed.

The awarding of first prize to Thomas's 'Fagan' in the *Collier's* competition might be attributed to a relative preference for the genre of 'local color' fiction by Page (a Southerner) and White (a Midwesterner) as compared to the high realist sensibilities of the Boston-bred Lodge. Witness Page's praise for the direct simplicity of 'Fagan', coupled with White's description of the story as 'biography', which suggest that the magazine editors could acknowledge the value of Thomas's regionalist particularity, whereas Lodge – who declined to explain his own aesthetic criteria – adhered doggedly to the bourgeois milieu and presumably universal, civic responsibility plot of 'The Best Man' without knowing the identity of its urbane, realist author.[2] This stark divide in judgement also resonates with what Nancy Glazener has observed as the 1890s-era decline of a Boston-based literary establishment – the so-called '*Atlantic* group' of magazines (heavily associated with editor and realist author William Dean Howells), which previously wielded tremendous 'power to construct and legislate the literary' (Glazener 1997: 230) – and the rise of a 'new group of mass-circulation magazines', centred in New York, which increasingly paired literary fiction with sensational, photo-rich journalism (236).

While Lodge (the oldest of the judges) may have preferred the literature of the New England-dominated era, his political investments benefited tremendously from the New York periodicals associated with William Randolph Hearst, Joseph Pulitzer and, indeed, *Collier's* magazine. After all, it was this New York group of muckrakers and yellow journalists that stoked the fires of popular imperialist sentiment in 1898. Still, the relative positions of the judges suggest that, however much periodical culture may have served the purposes of empire-building in this period, literary tastemakers were not always in step with the desires of politicians. As domestic magazine editors, Walter Hines Page and William Allen White's relative insulation from contemporary transpacific affairs might explain their continuing regard for 'local colour' and 'plantation-school' fictions as resilient prisms through which to imagine American race relations after Reconstruction. By contrast, Lodge's rejection of Thomas's story intimates some disturbance at how 'Fagan' – which re-litigates sectional tensions and invites a degree of sympathy with Fagen's desertion – disrupts the integrity of American national identity during an epoch fraught with colonial desires and anxieties about immigration ('Opinions' 1905: 14). That Lodge agreed to judge the contest in the first place would seemingly owe to the fact that *Collier's* had been 'a strong proponent for American intervention in Cuba' and the war with Spain (Cole 2010: 205). Quite probably, therefore, he would have been filled with ironic dismay to learn that the winning story evoked some sympathy – albeit a sympathy soaked in racist paternalism – for a real, subversive case of Black desertion from US imperial service. Within this context, we can see how aesthetic disjuncture among the judges actually exceeds the scope of literary genre and appreciation, troubling the boundaries of both race and citizenship as genres of social organisation.

Addressing this disjuncture allows us to reverse Harilaos Stecopoulos's argument that 'imaginative writing of the modern US South emerged in part through a dynamic engagement with an expansionist state' (Stecopoulos 2008: 14). Specifically, 'Fagan' and its unique circumstances collectively illustrate how an instance in the literature of American overseas empire, adapted from a regionalist form associated with the Reconstruction-era South, was manipulated to accommodate new political conditions. Thomas's adaptation focuses the overlapping concerns of aesthetics and politics, opening an uncomfortable literary vista into the changing nature of American racial thought as the nation acquired new overseas territories. What Senator Lodge's dissent suggests, and what Thomas's later, revised and extended version of 'Fagan' further implies, is that the transpacific repurposing of plantation-school literature had its breaking point – a point of rupture that reveals the central role of the aesthetic in the makings of race and empire.

Fagen's Desertion, African American Soldiers and the Prospect of Solidarity among 'Dark Races'

Before appraising this revelatory rupture, however, we should address the stakes of the real David Fagen's desertion for Black readers and writers. Fagen deserted the US Army's Twenty-Fourth coloured regiment in November 1899, having come into conflict with his superiors and having been repeatedly fined, confined and made to perform hard labour. While personal conflicts may have played some role in his actions, biographer Michael Morey 'maintain[s] that [Fagen's] desertion was a conscious political act, evidenced by his subsequent unwavering loyalty to the revolutionary cause. Fagen did not desert simply for personal reasons. He deserted to make war on white Americans in concert with the Filipino revolutionaries' (Morey 2019: 108–9). At any rate, Fagen soon attained a prominent position among the freedom fighters, rising to the rank of captain and perhaps even that of major (Morey 2019: 145–6, 179). According to General José Alejandrino, he 'spoke Tagalog very vividly' and, as represented in Thomas's story, married a Filipina (Alejandrino 1949: 176). Newspaper accounts of Fagen appear periodically throughout the first two years of the twentieth century, often misreporting actions that – despite fragmentary documentation – Morey and others have verified through analysis of military reports.[3] Fagen's death was proclaimed numerous times, most convincingly in December 1901, when the *Manila Freedom* and *Manila Times* newspapers announced that he had been beheaded by a Filipino bounty hunter named Anastacio Bartollomé. According to Morey, 'hundreds of newspapers covered the story' (Morey 2017: 262). Fagen's body was not identified beyond a shadow of a doubt, however, and in 1906 the *Washington Post* ran a *Manila Times* story with the headline 'Fagan Again on Warpath', attributing its source to the Bureau of Insular Affairs and reporting Fagen's involvement with banditry and carabao-rustling (cattle theft).

While the circumstances of Fagen's death cannot be definitively settled, we can at least gauge how one African American newspaper answered reports that the renegade's career had come to an end. On 14 December 1901, the Indianapolis *Freeman* announced Fagen's 'behead[ing] by the natives' and provided what is perhaps the closest thing to a eulogy in the era's Black press. 'Fagin [*sic*] was a traitor, and died a traitor's death,' it reads. 'But he was a man, no doubt, prompted by honest motives to help a weaker side, and one to which he felt allied by ties that bind. Fagin [*sic*], perhaps, did not appreciate the magnitude of the crime of aiding the enemy to shoot down his flag. He saw, it may be, the weak, the strong, he chose, and the world knows the rest' ([No Title] 1901: 4). The article intimates a tension between official nationalism and a cross-racial sympathy it declines, directly, to disclose. Showcasing the dilemma endemic to Du Bois's formulation of 'double consciousness', it invites a very different kind of sympathy than that of Thomas's 'Fagan'. Whereas the *Collier's* story encourages the sympathy of white condescension towards a Black man-child's moral confusion, the *Freeman's* obituary invites sympathy for Fagen's unpatriotic, yet still ethically sound impulse to stand with another oppressed race.

If such language indexed the fault line separating African Americans from a white supremacist imperial cause, it reiterated a truth well known to Filipino freedom fighters in the late nineteenth century. An 1899 propaganda placard addressed 'to the Colored American Soldier' and reproduced in the African American newspaper *Richmond Planet* showcases this knowledge:

> It is without honor that you are spilling your costly blood. Your masters have thrown you into the most iniquitous fight with double purpose – to make you the instrument of their ambition and also your hard work will soon make the extinction of your race. Your friends, the Filipinos, give you this good warning. You must consider your situation and your history. And take charge that the blood of your brothers Sam Hose and Gray proclaim vengeance. ('War in the Philippines' 1899: 8)

While the placard certainly seeks to sow dissent in the ranks of the US Army, it also showcases the Filipino guerrillas' attention to specific instances of lynching and racialised violence in the Reconstruction-era South (Hose and Gray) and their intimation of a transpacific sensitivity to African Americans' divided sense of identity.

Surveying Willard B. Gatewood Jr's *Smoked Yankees,* an invaluable collection of letters published in contemporary Black newspapers, one finds a subcurrent of sympathy for the Filipinos among some African American troops. This sentiment is overtly captured in an unsigned letter to the Wisconsin *Weekly Advocate*, whose author opines that the Filipino insurgents have a 'just grievance' against American forces and especially White soldiers, who, in 'apply[ing] home treatment for colored peoples', 'curs[e] them as damned n*****s, steal [from] and ravish them, rob them on the street of their small change . . . and after fighting began, loo[t] everything in sight, burning, [and] robbing the graves' (quoted in Gatewood 1971: 279–80). More common, however, are letters like that of Captain W. H. Jackson, published in the *Colored American Magazine*: 'The insurgents even sent out placards to the colored officers and men,' he writes, 'Asking us not to fight against them, because we were of the same color. But we only laugh, for we are U. S. soldiers, and all the enemies of the U. S. government look alike to us, hence we go along with the killing, just as with other people' (Jackson 1900: 149). Black soldiers of lower rank voiced similar sentiments. Writing to the Indianapolis *Freeman*, Sergeant M. W. Saddler states, 'We are now arrayed to meet what we consider a common foe, men of our own hue and color. Whether it is right to reduce these people to submission is not a question for the soldier to decide' (Gatewood 1971: 248). Likewise, P. C. Pogue asserts to the Cleveland *Gazette* that 'colored Americans are just as loyal to the old flag as white Americans and it will always be so' (Gatewood 1971: 259). In such statements, there is a notable displacement of personal sentiment onto patriotic signifiers – that is, a suspension of political morality premised on one's status as a soldier fighting beneath the American flag. Allusions to the flag, in particular, resonate with the conclusion of Sutton E. Griggs's popular 1899 novel *Imperium in Imperio*, in which a Black community leader struggles valiantly against white supremacist violence but balks at supporting African American separatism. Before a firing squad comprising members of the 'Imperium in Imperio', a clandestine Black government, he states, 'Tell posterity . . . that I loved the race to which I belonged and the flag that floated over me; and, being unable to see these objects of my love engage in mortal combat, I went to my God' (Griggs 173). After his execution, he is buried and 'shrouded in an American flag' (Griggs [1899] 2003: 174).

Whether or not an individual Black soldier would self-describe as a patriotic supporter of the war, we are confronted with the basic reality that most Black troops remained loyal to their units and often framed that loyalty – idealistically or pragmatically – as a guarantor of citizenship. It is instructive, therefore, to read and understand these loyalty affirmations against the backdrop of an era marked by Jim Crow laws, newly emergent forms of structural racism and extralegal acts of lynch terrorism, which converged to 'erase evidence that African Americans could be modern citizens' (Mitchell 2011: 14). In literary culture, Koritha Mitchell has shown how, in the years immediately following the First World War, the figure of the Black soldier would soon become integral to the formation of Black-authored lynching dramas that centred affirmations of Black citizenship. 'Whether he died valiantly in battle or returned home demanding the rights for which he fought,' she explains, '[t]he black soldier personified African Americans' admirable character and valid claim to full citizenship' (82).

Unfortunately, however, efforts to assert Black citizenship sometimes came at the expense of other racialised and oppressed groups. Hence, the printed correspondence of Black American soldiers in *Smoked Yankees* largely reverberates with Helen Heran Jun's analysis of 'black Orientalism' (Jun 2011: 17) in African American newspapers of this era, which sought to secure national identity through an 'Orientalist dis-identification with Chinese immigrants' (28). White supremacist enterprises both at home (e.g. the Chinese Exclusion Act) and abroad (e.g. colonisation of the Philippines) would therefore exert powerful constraints – vis-à-vis the lure of citizenship – on the formation of Afro-Asian solidarities in this period.[4] Still, if Afro-Asian solidarity in the Philippines remained a fugitive practice, its prospects seemed threateningly vivid to anxious White American observers of the period. After the war, in 'The Negro Soldier in War and Peace', war correspondent Stephen Bonsal stated, 'Many observant officers expressed the opinion that the color line had been drawn [in the Philippines] again to our disadvantage, and that the negro soldiers were in closer sympathy with the aims of the native populations than they were with those of their white leaders and the policy of the United States' (Bonsal 1907: 321). More significantly, William Howard Taft, in his capacity as the first colonial governor of the Philippines, also rued the fact that Black soldiers 'got along fairly well with the natives' and sent Black regiments home in advance of other units (quoted in Gatewood 1971: 243). Such comments intimate that, despite the ambivalence of Black soldiers and domestic observers, Fagen's desertion dramatically registered the tenuousness of the global colour line. With this tenuousness in mind, we can now address the following question: Was it necessary for US imperial institutions to consider Black men – however contingently – as White, if they 'took up the White Man's Burden' in the Philippines? This is the very question Rowland Thomas circumambulates in the revised 1909 version of 'Fagan'. An analysis of this dissonant proposition requires some reconsideration of methodological tendencies in transnational American Studies, as well as in studies of comparative racialisation in the US.

The Revised 'Fagan', Comparative Racialisation and the Rupture of Racialising Aesthetics

Rather than magnifying Fagen's defection as a marginal act of anti-imperialist Afro-Asian solidarity, which we cannot easily extrapolate to a broad Afro-Asian community sensibility in this period, I will address how Thomas's story 'Fagan', as an index of the dominant literary establishment (sanctioned in *Collier's*), exposes the workings of comparative racialisation in a manner useful to future forms of solidarity.[5]

Although scholars have addressed Afro-Asian interactions 'amid the interracial tensions and varied race legislation of the late nineteenth century', Hsuan Hsu observes that 'we need a better understanding of how this dynamic field of cross-racial analogies and tensions played out in literary form' (Hsu 2015: 8). Until recently, American Studies scholars have tended to emphasise how Blacks and Asians have been differently racialised in accordance with a 'dialectic of black inclusion/Chinese exclusion' from the Reconstruction era through the Second World War, or, more recently, how these groups have been pitted against one another vis-à-vis the divisive concept of the model minority (Wong 2015: 3).[6] Less has been said, however, concerning fluctuations of the colour line in the context of the Philippine-American War. What I would like to highlight, therefore, in analysing how the aesthetics of racism come undone in Thomas's revised 'Fagan', is how this unusual story registers the Philippine-American War as what Shu-Mei Shih terms a 'chronotope[e] of racialisation': a transpacific 'interarticulation' of regions, peoples and their presumed positions on a timeline that culminates in White Western modernity (Shih 2008: 1358).

In a longer 1909 version of 'Fagan', published in Thomas's collection *The Little Gods*, the story begins and ends with an Igorot tribesman bearing Fagan's severed head to US troops and claiming a reward. Although the historical Fagen was allegedly beheaded, the addition of decapitation to 'Fagan' in 1909 suggests the deep irony of Rowland Thomas's capitalisation on the life and death of the titular Black rebel. The Igorot, described as 'squat, huge-muscled, [and] naked' comes into the small Philippine town 'with a head-axe . . . thrust through his belt, and at his back a bag, swollen as if it held something big and round' (Thomas 1909: 10). The object in the bag, we learn, is Fagan's head. With this identification, the Igorot 'savage' replies 'Me got . . . *mucho dinero. Mucho mucho dinero*. Me got' (38–9). Disgusted with this sight, a White American officer states, 'I'm not in favor . . . of payin' gu-gus for killin' white men, no matter whether they're white or black. It's a catchin' habit' (39). This uncommon remark, in which Fagan is marked as a White man distinct from Filipino 'gu-gus' (a racist term used by US troops during the War), discloses a rupture in the primary aesthetics of racism.

What do I mean by the 'primary aesthetics of racism'? As Michael Omi and Howard Winant observe, in America, race has become '"common sense" – a way of comprehending, explaining, and acting in the world' (Omi and Winant 2015: 127). Their use of 'common sense', here, follows from Antonio Gramsci, referring to the process by which a social class attains hegemony by rhetorically defining (or redefining) what is intuited as the simply given: that is, the unphilosophical reasoning common to all (Gramsci 1971). However, the term 'common sense' – sometimes rendered *sensus communis* – is also a central concern in the domain of aesthetics, which, despite a long history of discursive quarantine from politics, has lately been reconsidered as mutually involved with the political.[7] In *The Difference Aesthetics Makes* (2019), Kandice Chuh insightfully applies Jacques Rancière's influential argument, 'that politics are constitutively aesthetic', to an analysis focused on how ideas of race and humanity emerge both within the arts and within society more broadly (Rancière 2004: 18).[8] 'Aestheticization', for Chuh, names an ongoing political project that 'produces a racial difference as sensible in both valences [of the term] – as reasonable (common sense) and as affectively available to apprehension' (Chuh 2019: 19).

With this notion of 'aestheticization' in mind, I argue that Thomas's 'Fagan' registers the failure of both plantation-school, local-colour fiction and turn-of-the-twentieth-century American 'common sense' perception to produce stable, ostensibly natural racial categories – what Sylvia Wynter evocatively terms 'genres of the human' – through the interpretive lens of the colour line, here understood as the key axis against which racial value was hierarchically plotted and made legible in this period (Wynter 2003). In both versions of his short story, Rowland Thomas gestures to this aesthetic rupture when Fagan – still a member of the US army – attacks Filipino soldiers shouting, 'Come on, boys . . . come on, kill the damn n*****s' (Thomas 1905: 17). In the *Collier's* version of the story, it is possible to read this dissonant moment at face value: that is, as an episode of racist comedy rooted in situational irony. It is only with the 1909 revision, and Thomas's confusion of racial signifiers in the dialogue of a white man, that 'Fagan' comes to underline the tortuous logic animating fin de siècle recalibrations of racial thinking in American culture.

Despite occasional notes of irony (for example, rendering the White soldier's self-contradicting racial terms in provincialising eye dialect), Thomas does not expose this rupture in racialising aesthetics to enact any subversive critique of power. Rather, his story works innovatively, if awkwardly, to suture an aesthetic rift by redirecting attention to a newly identifiable figure of racial difference in contemporary American popular culture. Indeed, what makes 'Fagan' stand out among the broader archive of stories about the Philippine-American War in this period is its redrawing of the colour line to create a symbolic space in which to reconcile the dynamic of White-Black antagonism through transpacific reference to the figure of the Igorot, an Indigenous racial Other. A critical context for understanding the Igorot figure is the 1904 Louisiana Purchase Exposition (held in St Louis, Missouri), in which a forty-seven-acre Philippine Reservation represented the event's most popular attraction and was visited by around 18.5 million people. As Beverly Grindstaff points out, the exhibit overrepresented the Igorot tribespeople as a synecdoche of a primitive Filipino nation. '[T]he final exhibit's emphasis was squarely placed on the Philippines' indigenous peoples,' she explains, 'and presented a narrow vision built from the seeming-objectivity of science, architectural gesture, and the language of popular press accounts, racial slurs and political metaphor' (Grindstaff 2009: 248). The appropriation of Igorot indigeneity as an index of Filipino primitivity was particularly useful to the interests of US empire as it provided spectacular distraction from an awkward, yet needed transformation in its animating discourse of 'Anglo-Saxon uplift' (Schleitwiler 2017: 11). As the military conflict of the Philippine-American War died down and a new, educational mission of Americanisation began, an abrupt revision took place in the dominant aesthetic and epistemological construction of the Filipino as colonial subject. Replacing the recalcitrant, treacherous Filipino – discernible in Thomas's characterisation of Patricia and popularly known as the figure of the 'insurrecto' or 'gugu' – came the pliant, infantilised 'little brown brother', eager for American tutelage.[9] In the 1909 version of 'Fagan', Rowland Thomas elides this profound rhetorical transition by diverting the reader's gaze towards an Indigenous figure, which, by dimly recalling the well-known, romanticised myth of the 'vanishing Indian', would allow for American soldiers – Black and

White – to share a provisional 'Whiteness' based on historical development and progress, rather than aesthetic perception.

Thomas's conclusion to the revised 'Fagan' thus illuminates what Omi and Winant (2015) might call a discreet 'racial project' emerging in this era – in which the US military, despite representing a nation that operated as a 'racial despotism' until the end of the Civil Rights Movement, actually prefigured a form of 'racial democracy' more characteristic of the US's present situation vis-à-vis race.[10] In this light, 'Fagan' should be read as imagining the US military's reification of a more inclusive, if entirely provisional and temporally constrained, notion of American identity under which segregated military units could be effectively aggregated and deployed. Whereas the racial state – especially in the American South – could operate despotically in its disenfranchisement and persecution of racial minorities in a relatively uninhibited manner, the US military could not exercise the same degree of impunity during wartime because, ultimately, it relied on Black volunteers to participate actively in combat manoeuvres for the cause of American imperialism. Hence, while some of Thomas's turn-of-the-century readers might well have taken cruel pleasure in the situational irony of Fagan brutally killing Filipinos he derides as 'n*****s', it was very much in the interest of the US military to promote Black identification with US imperialism – a White supremacist cause – in and through the protean cipher of American citizenship that, domestically, was being ruthlessly legislated as the preserve of Whites.

CONCLUSION

The provisional, bad-faith extension of Whiteness to Black soldiers imagined at the end of Rowland Thomas's 'Fagan' represents a moment of African American inclusion at the expense of Asian exclusion that is at once resonant with and distinct from Justice John Marshall Harlan's written dissent from the Supreme Court's ruling in favour of segregation in *Plessy v. Ferguson* (1896). Harlan's dissatisfaction with the ruling hinged partly on his outrage that 'a Chinaman [could] ride in the same passenger coach with white citizens of the United States' while Black citizens, 'many of whom, perhaps, risked their lives for the preservation of the Union', could not (quoted in Lwin 2006: 20). As Sanda Mayzaw Lwin points out, Harlan's dissent 'configures both citizenship and membership in the American nation as a right one can earn by proving loyalty to the nation-state', which, as I have noted in the letters of African American soldiers above, proved an alluring if generally unfruitful logic for Black Americans to assimilate (Lwin 2006: 21). By focusing on how Thomas's revisions to 'Fagan' register the shifting exigencies of US state power vis-à-vis the contours of racial formation, we gain a sense of how turn-of-the-century American literary crossings provided a space within which to experiment with more inclusive forms of American identity while, at the same time, working to obfuscate the prospect of subversive Afro-Asian affinities. By appreciating how these revisions also expose racialising aesthetics as artificial and politically interested constructs of the dominant racial class, however, we may improve our understanding of how intersectional attachments operate vis-à-vis notions of identity and unequal structures of power.

WORKS CITED

'$5,000 for a Short Story' (1904), *Collier's*, 21 May, p. 19.

Alejandrino, Jose M. (1949), *The Price of Freedom: Episodes and Anecdotes of Our Struggles for Freedom*, Manila: M. Colcol.

Bonsal, Stephen (1907), 'The Negro Soldier in War and Peace', *The North American Review*, 7 June, p. 321.

Cheah, Pheng (1998), 'Given Culture', in Pheng Cheah and Bruce Robbins (eds), *Cosmopolitics: Thinking and Feeling Beyond the Nation*, Minneapolis: University of Minnesota Press, pp. 290–328.

Chuh, Kandice (2019), *The Difference Aesthetics Makes*, Durham, NC: Duke University Press.

Cole, Jean Lee (2010), 'The Hideous Obscure of Henry James', *American Periodicals* 20(2): 190–215.

Du Bois, W. E. B. (1906), 'The Color Line Belts the World', *Collier's*, 20 October, p. 30.

— [1903] (1986), *The Souls of Black Folk*, in *Writings*, ed. Nathan Huggins, New York: Library of America.

— (2014), 'The Present Outlook for the Dark Races of Mankind', in *The Problem of the Color Line at the Turn of the Twentieth Century: The Essential Early Essays*, ed. Nahum Dimitri Chandler, New York: Fordham University Press, pp. 111–37.

'Fagan Again on Warpath' (1906), *Washington Post*, 28 June, p. 11.

Gaines, Kevin (1996), *Uplifting the Race: Black Leadership, Politics, and Culture in the Twentieth Century*, Chapel Hill: University of North Carolina Press.

Gatewood, Willard B. Jr, ed. (1971), *'Smoked Yankees' and the Struggle for Empire'*, Champaign: University of Illinois Press.

Glazener, Nancy (1997), *Reading for Realism*, Durham, NC: Duke University Press.

Gramsci, Antonio (1971), *Selections from the Prison Notebooks*, ed. and trans. Quintin Hoare and Geoffrey Nowell Smith, London: International Publishers.

Griggs, Sutton E. [1899] (2003), *Imperium in Imperio*, New York: Modern Library.

Grindstaff, Beverly (2009), *Anthropology Goes to the Fair: The 1904 Louisiana Purchase Exposition*, Lincoln: University of Nebraska Press.

Hinderliter, Beth, Vered Maimon, Jaleh Mansoor and Seth McCormick (2009), *Communities of Sense: Rethinking Aesthetics and Politics*, Durham, NC: Duke University Press.

Hoffmann, Phillip W. (2017), *David Fagen: Turncoat Hero*, Staunton, VA: American History Press.

Hsu, Hsuan L. (2015), *Sitting in Darkness: Mark Twain's Asia and Comparative Racialisation*, New York: NYU Press.

Jackson, W. H. (1900), 'From Our Friends in the Far East', *Colored American Magazine*, August, pp. 146–9.

Jun, Helen Heran (2011), *Race for Citizenship: Black Orientalism and Asian Uplift from Pre-Emancipation to Neoliberal America*, New York: NYU Press.

Lwin, Sanda Mayza (2006), '"A Race So Different from Our Own": Segregation, Exclusion, and the Myth of Mobility', in Heike Raphael-Hernandez and Shannon Steen (eds), *AfroAsian Encounters: Culture, History, Politics*, New York: NYU Press.

Lye, Colleen (2008), 'The Afro-Asian Analogy', *PMLA* 123(5): 1732–6.

Melamed, Jodi (2011), *Represent and Destroy: Rationalizing Violence in the New Racial Capitalism*, Minneapolis: University of Minnesota Press.

Mitchell, Koritha (2011), *Living with Lynching: African American Lynching Plays, Performance, and Citizenship, 1890–1930*, Champaign: University of Illinois Press.

Morey, Michael (2019), *Fagen: An African American Renegade in the Philippine-American War*, Madison: University of Wisconsin Press.

Mott, John Luther (1957), *A History of American Magazines: 1885–1905*, Cambridge, MA: Belknap.

Ngozi-Brown, Scot (1997), 'African-American Soldiers and Filipinos: Racial Imperialism, Jim Crow, and Social Relations', *The Journal of Negro History* 82(1): 42–53.

[No title] (1901), *The Freeman*, 14 December, p. 4.

Omi, Michael, and Howard Winant (2015), *Racial Formation in the United States*, 3rd ed., New York: Routledge.

'The Opinions of the Judges' (1905), *Collier's*, 11 February, pp. 13–14.

Rancière, Jacques (2004), *The Politics of Aesthetics*, trans. Gabriel Rockhill, New York: Continuum.

Rockhill, Gabriel (2014), *Radical History and the Politics of Art*, New York: Columbia University Press.

Schleitwiler, Vince (2017), *Strange Fruit of the Black Pacific: Imperialism's Racial Justice and Its Fugitives*, New York: New York University Press.

Shih, Shu-Mei (2008), 'Comparative Racialisation: An Introduction', *PMLA* 123(5): 1347–62.

Stecopoulos, Harilaos (2008), *Reconstructing the World: Southern Fictions and US Imperialisms, 1898–1976*, New York: Cornell University Press.

Thomas, Rowland (1905), 'Fagan', *Collier's*, April.

— (1909a), 'The Little Gods', *Dallas Morning News*, 11 July.

— (1909b), *The Little Gods*, New York: Little, Brown, and Co.

'War in the Philippines' (1899), *Richmond Planet*, 11 November, pp. 1 and 8.

Wesling, Meg (2011), *Empire's Proxy: American Literature and US Imperialism in the Philippines*, New York: NYU Press.

Wong, Edlie L. (2015), *Racial Reconstruction: Black Inclusion, Chinese Exclusion, and the Fictions of Citizenship*, New York: NYU Press.

Wynter, Sylvia (2003), 'Unsettling the Coloniality of Being/Power/Truth/Freedom: Towards the Human, After Man, Its Overrepresentation – An Argument', *CR: The New Centennial Review* 3(3): 257–337.

1. The historical person was David Fagen. His name was sometimes misspelled as 'Fagan' or 'Fagin'.

2. By 'high realism', I refer to Nancy Glazener's analysis of how *Atlantic*-group magazines produced a readerly understanding of realism as a literary form that 'emphasized some combination of philanthropic national citizenship and connoisseurship' (Glazener 1997: 43). While high realism championed 'the common man and woman' as characters in fiction, it disparaged popular aesthetic taste (48).

3. Relatively little information about Fagen exists, but Morey's recent biography (2019), as well as Phillip W. Hoffman's *David Fagen: Turncoat Hero* (2017), reveal much that was previously unknown.

4. I register these rather unpleasant circumstances of intersectional discord not to 'dismiss [Black soldiers] as complicit' or to 'vindicat[e] or condem[n] them as unaware', but rather to clarify the structural dynamics of racialisation in which these historical figures were so often immured. In doing so, I concur with Schleitwiler about the value of 'approach[ing] them as [subjects] caught in a different location within a predicament [we] share, of structural complicity within an imperialism whose power extends in the name of justice' (Schleitwiler 2017: 90).

5. Again, I do not intend to downplay the significance of Fagen's solidarity with the Filipino freedom fighters. Rather, I wish to acknowledge that, as a communal premise, the form of cross-racial solidarity Fagen's actions entailed were practically unavailable to most Black soldiers and to Black Americans, generally. In doing so, I am partly informed by Pheng Cheah's critique of Homi Bhabha's synecdochal preoccupation with colonial migrants in his famous theorisation of transnational, postcolonial hybridity. As Cheah puts it, 'Bhabha's picture of contemporary globalization is virulently postnational because he pays scant attention to those postcolonials for whom postnationalism through mobility is not an alternative' (Cheah 1998: 302).

6. See, for examples, Edlie Wong's *Racial Reconstruction* (2015), Helen Heran Jun's *Race for Citizenship* (2011), Colleen Lye's 'The Afro-Asian Analogy' (2008) and Claire Kim's 'Racial Triangulation of Asian Americans'.

7. See, for examples, Jacques Rancière's *The Politics of Aesthetics* (2004), Beth Hinderliter et al.'s collection *Communities of Sense: Rethinking Aesthetics and Politics* (2009) and Gabriel Rockhill's *Radical History and the Politics of Art* (2014).

8. Rancière argues that 'there is . . . an "aesthetics" at the core of politics', which can be understood as a 'system of a priori forms determining what presents itself to sense experience' (Rancière 2008: 13). He terms this system 'the distribution of the sensible', an always unequal apportionment of seemingly 'self-evident facts of sense perception' that reveal how 'politics revolves around what is seen and what can be said about it, around who has the ability to see and the talent to speak, around the properties of space and the possibilities of time' (12–13).

9. As Meg Wesling points out, this shift is symbolically captured in the repurposing of the US transport ship *Thomas* from carrying troops to carrying 509 American teachers (dubbed 'Thomasites') to the Philippines. 'A highly performative gesture', Wesling observes, 'The arrival of this "educational army" eclipsed Filipinos'

continued struggle for independence against the United States by announcing the finality of American sovereignty in the islands and adopting as charges America's new "little brown brothers"' (106).

10. This transition can be considered a process – albeit an incomplete and inconsistent one – whereby 'hegemonic forms of racial rule – those based on consent – eventually came to supplant those based on coercion' (Omi and Winant 2015: 132). Jodi Melamed provides a distinct but related account of a transition from 'white supremacist modernity' as a dominant racial project in the early twentieth century to a 'formally antiracist, liberal-capitalist modernity', still operating in our present moment (Melamed 2011: 12).

6

WHITE/NOT-WHITE: ROBERT MONTGOMERY BIRD'S RACIAL TRANSFORMATIONS, 1839

HANNAH LAUREN MURRAY

In the middle of Robert Montgomery Bird's *The Adventures of Robin Day* (1839), racial transformation is an unusual yet necessary mode of survival. After deserting the British army during the War of 1812, downwardly mobile Robin reunites with Captain Brown, a pirate who previously tricked him into committing burglary. In order to escape detection and execution, Brown convinces Robin he must masquerade as an East Indian mystic doctor called Chowder Chow whom Brown has enslaved. Knotting Robin's hair, making a turban out of a handkerchief and darkening his complexion with a chunk of damp tobacco, Brown educates Robin on speaking and acting 'Injun' (Bird [1839] 1877: 193).

> 'Harkee, my skilligallee; can you say *Holly-golly-wow*?'
> 'Yes,' replied I, repeating the mystic word, 'but I don't know what it means.'
> 'And *Sammy-ram-ram*?' quoth Captain Brown.
> '*Sammy-ram-ram*,' said I.
> 'Bravo!' said Captain Brown, with another explosion of merriment, 'that will do. Them two words will make a man of you; and hearkee, my hearty, they are the only ones you are to speak. You don't understand English, d'ye see, and speaks only in your native lingo.' (193–4)

Taking on this darkened appearance and invented language, Robin performs orientalist stereotypes of exotic indecipherable intelligence. As the two travel to a Virginia plantation to ply quack medical cures, Robin inhabits a liminal position in the racial hierarchy – not treated the same as the enslaved Black men and women he encounters yet very much no longer White. With his tanned complexion, he blurs the boundaries between White and non-White in racial categorisation. In this novel, racial transformation articulates both the stratification of race as a social category and the feared precarity of Whiteness itself.

In the 1830s, Bird wrote a trio of racial transformation novels – *Sheppard Lee* (1836), *Nick of the Woods* (1837), and *Robin Day* – each of which makes political statements on racial tensions in early national America, and more specifically, White male desires to maintain social and economic power. In *Nick of the Woods*, a peaceful Quaker on the Kentucky frontier transforms into 'The Jibbenainosay', who speaks fluent Shawnee, dresses in 'Indian garments' and scalps Native Americans to avenge the murder of his family (Bird [1837] 1967: 342). Bird celebrates this violence as part of a righteous campaign against 'the barbarities of the savages' and positions Nick's extreme 'metamorphosis' as due to familial trauma (34, 226). He frames Nick's revenge in Indigenous markers to show how far he has fallen from Christian Whiteness due to the Native violence inflicted upon him, and he reflects earlier environmentalist theories that White men could degenerate from life along the frontier. In the more experimental endeavour *Sheppard Lee*, the White protagonist enters the bodies of six recently deceased men and takes on, to varying extents, their personalities, values and behaviours. Bird draws on the prevalent blackface minstrelsy culture around him to dare his readers to identify with and desire Blackness. Sheppard's transformation into childlike and lazy enslaved Tom temporarily offers a respite from the oppressive market economy in the novel, before an abolitionist pamphlet incites a failed slave rebellion that results in Tom's execution. The prospect of rapid physical movement from one body to another articulates the fear of unstable social movement and a growing politically active Black population outnumbering and subjugating White Americans.

In *Sheppard Lee*, medically trained Bird employs racial metempsychosis in part to probe mind-body dualism and understand the root of individual consciousness. By 1839, his views on race had hardened: he was no longer interested in the psychological questions of racial interiority but still committed to employing racial transformation to show Whiteness under threat. The 'Injun' transformation Robin undergoes aids our understanding of race and Whiteness in Bird's fiction in two ways. First, the choice to turn Robin into an Indian mystic indexes thinking about race beyond Black/White and Indigenous/White binaries in the 1830s. Indians were seen as both a grouping or 'family' of similar yet stratified ethnicities along a spectrum within the 'Caucasian Race' and a monolithic population outside Whiteness (Morton 1839: 5). Written in the context of public discussions of the Indian caste system, race becomes more finely delineated and social in the novel as stereotypes of national character dictate social standing and freedoms.

Second, Robin's transformation reinforces anxieties in Bird's fiction that White men could be oppressed akin to – and by – people of colour in the United States. In writing episodes of racial crossing, Bird formulates a metamorphic Whiteness in which one could become less-than-White. Fears of losing Whiteness and its attendant rights are palpable throughout the text. In appropriating the language and bodies of slavery, Robin's temporary loss of Whiteness emphasises pressing anxieties of White precarity and marginalisation in the new nation. In other words, *Robin Day* imagines that White men are the real slaves in the early US. Racial transformation exaggerates the empathic possibility of fiction to cross racial boundaries and imagine the experience of others across the colour line. However, in *Robin Day*, temporary enslavement does not call for empathy towards the enslaved but rather towards a lower-status white man without financial or social capital who is continually at risk of losing his autonomy. Texts such as Bird's transform White citizens into less-than-White noncitizens to consider how Whiteness can be lost rather than just gained. Reading with a critical Whiteness lens, Bird's writing shows a genealogy for emboldened White supremacy in the contemporary moment that voices its anxieties through the language of loss and oppression.

Critical Whiteness studies employs three modes of the 'critical': one, to draw attention to Whiteness as a site of critique; two, to criticise structures of Whiteness in an anti-racist framework; and three, which I return to at the end of the essay, to be critical – both necessary and urgent – to our understanding of how Whiteness operates and dominates today. The initial aim of critical Whiteness studies, put forward by Black writers such as W. E. B. Du Bois, James Baldwin, Audre Lorde and bell hooks, has been to invert the expectation that Whiteness – and male Whiteness specifically – is the invisible yet expected default position in society against which all other groups stand out, particularly Black people. But Whiteness is not an absence of identity and this default abstraction is a form of identity politics itself. Whiteness is not an innate biological condition, but a social construct: not simply phenotype, but 'a way of "doing identity"' (Levine-Rasky 2013: 18). To appear as unmarked, when all other groups are marked (by race, gender, disability, sexuality) is still a distinct category. George Yancy isolates Whiteness in *Look, a White!*, arguing that making Whiteness visible 'returns to white people the problem of whiteness' so they can recognise the social and material conditions that produce Whiteness as an identity, conditions already visible to – and understood by – non-White groups (Yancy 2012: 6).

The socially marginalised non-White body has long been understood as a negative counterpoint to enfranchised White male citizenship in nineteenth-century America: a hyper-visible example of dependency, irrationality and brutishness compared to the autonomous, rational and respectable model White male citizen (Morrison 1992; Castronovo 2001; Dayan 2011). Whiteness depends on this negative example in order to unite and privilege those who perform desired personal and civic values and exclude those who appear to deviate from or fail to demonstrate them. The cohesive power and protection of Whiteness is a '"straightening" device' that makes bodies 'line up' to show and share expected behaviours – to be like everyone else who appears White (Ahmed 2007: 159). It is a shifting social category that expands or contracts in different contexts, therefore placing individuals along and outside its limens. In the nineteenth century, people could be considered not White despite appearing so: Germans, the Irish, Italians, Eastern Europeans and Jews gradually become White through changing attitudes that non-Anglo populations could possess White-coded values (Jacobson 1999). At the same time, rural and poor White groups were described as 'not quite white' for lacking respectability and industriousness (Wray 2006). As a result, these groups have often lost their Whiteness in literature of the early US, pushed closer to the physical and behavioural descriptors of non-White groups.

Critical Whiteness studies has often focused on the construction and maintenance of Whiteness, but has paid less attention to the reverse, that if Whiteness can be established or bestowed on groups, then its loss or removal can be threatened. Episodes of racial transformation in early US fiction are not just a commentary on the stereotyped non-White groups that White characters masquerade as, but also speak to the precarity of Whiteness itself. The temporary performance of non-White groups in these texts is not White men standing in for those groups, but rather the possibility that White men could lose hold on a valued social position and be treated as if they were no longer White. These episodes make visible through the metamorphosed body a larger figurative concern in early US fiction in which White authors use the language of loss, exclusion and degradation to express fears of social precarity for White men. Many early US authors are preoccupied with how citizens are at risk of returning to subjects. In Bird's work, and specifically *Robin Day*, physical racial transformation is an embodied expression of a cultural anxiety that in a turbulent and exploitative economy, White men could lose the rights of Whiteness and become less-than-White noncitizens.

'SHIVER MY TIMBERS, HE'S A MAGI!': ROBIN DAY'S INDIAN TRANSFORMATION

Circulating through Philadelphia, Southern plantations, the frontier and the Gulf Coast, Robin Day appears in a number of guises across profession, class and race; he transitions between indentured child servant, young middle-class gentleman, soldier, 'Hindoo' mystic and pirate. In this picaresque novel, Bird draws on stereotypes found in early US performance culture. Shortly after training as a physician, he turned to playwriting in 1827. Both his tragedies and comedies feature stock characters along lines of race, nationality, profession and class. Furthermore, he wrote roles in which racial transformation was expected. In *The Gladiator* (1831), *Oralloosa* (1832) and *The Broker of Bogota* (1834), the central characters are less-than-White historical heroic figures safely removed from contemporary racial issues. Edwin Forrest's tanned and muscular Spartacus in *The Gladiator* was an exotic figure on the stage: a violent enslaved man with a swarthy appearance, yet one who spoke with both eloquence and raw power.[1] While this dramatic portrayal was intended to foster White audience sympathy with a racially ambiguous Other, Bird's unpublished *The City Looking Glass* (1828) makes race hyper-visible for comic effect. In one scene a character is tricked into escorting a veiled Black woman, who reveals her face to his horror and the audience's amusement (Bird [1828] 1933: 43). As in many Yankee comedies, Bird envisaged that the White actor would use burnt cork and lard to transform themselves: one of the beginnings of blackface minstrelsy. In *Sheppard Lee*, the supernatural plot device of metempsychosis enables Bird to turn the performance of blackface minstrelsy into real and complete racial transformation.

Rather than burnt cork and lard, in *Robin Day* Captain Brown resorts to 'moistened tobacco' to disguise Robin as Chowder Chow, and he instructs him to perform as a mystical doctor and utter nonsense to impersonate Indian speech (Bird [1839] 1877: 191). A fascination with Indian performance culture can be found in 1830s newspaper pieces on jugglers, magicians and mystics. Several accounts of disappearance and replacement tricks evince 'the powers of deception to which the race of jugglers has attained' (*Star and Banner* 1839). Bird draws on this popular perception of Indian culture in the novel. When a stranger asks Captain Brown, 'where did you come by him?', the pirate responds:

> 'You've heard tell of them Magi breed? – the great wise fellers in the Injies, that knows all things – can eat fire, chaw swords, find money, read the stars, raise the devil, cure the consumption and draw rum out of a beer-barrel. Well, shiver my timbers, he's a Magi!' (Bird [1839] 1877: 197)

Bird's characters collapse specific national cultures into a homogeneous orientalist Other, extending from the Ottoman Empire to East Asia. We see this in Brown's naming Robin 'Chowder Chow', a Sinophobic epithet, yet asking him to perform as a 'Maji', a Persian term. The Feverage siblings, adult children of the plantation owner, further conflate India and the Near East. The brother groups 'all the East Indians' as belonging to 'a kind of half-man, half-monkey family', whereas the sister replies, 'I thought all the Oriental people were handsome, like the princes we read of in the Arabian Nights' (220). Bird balances specific popular understanding of Indian performance culture with broader amalgamation of ethnicities that sat outside the Black/White dichotomy in the early US.

Bird's choice of racial type in the novel is apt commentary on the construction of race and socio-racial relations in the period. The Feverage siblings attempt to comprehend race in a hierarchical system in which inhabitants of India occupied a broad and often contradictory position, shifting between pale and dark, educated, aristocratic and beautiful, irrational, savage and ugly. Race scientist Samuel George Morton – a 'warm personal friend' of Bird's and colleague at Pennsylvania Medical College – described 'Hindoo' complexion varying 'from an absolute black to a clear and beautiful brunette; but the different shades of olive are predominant' (Foust 1919: 123; Morton 1839: 32). In *Crania Americana* (1839), he portrays the 'Indostanic Family' as a 'half-civilised' group within the broader 'Caucasian Race' shared with groups from Europe, the Caucasus, the Middle East and North Africa (33, 5). They are above the 'Ethiopian' and '[Native] American' races and not fully barbarous due to their focus on education, but not enlightened like (White) Christian nations, due to 'their love of the marvellous', such as snake-charming, sword-swallowing, juggling, magic (33).

White does not appear as a category in Morton's work – only mentioned as an epithet for pale skin or as a colour – but in the early US, as Bird's novel evinces, Whiteness is constructed to attach social meaning to already arbitrary categories. In primarily uniting those from Northern Europe and excluding all others, Whiteness further delineates between groups of people to afford and deny social rights and power based on assumptions of 'physical and moral character' that Morton catalogues (4). Chowder Chow's tanned complexion and nationality cross the boundaries of race as a social categorisation in the United States by existing both between and apart from African Blackness and European Whiteness. He is Caucasian but he is not White. Constructing their backstory, Brown says he purchased Chowder Chow in the East Indies: the Magi is human property yet elevated above the enslaved Black men and women on the Feverage plantation. Initially mistaken as Black, Mr Feverage contends Chowder Chow is 'no common blackey . . . take him to the housekeeper's pantry, and there feed him like a white-man' (217). Robin acknowledges that his fraudulent nationality 'favorably distinguished me from the sons of Africa' and he escapes physical violence and 'slavish occupations' of servitude (227). He is a 'blackey' but not Black; his performance of mystical untranslatable intelligence saves him from complete subjugation but neither his enslavement nor debasement is questioned. As he is 'like a white-man' he sits between Blackness and Whiteness: Black enough in appearance to be purchased, White enough in perceived behaviour to sit apart from the enslaved.

In addition to the construction of an ambiguous foreign racial type that characters try to fit into the American plantation system, the 'Injun' reflects a complicated relationship between social mobility and race in the novel. Although there is no conversation on caste in the novel, Bird writes in the context of cultural conversations on the interrelation between profession, religion, class and appearance in which Americans understood caste, a term inextricable from India. In

Crania Americana, Morton lists the 'four great divisions [. . .] each designed to be isolated and exclusive in all relations' that make up caste in India: Brahmins (priests), Rajahs (soldiers), Vaisya (merchants) and Sudras (slaves) (1839: 35). Morton adds, 'the Brahmins, and perhaps the Kishatriya and Vaisya castes were originally a race of northern conquerors of fair complexion; while the Sudras and other inferior tribes were an aboriginal and darker race' (36–7). Skin colour therefore indicates social category, which cannot be transgressed. In the US, early usage of 'caste' omitted discussion of skin colour to group White Americans in social categories. One magazine article from *The Ariel* in 1829 states:

> [S]ociety in America is divided into castes, as completely as in India . . . The poor do not associate with the rich . . . In India, a person born to a particular caste cannot leave it, without losing his character. In America, every man is respectable who is virtuous, and may expect some day to belong to the highest caste or rank. (Ryan 2017: 207–8)

The writer's optimistic suggestion of social opportunity, in contrast to fixed Indian caste, excludes those enslaved in America and ignores the race-based legal barriers preventing millions achieving a higher rank. Later usages from antislavery and anti-racism writers continued to use India as a negative example, but did make caste racial: both Mary Hayden Green Pike's *Caste* (1856) and Julia C. Collins's *The Curse of Caste* (1865) employ the term to refer to light-skinned African American women prevented from progressing in White society due to *partus sequitur ventrem* and the one-drop rule. Robin's transformation into an Indian sits between both these US interpretations of caste. He suffers the debasement of enslavement because of his temporary skin colour, but throughout the novel his attempts to progress as a White man are also frequently unrewarded by the social mobility the optimistic *Ariel* writer suggests. Robin's improbable masquerade and enslavement is one part of a series of escapades in which he is debased, demeaned and feels less than White. His temporary transformation into a degraded figure of two fixed systems (Indian caste, American chattel slavery) is a hyperbolic episode that employs visible signs of race to mark a lower-status White man's fragile grasp on free White citizenship and its accrued rights.

In these Virginia scenes the novel temporarily turns into a slave narrative as Robin narrates his demeaning enslavement. While he at first suffers the indignation of having to pretend to be enslaved and is 'ashamed' of his appearance, he is soon trapped in the 'horror' of actual bondage (Bird [1839] 1877: 191, 223). Brown absconds from the plantation, selling Chowder Chow to Mr Feverage, who has no problem with purchasing him and putting him to work in the house. Robin faces the dilemma of speaking English to reveal his Whiteness, therefore leading to his arrest for desertion, or continuing to feign ignorance and remaining subject to a life of degradation. He chooses instead to run away, attempting to poison the Feverage family and escape towards the West, to which he attaches the 'ideas of freedom and independence'. The Western states are 'the direction in which no fugitive slave would be believed to bend his steps' as due to the Fugitive Slave Act of 1793 they are only free for the White man, which Robin can easily return to by washing his face (230).

Bird draws on the texts of fugitive slavery as a creative resource; after absconding, Robin sees a newspaper 'offering a reward for the capture of the slave Chowder Chow' under the title 'Stop the Villain', which replicates the language of fugitive adverts (Bird [1839] 1877: 240). However, Bird plays with the slave narrative genre to redirect sympathy away from enslaved African Americans. Slave narratives used first-person voice to emphasise the humanity of the enslaved and encourage identification from sympathetic abolitionist readers across the colour line. As Christopher Castiglia argues, abolitionists such as William Lloyd Garrison spoke of taking on the emotional pain felt by enslaved Black men and women in order to propose 'a way for whites and blacks to merge through the imagination' and share an 'affective "sameness" once the burden of marked bodies is removed' (Castiglia 2008: 124). Episodes of White enslavement in abolitionist literature supported these aims by encouraging White readers to imagine the degradation of enslavement happening to them. In *Picture of Slavery in the United States of America*, George Bourne gives the frightening example of a young White boy 'stolen from his parents . . . tattooed, painted, and tanned' and sold into slavery as a 'non-descript', no longer White American (Bourne 1834: 145). Expanding the threat of enslavement to White Americans who could have their physical Whiteness erased, Bourne encourages his readers to identify with and protest against the suffering of a Black potential citizen. These abolitionist imaginaries of White enslavement privilege White feelings over Black testimony in order to garner support for antislavery movements. Bird too imagines a forced loss of physical Whiteness but has no abolitionist purpose. In *Sheppard Lee*, he dares the reader to identify with the limited psychology of the Black noncitizen of minstrel culture, rather than the potential Black citizen of abolition. In *Robin Day*, he centres White feelings to call attention to the degradation of slavery, but only for his White protagonist. He caricatures the fleeting Black characters on the plantation as lazy frauds; at no point does Robin sympathise with the enslaved men and women on the plantation, nor does Bird ask his readers to. Instead, Bird employs temporary racial crossing and enslavement to emphasise how fragile and precarious Robin's own experience is as a lower-status White man in the early US.

'ALMOST A CITIZEN': WHITE PRECARITY IN *ROBIN DAY*

Although Robin's racial performance is transitory, his accidental enslavement exposes the threat of White subjugation in the new nation. The Indian metamorphosis is the most dramatic and painful transformation in the novel but the fear of White unmaking and degradation is palpable throughout the text. From early in the novel Robin has felt enslaved and the frame of the slave narrative extends beyond his masquerade as Chowder Chow. As a baby, Robin washes up on the shores of New Jersey from a shipwrecked West Indian ship containing slavery's consumables, 'a rich freight of rum and sugar' (Bird [1839] 1877: 10). He is seen as property (an item of 'goods and chattels') by his pirate master and feels as 'his most helpless slave' (13, 14). Following adoption by a middle-class family he flees to Philadelphia as an adolescent after setting fire to his school. On arrival he is mistaken for a runaway servant by an innkeeper who sneers 'they never harboured runaway 'prentices', turning Robin away and leaving him distraught (97). Robin's scruffy appearance signifies he is what Simon Newman calls a 'lower sort' body – a man without property, capital, inheritance or profession who is continually at risk of having his labour extracted and his autonomy robbed (Newman 2003: 8). Throughout the novel, Robin continually takes on new exploited social positions (servant, soldier, slave, pirate) moulded by the scheming figures around him. *Robin Day* is a novel of circulation but not progress – seemingly stripped of self-determination, Robin gets into the same degrading scrapes over and over again, only saved by luck or the beginning of another dangerous scheme. He is always at risk of losing his claim on the rights of Whiteness, whether or not his skin colour changes.

In *Robin Day*, Robin's experience of 'Injun' plantation slavery actualises the figurative language of White slavery in the antebellum period. Lower-status White workers spoke of themselves as experiencing a form of oppression – 'wage slavery' – worse than the life of easy dependence they believed many plantation slaves enjoyed (Roediger 1991: 65–74).[2] In framing themselves as enslaved, White workers emphasised their drudgery yet refused interracial solidarity. Enslaved Black work was a point of contradistinction for White workers: the figurative language of slavery articulated a belief that they suffered yet were racially superior and alone in deserving legal and political rights – rights under threat from a growing politically active Black population in the North. For Bird, co-opting the language of slavery extends beyond manual and mechanical labour to frame all paid work and urban living. In his short story 'A Night on Terrapin Rocks', the narrator seeks to escape 'the slavery of a city life, not to speak of the more intolerable bondage of trade', and 'to throw off my chains' (Bird 1838: 21). By expanding slavery to include White citizens who are legally free, yet constrained by economic or social conditions, Bird articulates a White privilege that clings onto assumptions of superiority while claiming oppression.

Encounters of disrespect and degradation where White figures treat him as less than White demonstrate Robin's precarity, but his encounters with non-White groups specifically emphasise these dual feelings of subjugation and superiority. The darkening of Robin's skin while 'Injun' places him outside Whiteness but treatment by non-white figures completes and compounds the racial transformation even when Robin is not masquerading. On the streets of Philadelphia, the 'almost a citizen' Robin is knocked about by free Black porters who shout at him, 'Git out of *my* way, will you?' Angered by the arrogance of the 'true aristocracy of the town', Robin is equally astounded by the 'general submissiveness' of genteel White citizens who meekly submit to the porters' yells (Bird [1839] 1877: 90). This seemingly small incident of jostling and shouting invokes such strength of feeling that the memory returns when Robin is later captured by Cherokee while fighting under Jackson. The same 'indignation and grief' emerge as when in Philadelphia; Robin recalls 'my adventures with the negroes in the streets of Philadelphia' when forced to run the Cherokee gauntlet (266–7). Bird articulates a potent anxiety of replacement: Black people acting as White free men; White free men subjugated and threatened with violence.

Concerned over rises in the Black demographic, with a pathological focus Bird considers the threat of Black power and the loss of White freedom in his personal notes. In one such note circa 1840, he calculates that the Black population could number at least '10 of 66 millions!!' by 1900 (Robert Montgomery Bird Papers f 305). Contending in a letter to his brother that 'there should be no negroes in the country' after emancipation, he formulates a plan for a domestic colony. Firmly segregationist, Bird argues that freed men and women should be transported past the Rocky Mountains and governed by a White head of state, putting up geographical borders to replace the existing political barriers to Black suffrage. When the population are able 'to take care of themselves' in a few generations, America should grant this colony independence and set a 'treaty of eternal amity'. Concluding the letter, Bird wonders if it 'would be easier or more effectual . . . to murder 'em all', revealing the extent to which he saw Black social mobility jeopardising the freedom, prosperity and even convenience of the White population (Robert Montgomery Bird Papers f 296).[3]

In *Robin Day*, 'Hindoo' racial performance and the slave narrative are modes not interested in interiority across the colour line or abolition, but rather the status of White male citizens. Episodes of blackening bolster rather than diminish claims on Whiteness for White men. Robin's journey into and out of states of enslavement strengthens his sense of entitlement to freedom, autonomy and prosperity, evinced by a neat conclusion in which he marries his estranged wealthy love and finds 'peace, and affluence, and happiness under my roof' (Bird [1839] 1877: 370). These are Robin's adventures – the plot has provided excitement for the reader in passing through numerous settings and scrapes before ending in traditional wealth transfer and social stability. Bird's novel articulates a particular strand of White privilege – the ability to temporarily imagine oppression in order to reclaim a centre that was never lost.

Fears of no longer being White permeate Bird's fiction, and these are ideas that re-emerge in the contemporary moment. Whiteness and male Whiteness has its own identity politics, which when under pressure rests on perceived victimhood as a result of increased rights for White women, people of colour, the LGBTQ+ community. We can see this most recently in the language of Trump's acolytes such as former Maine governor Paul LePage. On the possibility that the US could abolish the electoral college, LePage commented the change would make him and other White Americans 'a forgotten people':

> 'Actually what would happen if they do what they say they're gonna do is white people will not have anything to say . . . It's only going to be the minorities that would elect. It would be California, Texas, Florida.' (Riga 2019)

This language is a continuation of antebellum anxieties that White men could be subjugated to the tyranny of socially mobile Black men in the North and rebellious enslaved men in the South. Echoing the demographic concerns that Bird raises in his personal notes, LePage fears the rise of Latinx American populations in the South and West of the nation. Furthermore, White people become the minority themselves, a twenty-first century 'vanishing Indian' – erased not through expansionist violence but through a democratic process that would more accurately reflect American citizens. The prospect of equality is presented as oppression.

Forgotten, lost, silenced – in this figurative language of oppression and violence, some White Americans feel similarly to Robin Day jostled and denigrated on the streets of Philadelphia. Repeatedly the fear of being treated as a minority, whether in the nineteenth or twenty-first century, finds form in the language of White exclusion, subjugation and replacement. These are not new narratives, and the victimhood language of contemporary White supremacy is a continuum not an aberration, but the resurgence and prominence of this language is why critical Whiteness studies is of urgent importance to nineteenth-century American Studies today, both in our research and teaching. A return to White authors that foregrounds Whiteness as an identitarian site of concern – expressed through literal and figurative erasures of Whiteness – rather than an absence or abstraction will help scholars to confront the genealogy for contemporary White supremacist imaginaries in early US fiction.

Works Cited

Ahmed, Sara (2007), 'A Phenomenology of Whiteness', *Feminist Theory* 8(2): 149–68.
Bird, Robert Montgomery (1838), *Peter Pilgrim: Or A Rambler's Recollections*, 2 vols, Philadelphia: Lea & Blanchard, II.
— [1839] (1877), *The Adventures of Robin Day*, New York: John Polhemus.

— [1828] (1933), *The City Looking Glass*, ed. Arthur Hobson Quinn, New York: The Colophon.

— [1837] (1967), *Nick of the Woods or The Jibbenainosay: A Tale of Kentucky*, ed. Curtis Dahl, Albany: New College and University Press, Inc.

— [1836] (2008), *Sheppard Lee: Written by Himself*, ed. Christopher Looby, New York: New York Review of Books.

Castiglia, Christopher (2008), *Interior States: Institutional Consciousness and the Inner Life of Democracy in the Antebellum United States*, Durham, NC: Duke University Press.

Castronovo, Russ (2001), *Necro Citizenship: Death, Eroticism, and the Public Sphere in the Nineteenth-Century United States*, Durham, NC: Duke University Press.

Dayan, Colin (2011), *The Law Is a White Dog: How Legal Rituals Make and Unmake Persons*, Princeton and Oxford: Princeton University Press.

'Extraordinary and Thrilling Feat of an Indian Juggler' (1839), *Star and Banner*, 29 July 1839.

Foust, Clement E. (1919), *The Life and Dramatic Works of Robert Montgomery Bird*, New York: The Knickerbocker Press.

Jacobson, Matthew Frye (1999), *Whiteness of a Different Color: European Immigrants and the Alchemy of Race*, Cambridge, MA, and London: Harvard University Press.

Levine-Rasky, Cynthia (2013), *Whiteness Fractured*, Abingdon: Ashgate.

Morrison, Toni (1992), *Playing in the Dark: Whiteness and the Literary Imagination*, Cambridge, MA: Harvard University Press.

Morton, Samuel George (1839), *Crania Americana: Or a Comparatif View of the Skulls of Various Aboriginal Nations of North and South America*, Philadelphia: J. Dobson.

Newman, Simon P. (2003), *Embodied History: The Lives of the Poor in Early Philadelphia*, Philadelphia: University of Pennsylvania Press.

Riga, Kate (2019), 'LePage: Eliminating Electoral College Would Make Whites "A Forgotten People"', *Talking Points Memo*, 28 February 2019, <https://talkingpoints memo.com/news/lepage-eliminating-electoral-college-whites-forgotten-people> (accessed 19 May 2020).

Robert Montgomery Bird Papers (1799–1946), Kislak Center for Special Collections, Rare Books and Manuscripts, University of Pennsylvania, Philadelphia.

Roediger, David R. (1991), *The Wages of Whiteness: Race and the Making of the American Working Class*, London: Verso.

Ryan, Susan M. (2017), 'India and U.S. Cultures of Reform: Caste as Keyword', in Anupama Arora and Rajender Kaur (eds), *India in the American Imaginary, 1780s–1880s*, Basingstoke: Palgrave Macmillan, pp. 199–227.

Wray, Matt (2006), *Not Quite White: White Trash and the Boundaries of Whiteness*, Durham, NC: Duke University Press.

Yancy, George (2012), *Look, a White! Philosophical Essays on Whiteness*, Philadelphia: Temple University Press.

Notes

1. Nevertheless, writing the play during Nat Turner's revolt in the summer of 1831, Bird was aware of its abolitionist connotations. He notes in his 29 August diary

entry, 'If *The Gladiator* were produced in a slave state, the managers, players, and perhaps myself in the bargain, would be rewarded in the Penitentiary!' (Robert Montgomery Bird Papers f 182).

2. Jim Jumble in *Sheppard Lee* is the clearest example of the perceived ease of enslavement in Bird's work. Offered emancipation by Sheppard at the beginning of the novel, he refuses because he knows 'the difference between living, on the one hand, a lazy life, without any care whatever, as my slave, and, on the other, labouring hard to obtain a precious subsistence as a free man' (Bird [1836] 2008: 20).

3. In another segregationist letter to John C. Groome in January 1837, an anxious Bird declares that the possibility of Black suffrage in Pennsylvania 'sharpens my desire to be off' (Robert Montgomery Bird Papers f 62).

7

ECOLOGY/RADICAL POLITICS: THOREAU'S SCIENCE OF CIVIL DISOBEDIENCE, 1849

MICHAEL JONIK

'Climate disorders are a vice inherent to civilized culture.'
Charles Fourier, *De la deterioration materielle de la planete*

'I am concerned to trace the effects of my allegiance.'
Thoreau, 'Resistance to Civil Government'

'The dissident . . . witnesses to the impossibility of continuing to obey.'
Frederic Gros, *Disobey!* (2020: 142–3)

INTRODUCTION

The radical politics of 'civil disobedience' which Henry David Thoreau advocates in his essay 'Resistance to Civil Government' (1849), and the ecological philosophy of *Walden* and his natural historical writings have each energised generations of scholars and activists. Yet, while often taken as separate aspects of Thoreau's work, the time is propitious to reconsider how Thoreau's calls to individual action in his anti-war and antislavery writings might be understood in tandem with the onto-ethics of relation, materialism and agency in his ecological work. What is at stake here is how such a 'crossing' between Thoreau's radical politics and ecology might afford new possibilities for individual and collective resistance, new modes of informed conducts of living, and a new concept of interactive responsibility past the constraints of liberal theorisations of justice.

The time is now! Environmental activists from Greenpeace to Extinction Rebellion understand civil disobedience as a necessary tactic both to disrupt the hegemonic forces of corporate capitalism that drive ecological degradation, and to fight for environmental justice for humans and nonhumans alike. The banner of civil disobedience has been raised over nonviolent acts of blocking access to fracking sites and forest protection, mass climate dissidence, as well as more openly combative acts of ecotage, property destruction and outright violent struggle. According to the *Guardian*, violent reprisals against ecological civil disobedience have reached a tragically high number in 2019, with 212 environmental activists murdered for defending the land against the degradations caused by agribusiness and resource extraction.[1] At the same time, although the Thoreau-inspired modes of resistance made famous by Gandhi and Martin Luther King Jr were oriented against colonialist and racist oppression, recent invocations of ecological civil disobedience have less often allied themselves with the cause of ending modern slavery. This is despite the fact that, first, it is antislavery and anti-war action that impels Thoreau's initial conception of civil disobedience and, second, an increasing body of research has asserted that climate-driven migration and the often violent conditions of resource extraction have exacerbated forms of forced labour, exploitation, debt bondage, sexual violence, detention and human trafficking. What is at stake is justice!

While addressing these issues would go well beyond the scope of this essay, I propose a Thoreauvian 'science of civil disobedience' that brings together his radical politics of resistance and abolition with his environmental ethics. First, contrary to the long tradition of reading Thoreau's civil disobedience as predicated on individual conscience, I argue that the term 'individual' in his work already implies a relational, 'transindividual' subjectivity in which action is only possible with and within the collectivities that form it and which traverse it. Individual action for Thoreau is always already interaction. Second, I extend his notion of a relational, divided conscience to *Walden*'s call for an 'intelligence with the earth' as core to Thoreau's political ecology. This would be 'an earth-conscience' that figures a relational ontology of collective agency as the ground of its ethics and politics. Here, I draw on and critique recent new materialist work on Thoreau, which explores understandings of agency as collective, distributed and inclusive of non-human actants, in order to reframe the act of individual political resistance. Thoreau's natural historical work, I argue, not only complements the concept of civil disobedience but reveals another dimension to its radical imperatives which can energise emergent ecological counter-conducts. Finally, I suggest that Thoreau's model for a performative, destabilising and interactive earth politics – centred on understanding the extent of one's own relationality and oriented towards the question of justice – not only informs his antebellum abolitionism, but can provide a model for thinking how to resist the complicities of environmental degradation and modern slavery in the present.

ACTION FROM PRINCIPLE AND THE EXTENT OF OUR RELATIONS

Civil disobedience has long been understood as an act of resistance undertaken by a rational, autonomous individual who decides on the basis of conscience.[2] Yet, in 'Resistance to Civil Government', Thoreau already asserts that the individual itself is divided in the act: 'Action from principle – the perception and the performance of right, – changes things and relations; it is essentially revolutionary, and does not consist wholly in any thing which was. It not only divides states and churches, it divides families; aye, it divides the *individual*, separating the diabolical in him from the divine' (Thoreau 1973: 72). 'Action from principle' is transformative and divisive. It involves enacting an understanding of justice that goes against the doxa, against conformity, against the state and church, or directly against others, even if it entails breaking the law, breaking up a family or risking violence. It separates us from ourselves insofar as it throws into relief which of our conflicting imperatives are oriented towards the right or have possessed us and led us to malevolence. As civil disobedience is not premised on a static understanding of the individual, neither is it premised on an individual conscience. Indeed, conscience is always already divisive, or is the dividing force at the centre of ourselves. Even in usual parlance, our conscience puts us at odds with ourselves. As Augustine writes, 'I have become a question to myself' (Augustine 2006: 217).

Conscience entails a self-scrutiny that upholds or denies prospective acts. It might impel us to ethical or 'moral' action, to hold the banner of the *summum bonum*; or it might decry our vices and doggedly pursue us, so many William Wilsons. In Heidegger's conceptual vocabulary, conscience is a call to 'care' for the world, an anticipatory resoluteness to 'authentically' comport ourselves towards the world and to our own finitude. It is a silent and directionless 'call' to recognise ourselves as finite beings amidst the ubiquity of the finite: our being-in-the-world. Even without taking up the mantle of Heidegger's ontological project, or with it the 'jargon of authenticity', conscience marks our becoming tangled in relations. For Thoreau, civil disobedience on the basis of conscience is likewise self-divisive, separating the diabolical from the divine.[3]

While he does employ the idealist/metaphysical language of higher laws, conscience for Thoreau is relentlessly oriented towards everyday practical justice. And, while he asserts the force of individual principled action against the state, the individual in Thoreau's conceptual vocabulary does not mean a lone autonomous subjectivity, but calls for a 'corporation of conscientious men' to pit themselves against the majority in the name of justice: 'But a government in which the majority rule in all cases cannot be based on justice, even as far as men understand it. [. . .] It is truly enough said that a corporation has no conscience; but a corporation of conscientious men is a corporation with a conscience. Law never made men a whit more just; and, by means of their respect for it, even the well-disposed are daily made the agents of injustice' (64–5). Both conscience and individual are given to their relations, self-divisions, allegiances and complicities. The division of the individual entails a new understanding of conscience which, if shorn of its ontotheological baggage, could name the awareness of the collectivities which form us and in which we participate. For Thoreau, political action, as both the perception and performance of right, is both a recognition of relations *and* an interruption or revolution in relations so that new relations can be made. Action from principle necessarily leads to a rethinking of how we perceive the world and the relations in which we are enmeshed. Thoreau articulates this question of relationality in his famous discussion of the effects of his 'allegiance' implicit in the act of refusing to pay his tax:

> I have never declined paying the highway tax, because I am as desirous of being a good neighbor as I am of being a bad subject; and, as for supporting schools, I am doing my part to educate my fellow-countrymen now. It is for no particular item in the tax-bill that I refuse to pay it. I simply wish to refuse allegiance to the State, to withdraw and stand aloof from it effectually. I do not care to trace the course of my dollar, if I could, till it buys a man, or a musket to shoot one with, – the dollar is innocent, – but I am concerned to trace the effects of my allegiance. (Thoreau 1973: 84)

Thoreau's 'quiet war with the State' is not declared in the name of a libertarian individualism if we take seriously that it is based on the political act of tracing the effects of his allegiance. His act of resistance is an act of withdrawing his allegiance such that he does not 'abet injustice'. The dollar itself is innocent. But as long as it supports a systemic injustice, there can be no justice; there can be no justice, that is, without understanding the collectivities in which we participate and rooting out even our indirect or distant complicities. His anti-war, antislavery message is meant thus to hit home:

> Practically speaking, the opponents to a reform in Massachusetts are not a hundred thousand politicians at the South, but a hundred thousand merchants and farmers here, who are more interested in commerce and agriculture than they are in humanity, and are not prepared to do justice to the slave and to Mexico, *cost what it may*. I quarrel not with far-off foes, but with those who, near at home, co-operate with, and do the bidding of those far away, and without whom the latter would be harmless. (68)

Thoreau's anti-war, antislavery stance is oriented against the economic conveniences for which people compromise their humanity. He quarrels not with the slave owners themselves, but with the merchants and farmers of Massachusetts who support the injustices of slavery through their cooperation with, which is to say non-resistance to, the slave system. Thoreau's formula for resistance, then, is 'to see . . . that I do not lend myself to the wrong which I condemn' (74). This formula is not merely a critique of the hypocrisies of his contemporaries, but underscores that the individual is always already a transindividual subject formed of relations, and given to the problem of dwelling-with.

As action from principle is self-dividing, it also entails the risk of a revolutionary loss of self. As Thoreau emphasises in *Walden*, to realise the 'extent' of our relations requires we lose ourselves: 'Not till we are lost, in other words not till we have lost the world, do we begin to find ourselves, and realize where we are and the infinite extent of our relations' (Thoreau 2004: 171). At the core of Thoreau's politics of resistance is, perhaps counterintuitively, not individual action but the division and disorientation of the individual through which one's relationality is made legible to oneself. In this context, in *Walden*, Thoreau recounts his famous night in jail:

> One afternoon, near the end of the first summer, when I went to the village to get a shoe from the cobbler's, I was seized and put into jail, because, as I have elsewhere related, I did not pay a tax to, or recognize the authority of, the state which buys and sells men, women, and children, like cattle at the door of its senate-house. I had gone down to the woods for other purposes. But wherever a man goes, men will pursue and paw him with their dirty institutions, and, if they can, constrain him to belong to their desperate odd-fellow society. (2004: 171)

Thoreau recalls this story here to trace the extent of his relations and, as in 'Resistance to Civil Government', to test that he does not partake in allegiances that might abet injustice. On this basis, he does not recognise the authority of the state, which for him is nullified by its unjust support for slavery: it is a government which buys and sells people like cattle at the door of its senate house. But what is also to be resisted is the form of power through which the state over-codes the system of relations: such that its 'dirty institutions' 'pursue and paw' individuals wherever they go. To resist (and here Thoreau is careful to note he could have resisted forcibly but did not) is to disallow oneself to be 'molested' by the state.

Here, 'Resistance to Civil Government' is in direct dialogue with Emerson's essay 'Politics', which makes a strong case for how the state, as 'founded on force', might be resisted by individual action. As Emerson writes, in phrases clearly reworked by Thoreau: 'Hence, the less government we have, the better, – the fewer laws, and the less confided power. The antidote to this abuse of formal Government, is, the influence of private character, the growth of the Individual; the appearance of the principal to supersede the proxy; the appearance of the wise man, of whom the existing government, is, it must be owned, but a shabby imitation' (Emerson 1983: 126). While Emerson privileges the individual as the 'antidote' to state power, it is important to remember that for both him and Thoreau the 'individual' does not signify a static or discrete subjectivity or personhood. The individual is not a cipher for selfishness, as 'there will always be a government of force, where men are selfish' (128). Rather, the individual is a figure for an open-ended process of moral perfectionism, and therefore a conduit for a 'moral sentiment' which undoes selfishness and empowers radical responsibility. The moral sentiment divides the individual from 'all party' and, in so doing, reconnects the individual to 'all humanity'. Emerson calls for one with 'sufficient faith in the power of rectitude, to inspire him with the broad design of renovating the State on the principle of right and love' (128).

In 'Resistance to Civil Government', Thoreau answers Emerson's call to deny the authority of law on the basis of the practising of the moral sentiment. Thoreau's action from principle prompts us to reconsider the interrelation of civil laws, ethical laws and natural laws – and of course the 'higher laws' that for him guide each of these. This interrelation of civil, ethical and natural law finds its philosophical precedent in Stoicism insofar as it suggests continuities between concepts of nature, everyday life and an ethics of self-cultivation. But what is key to Thoreau's politics of conscience is less its metaphysical ground in a higher law than the tracing of relation that, as he details in *Walden*, drives his attempt to 'live deliberately' and to 'front the essential facts of life'. This is because the essential facts of life – how one feeds, clothes and shelters oneself – are themselves functions of material relations, relations with hidden or buried complicities. As such, the function of Thoreau's home economics in *Walden* is to trace where he gets his food (eating locally, planting his own beans); where he gets the materials to make his house (buying out and reusing the materials from the shanty of James Collins and family, or the tools he borrows to build it), or where he gets his clothes (rejecting clothes made of cotton which was once picked using slave labour or milled in a Lowell factory which exploits its workers). Apropos the latter, he writes: 'I cannot believe that our factory system is the best mode by which men may get clothing. The condition of the operatives is becoming every day more like that of the English; and it cannot be wondered at, since, as far as I have heard or observed, the principal object is, not that mankind may be well and honestly clad, but, unquestionably, that corporations may be enriched' (2016: 27). In short, Thoreau has us ask ourselves if the maintenance of our 'vital warmth' aids or is inimical to a just society. From this perspective, civil disobedience happens not just in discrete acts of protest, but in disobediences to the conformities and unjust allegiances which suffuse our daily lives.

Justice for Thoreau is the practical effect of living a life *with* principle and a life *with* others. Justice is not an end in itself. It is performative, relational and contingent. The law, by contrast, is an 'agent of injustice' when it facilitates even the well-disposed to act against themselves and others. One might disobey in order to counter the intolerability of personal relations; but only when one becomes an agent of injustice does Thoreau advise breaking the law. Breaking the law for just reasons undoes the system of unjust relations. As civil disobedience implies a collective act, the scene of resistance is the mass withdrawal of allegiance. Justice, then, is only possible through a collective action of conscience, or the formation of a corporation of conscientious persons. For Thoreau this leads to a 'peaceable revolution':

> If a thousand men were not to pay their tax-bills this year, that would not be a violent and bloody measure, as it would be to pay them, and enable the State to commit violence and shed innocent blood. This is, in fact, the definition of a peaceable revolution, if any such is possible. If the tax-gatherer, or any other public officer, asks me, as one has done, 'But what shall I do?' my answer is, 'If you really wish to do any thing, resign your office'. When the subject has refused allegiance, and the officer has resigned his office, then the revolution is accomplished. But even suppose blood should flow. Is there not a sort of blood shed when the conscience is wounded? Through this wound a man's real manhood and immortality flow out, and he bleeds to an everlasting death. I see this blood flowing now. (1973: 76–7)

In answer to Chernyshevsky's question 'What is to be done?', Thoreau would have us kill the messenger. The messenger, in the form of the tax-man, or in the form of any representative of an unjust state, must resign and therefore withdraw allegiance. A thousand people withdrawing their allegiance foments a peaceable revolution. Even if violence would occur (and Thoreau will support John Brown's righteous violence), it is better that blood flows than injustice be allowed to continue unchecked. What is to be done? Withdraw your allegiance.

If action from principle changes things and relations, in turn, the task of conscience is to constantly rethink the collectivities in which we participate, and to cultivate an interactive and just politics of dwelling-with. Action from principle invokes a broad ecology of relations. The scene of 'individual' action is at once divided, rendered heterogeneous, extended and multiplied. The choice, then, is never between action and inaction. All action is *interaction*. There is no inaction per se, as we are always already entangled and formed by relations, the extent to which we may be hardly aware. Interaction instead becomes a life-labour of finding ever novel ways of realising the extent of our relations in world that is indeterminate and volatile, plural and wild. As individuals divided by action from principle, it is also to find ways to reconfigure the grid of our relations, and thus the grid of the possible, such that incipient events cannot be appropriated by the state for the state's ends. What is to be done? 'Let your life be a counter friction to stop the machine' (1973: 73–4).

EARTH-CONSCIENCE

Proposing 'a science of civil disobedience' prompts us to situate Thoreau's 'Resistance to Civil Government', as well as his other political works like 'Slavery in Massachusetts' or 'A Plea for Captain John Brown', in the broader context of his work on natural history and ecology. It is to understand these together with the politics of the earth that emerges from *A Week on the Concord and Merrimack Rivers* and *Walden*, with their sustained meditations on nature and the ethics of everyday life, to his natural history essays, journals and letters. Thoreau's ecological work reveals a political dimension to resistance pertinent to today's heated debates over global climate change, energy, sustainability, species extinction and biodiversity. To begin with, in 'Ktaadin', written about the same time (1846–7), Thoreau again renders the individual subject as divided and relational. When faced with 'primeval, untamed, and forever untameable *Nature*', with an earth 'made out of Chaos and Old Night', he remarks, 'I stand in awe of my body, this matter to which I am bound has become strange to me' (Thoreau 1972: 69, 70). He finds himself in a place 'to be inhabited by men nearer of kin to the rocks and wild animals than we' (71). Contact with the inhuman force of nature becomes *ek-static*, a standing outside of himself, such that he is estranged from his own body. For Robert D. Richardson, the juxtaposition of 'Resistance to Civil Government' to 'Ktaadin' shows that Thoreau's call to political resistance on the basis of individual conscience is 'balanced' by a dissolution of individuality when confronted with the inhuman force of nature (Richardson 1986: 183).

But rather than merely balancing individual conscience, a dissolved or relational (in)dividuality can serve as the basis for politics of dwelling-with. If in 'Resistance to Civil Government', the action and performance of right changes relations and perceptions, across Thoreau's work, terms like 'perception' and 'relation' inscribe modes of dwelling-with into broader scientific or ecological significances. Thoreau develops an ecological perception across his career, which becomes manifest in a series of nonanthropocentric figures and collectivities of natural relations. Paradigmatically, as he asks in *Walden*, 'Shall I not have intelligence with the earth? Am I not partly leaves and vegetable mould myself?' (Thoreau 2004: 138). Having intelligence *with* the earth, is to configure ourselves – and our perceptions – as interlinked into a network of earth processes and non-human intelligences, including plant intelligence. To have intelligence with the earth is disorienting or estranging, as one's human subjectivity is de-privileged. This is less a metaphysical or poetic loss of self, than for

Thoreau a way to think the interactive network or a web of collective agencies we inhabit and which inhabit us, such that each action transforms the other actors and actions. Thoreau's work could be said to catalogue such interactive transformations, an archive of instants of 'withness'.

With such moments in mind, Bennett takes Thoreau as a touchstone to develop her new materialist political ecology. In *Thoreau's Nature: Ethics, Politics, and the Wild* she finds Thoreau to 'slip across the border of nature and self, to achieve a moment of contact, even intimacy, with that which is wild and non-human'. She finds Thoreau to be a 'part and parcel of nature' (Bennett 1994: 108). In *Vibrant Matter*, Bennett unfolds how Thoreau's notion of the wild plays an important role for how she conceives of thing-power. Wildness denotes the process of losing ourselves in or to the plural world of inhuman relations, it is the othering force of the inhuman that 'addles or alters' human and non-human bodies (Bennett: 2010: 2). And again, in *Influx and Efflux: Writing Up with Walt Whitman*, Thoreau's figures of intelligence with the earth inform her onto-ethics:

> If we were to expand upon Thoreau's half-winking claim that his inner mould has 'intelligence' with vegetal kin living abroad, we might describe what happened that delicious evening as a *trans-species nod*. This is not the intersubjective recognition pursued by Hegel, wherein two human individuals become self-conscious of themselves in the process of recognizing 'themselves as mutually recognizing that the other being is, like itself, more than an object in its capacity to reflect upon its own existences'. We would have here instead a species-crossing acknowledgement that gives witness not to shared personhood but to asubjective affinities between resonant materials. The 'recognition' is more like heliophile than an inter-human recognition initiated and enacted in psyches. (Bennett 2020: 100)

This moment of 'species crossing acknowledgment' is not reterritorialised into an interhuman, intersubjective relation or a Hegelian politics of recognition between formed subjectivities. Rather 'asubjective affinities between resonant materials' afford new relations to mutually emerge.

Intelligence with the earth, as an interactive instant of shared affinities, might be extended to the sense of dividual 'conscience' staked out in 'Resistance to Civil Government' into what could be called an 'earth-conscience'. Indeed, if we take literally conscience as a 'knowing-with' (*con-science*), it becomes strikingly resonant with the intelligence with the earth Thoreau calls for in *Walden*. Throughout the 1850s and early 1860s, in turn, Thoreau develops an earth-conscience across the vast open-ended canvases of his journals and 'Kalendar' project. In so doing, he increasingly embraces science and scientific practices. He relentlessly catalogues the blooming of plants, the dispersion of seeds, processes of forest succession or the growth of wild apples, and assiduously documents the events of embodied perception he experiences in the 'maze' of natural phenomena. A central passage in his journal on 5 November, 1857 restates the dynamics of contact in terms of an individual subject dissociated by the direct experience of objects: 'I find that it is not they themselves (with which the men of science deal) that concern me; the point of interest is somewhere between me and them (i.e. the objects)' (Thoreau 1906: 1223). Such an interactive movement underlies Thoreau's approach to phenomena throughout his work.

But as Thoreau's incipient radical empiricism offers an ecological thinking of relation, the question arises as to what extent it can also provide a topology for the form of polity Thoreau calls for at the end of 'Resistance to Civil Government': a polity that would go past 'a true respect for the individual', and effect a politics no longer, human, all-too-human (Thoreau 1973: 89). As many have noted, resisting anthropogenic climate change demands more than a politics of the agora. It demands a politics of the earth, with the earth. Thoreau's politics of the earth, positioned at the beginning of the event of the Anthropocene, prompts us to break up any monolithic idea of Nature with an idea of natures in the plural – a multitude of fluid relations that resist ready-made deployment, and demand the recognition of different co-constructions of nature. Understanding natures is to find ourselves gathered in a heterogeneous world of seeds and stones, flesh and fluid, friends and foreigners. Such a multiplication of nature also multiplies (if not dissociates) how we understand the individual or the person – not as monadic and isolated but as enmeshed in extensive webs of relation. As Whitehead writes in *Adventures of Ideas*:

> an animal body is a society involving a vast number of occasions . . . Each living body is a society, which is not personal . . . and all vegetation, seem to lack the dominance of any included personal society. A tree is a democracy. Thus living bodies are not to be identified with living bodies under personal dominance. There is no necessary connection between 'life' and 'personality'. A 'personal' society need not be 'living', in the general sense of the term; and a 'living' society need not be 'personal'. (Whitehead 1961: 207)

Deleuze and Guattari go even farther to posit that 'each individual is an infinite multiplicity, and the whole of Nature is a multiplicity of perfectly individual multiplicities . . . its pieces are the various assemblages and individuals, each of which groups together an infinity of particles entering into an infinity of more or less interconnected relations' (1987: 254). The individual becomes a dividual.[4] Any politics that we might infer from this would seemingly traverse the boundary of the human and inhuman, organic and inorganic, personal and impersonal. It would be a politics of 'plurivocity, metamorphosis and contamination' that 'brings into relation heterogeneous terms – like a human being, an animal, and a micro-organism; but even a tree, a season, and an atmosphere' (Esposito 2012: 150). In *Vibrant Matter*, Bennett similarly describes human political and ethical responsibility in terms of the assemblages that individuals participate in and are formed by. She writes: 'Perhaps the ethical responsibility of an individual human now resides in one's response to the assemblages in which one finds oneself participating: Do I attempt to extricate myself from assemblages whose trajectory is likely to do harm? Do I enter into the proximity of assemblages whose conglomerate effectivity tends toward the enactment of nobler ends?' (Bennett 2010: 38).

To be sure, the de-anthropocentric gesture at the heart of recent ecological politics has been key to opening new realms of earth-conscience, including the move from recognising climate change anthropogenically to enacting new political policies that place nonhumans at their centre. If the environment had long been that part that plays no part, to adapt Rancière's formulation, then now it has found a putative 'voice'. However, can positing a world of relations and differences, becomings and multiplicities, which blurs such distinctions, break the double grip of the Anthropocene and neoliberal capitalism? Have recent responses to the event of the Anthropocene taken for granted a move from a flat or immanentist ontology and collective forms of agency to an emancipatory politics (a move common to recent Deleuze-inspired critical approaches such as new materialism and posthumanism)? Does an immanentist ontology of earth's multifarious acting, or even such 'cross-species acknowledgements' as Bennett celebrates, guarantee political transformation? Although Bennett's human dividual is relational, the question remains how we might understand the decision to exit or enter assemblages as other than an individual act and articulate a politics on the basis of it. Or, how does the 'onto-ethics' of gestures, nods, tendencies and sympathies which she details in *Influx and Efflux* open into the domain of politics?

At the centre of these questions remains the relationship between the act of resistance and a notion of distributed agency of interconnected networks of nonhuman actants and causalities. For Thomas Lemke, effective resistance and transformation require something more than the cross-species acknowledgement, or even the acknowledgement of the vital capacities of matter and the assemblages in which we participate. Radical politics does not merely need to acknowledge but rather to root out how vitalities of matter and assemblages of actants come to be determined. Lemke, in turn, quotes Bruce Braun, who argues for a politics based not on publics, but on how events of materiality are actualised: 'politics does not name the formation of publics as such, but rather the *determination* of incipient events, the ongoing and ever renewed work of turning contingency into necessity. . . . Politics, then, is perhaps not *equivalent* to the vitality of matter, rather it consists in *rejoining* this vitality, in contributing to its ongoing and ever-renewed determination' (Braun 2011: 392, cited in Lemke 2018: 42). If politics happens at the level of relations of matter and the determination of incipient events, then an ecological politics demands more than the mere recognition that humans are participants in assemblages – noble or nefarious, divine or diabolical. Political ecology names praxes of justice appropriate to how material interdependencies are determined at both the local and global scales.

Thoreau's work, in cultivating praxes of ecological justice, is poised precisely at this coincidence of the local and global. He offers a guidebook to construct an eco-social pluriverse that takes ecology as a discipline that traverses the biological and the political, and the human and natural sciences. His performative, destabilising and interactive ecology is focused on the question of justice. Coupling the concept of civil disobedience with Thoreau's ecological thinking of relations and particularities, then, offers a way to understand real struggles, including the real struggles today for which civil disobedience increasingly serves as a tactic. All around, disobedience is being invoked to empower direct action as issues of global climate change, sustainability, energy, toxification, extinction and biodiversity have become thrust to the forefront of our attention. With uncertain results from climate summit after climate summit, retrogressive movements from major players like the US, China or Russia, and the machinery of large capital still determining climate policy, green activism has become ever more urgent and must cut deeply into the paranoid structure of neoliberal geo-politics. Any politics of the earth must involve civil disobedience; obedience means complicity in ecological degradation and injustice. Or, John Jordan says, 'life on this world of ours may well be terminated because of too many acts of obedience' (qtd in Klein 2010).

'THE ODOR OF YOUR ACTIONS'

For Thoreau, tracing the effects of his allegiance as a form of resistance to unjust laws only became more urgent with the passage of the Fugitive Slave Law, which prompted his invective 'Slavery in Massachusetts'. There, he entreats Americans to realise that 'whatever the human law may be, neither an individual nor a nation can ever commit the least act of injustice against the obscurest individual without having to pay the penalty for it' (Thoreau 1973: 96). To commit the least act of injustice against the obscurest person is to support a system of injustice, and any government which perpetuates injustice is illegitimate. The state's laws do not ensure justice, for Thoreau, but protect entrenched complicities which foster injustice. In a reductio ad absurdum reminiscent of Marx's discussion of *Capital*'s literal grinding up of the bodies of exploited workers, Thoreau bitterly rebukes those who misunderstand the real effects of the Fugitive Slave Law:

> Much has been said about American slavery, but I think that we do not even yet realize what slavery is. If I were seriously to propose to Congress

to make mankind into sausages, I have no doubt that most of the members would smile at my proposition, and if any believed me to be in earnest, they would think that I proposed something much worse than Congress had ever done. But if any of them will tell me that to make a man into a sausage would be much worse – would be any worse – than to make him into a slave – than it was to enact the Fugitive Slave Law – I will accuse him of foolishness, of intellectual incapacity, of making a distinction without a difference. The one is just as sensible a proposition as the other. (96–7)

It might sound absurd to propose to Congress that they make humans into sausages, but the Fugitive Slave Law, by furthering the reach of a system which effectively serves to grind down Black bodies, does just that. With the protection of the law, Black bodies are made indispensable to slavery's reproduction, yet at the same time disposable and given to crushing work, violence and murder. 'Slavery in Massachusetts' brings home the reality of slavery, and enjoins New Englanders to confront directly the injustices they abet. Again, this does not mean 'combat' with far-off foes, but with local farmers and merchants, and the tax-man himself. To be a good neighbour, to those close and far away, is inconsistent with being a law-abiding citizen. With bitter irony directed towards the Fugitive Slave Law, he writes: '[t]he law will never make men free; it is men who have got to make the law free' (98).

For Thoreau, however, slavery is not only a crime against morality but also against nature. The model of moral rectitude offered by nature – in its beauty and purity – stands in contradiction to the slave system. 'Nature has been partner to no Missouri Compromise. I scent no compromise in the fragrance of the water-lily' (108). As James Finley suggests, Thoreau's support for the Free-Soil Movement posits his antislavery work as literally 'grounded' in the question of slavery's territorial expansion. Slavery is a 'moral earthquake' in both ecological and political terms. For Finley, Thoreau charts 'the wide-ranging ecological consequences of social injustice' to the extent that 'the slave system pollutes everything, including agricultural land, wilderness, labor conditions, politics, and interpersonal relationships' (Finley 2013: 5). Slavery thus does not respect topographical, physical or even political boundaries. Cash crops like tobacco and cotton dominate both ecosystems and the bodies of the enslaved. Yet nature provides a guide for a moral action to combat this pollution. As Thoreau writes: 'behave that the odor of your actions may enhance the general sweetness of the atmosphere, that when we behold or scent a flower, we may not be reminded how inconsistent your deeds are with it; for all odor is but one form of advertisement of a moral quality, and if fair actions had not been performed, the lily would not smell sweet' (Thoreau 1973: 109). To behave that the odour of your actions may enhance the general sweetness of the atmosphere serves as a Thoreauvian categorical imperative that takes as its ground a relational earth-conscience. While Thoreau's idealist natural philosophy often seeks to evince a higher law of morality from the natural beauty of the lily, at the same time, the natural serves as a seeming antidote to the material and social derogation of slavery, both locally and across a network of relations.

For Cristin Ellis, Thoreau's philosophical exploration of 'agency within a materialist system' in his late natural historical work is central to his late antislavery work, as well. They each explore, that is, how models of attenuated agency problematise the role of individual actants, and might thus offer a more complex picture of acts of political resistance. While the figure of John Brown might be taken as emblematic of the power of individual acts of conscience, Ellis argues that Thoreau's speeches and essays in defence of Brown '[derive] more immediately from his late naturalistic studies, and in fact [mark] a significant departure from his earlier antislavery thought' (Ellis 2018: 91). Thoreau's increased interest in collective agency and his receptivity to Darwinism shifted the emphasis in his thinking away from the individual actant as a catalyst for change, to the species, ecological systems and the *longue durée* of multi-agent biological and historical processes. As Ellis puts it: '[t]he transference of this ecological model of change into his antislavery writings inspires his expanded conception of political action, and the result seems less an elaboration than a displacement of his earlier politics' emphasis on the revolutionary power of individual moral agency and the possibility of immediate political conversion' (92). If reading Brown's actions in the context of Thoreau's natural historical thought 'reduces' Brown's 'intentional scope', one could also argue that it provides a ground for a more complex and capacious understanding of action taken in the name of political justice. Thoreau's strident celebration of Brown, as many have argued, lends him a posthumous agency: he was 'successful' in both the 'urgency of now' in furthering the cause of justice by threatening the order of slavery, *and* he planted the seeds to cultivate future righteous insurgencies. For Thoreau, Brown duly serves as an enduring model of action against any 'audacious government' that imposes on its citizens unjust and intolerable circumstances.[5]

Yet Brown also offers a way to understand transindividual subjectivity as a forceful site of resistance in itself. Brown's intervention is premised on his being overtaken by a powerful force of justice and life that cannot be reduced to the free will of an autonomous individuality. As Thoreau writes:

> He did not value his bodily life in comparison with ideal things. He did not recognize unjust human laws, but resisted them as he was bid. For once we are lifted out of the trivialness and dust of politics into the region of truth and manhood. No man in America has ever stood up so persistently and effectively for the dignity of human nature, knowing himself for a man, and the equal of any and all governments. (Thoreau 1973: 125)

While we might question the value of metaphysical truth and ideal masculinity that Thoreau finds in Brown, he nonetheless renders the concept of individual free will to be a fiction: Brown is 'bid' to sacrifice his bodily life in the name of a justice that comes from outside of him and overtakes him. Brown does not will his actions, but he draws his power by refusing to deny the forces that overtake him, which do not accede to the rules of prescribed morality or racial difference. His actions, though themselves violent, seek to nullify unjust laws of an audacious government, which for him are more violent and destructive than the righteous violence he performs. He counters destructive and subordinating force of the order of slavery with an affirmative force of justice performed in the name of the vulnerable and the vanquished. For Thoreau, Brown shatters the self-serving illusions of a liberal conception of justice centred on the individuality of action, and indeed reveals 'individual action' to be a tool that reinforces despotism. As Daniel Colson holds, 'free will makes human individuals responsible for their actions (before God, the law, society) and thus culpable for all of the forces and desires that actually constitute it as a subject . . . which it is always forced to repress, to experience as realities as external to itself' (Colson 2019: 95). While it's tempting to see Brown as an apotheosis of individual conscience, Thoreau's Brown shows how the forces which constitute him exceed his subjectivity; instead of repressing or restraining the excessive force of justice that overtakes him, he relentlessly follows his desire, like Antigone, to effect justice against the systemic injustice that will render him responsible for resisting that which he found intolerable.

At stake, then, in the combination of Thoreau's conceptions of civil disobedience, his ecological thought and his abolitionism is a notion of collectivised political agency that is relentlessly oriented towards justice: 'The only government that I recognize . . . is that power that establishes justice in the land, never that which establishes injustice' (Thoreau 1973: 129). The problem of justice undoes any solipsism at the basis of individual action insofar as it implies a collectivity of agencies to effect it. As such, we must rethink the notion of individual conscience that has long been the cornerstone of the liberal understandings of civil disobedience. To achieve justice, all calls to action are calls to interaction: for a revolution in our conduct of life, a revolution in our perception and our relations, a revolutionary division we allow to cut us down to the level of the individual. There is no such thing as inaction in a Thoreauvian 'science of civil disobedience', because choosing to do nothing about injustice is action through complicity – the pledging of allegiance. At the same time, action, when it is taken, is not an expression of individual subjectivity or agency because it is historically and politically determined. These two aspects are not only generative for tracing the relation between the political and the ecological, they are at the core of Thoreau's abolitionism. Like for Brown, to resist slavery is to find intolerable slavery's systems of relations: both the horrific chains that bind people to the plantation earth and the supply chains their forced labour originates, the material and economic flows slavery makes available to the extremities of its relations.

Thoreau's political ecology, premised on an earth-conscience, investigates how relations between actants and materialities come to be determined. It attends to the interactive instants of dwelling-with, and the processes by which modes of dwelling-with take shape. As such it marks the becoming-political of social and material forces, and demands a life-labour of finding novel modes of interactivity. It takes its pertinence in how it continues to inform counter-conducts in relation to our material interdependencies. Ecological civil disobedience today is oriented towards environmental justice as not only a question of individual action, but of collective action: in the effectivity of revolutionising everyday relations or small acts that add up to thwart corporate greed, or in large-scale events like mass climate protests. Acts of ecological civil disobedience seek to reconfigure the material relations that subtend and make possible the essentials of human lives in a global capitalist system. 'Resistance to Civil Government' is a call to end our own complicities in systems that foment injustice, and calls for a form of polity that would go past 'respect for the individual' to offer a more capacious model of distributed agency necessary for a just society for humans and nonhumans alike. It calls us to trace the allegiances of our dollars, or to conduct life-histories of commodities or material-flow analyses to find out how the objects that surround us are produced (our food, our clothing, our shelter, our fuel), in what eco-social networks they are imbricated, and where they are ultimately going (as repurposed, as waste).

Distributed agency is not distributed responsibility. If it diminishes the anthropocentric arrogance of individual action, it reinscribes action into a more complex network of agencies that demand an even higher level of political awareness and responsible intervention. Responsibility becomes radical in that it must trace its roots in seemingly all directions, to ask how to lend one's body in support, or to withdraw allegiances that abet injustice. This is what makes the combination of Thoreau's concept of civil disobedience, his ecology and his antislavery activism so necessary now. As we root out our interdependencies, we must also trace the course of our dollars to see if they lead to the forced labour of persons or the degradation of ecosystems, and to act against our own complacencies and conveniences.

In Thoreau's time, slavery came to Massachusetts not only with the Fugitive Slave Law, but was long there in the economic dependencies northern industries had on plantation slavery. Slavery in Massachusetts – or in the United States – did not end with emancipation or with the thirteenth amendment. It rather became 'reformed' and even legalised in the form of Jim Crow, segregation and, now, the systemic injustices of mass incarceration and criminalisation of African Americans and Latinos. In the USA and in the world, slavery still exists, as over forty million people in the world endure debt bondage, forced labour, exploitative labour practices and child labour. Modern slavery is often hidden in the plain sight of our everyday world of consumer products: in the supply chains of our food, our clothing and our electronics. There is slavery in California, in Texas, in Florida, or in Virginia, in the form of prison work programmes which inmates are forced to undertake in the name of public safety, education and reduced rates of recidivism. To be sure many prisoners benefit from the vocational programmes prisons offer. But many are also made to work in harsh conditions about which they have little choice, and for which they earn little or no recompense. In California, through the private company CALPIA, prisoners make not only licence plates and street signs, but everything from retail clothing, furniture and food products to face masks and hand sanitiser. Following Thoreau's injunction to trace our dollar should it lead to injustice, trace your dollar to find out what products we buy are fabricated in prisons using prison labour, and ask who profits from prison labour. More extensively, trace your dollar to find out if everyday electronics abet injustice in the Democratic Republic of Congo, where coltan resources are extracted, or in China, where many such products are fabricated.

While climate civil disobedience and the cause of ending modern slavery are not yet firmly allied movements, it is clear that climate-induced migration and the societal vulnerabilities that drive human trafficking will call for new expansive and creative forms of resistance. As scholars are just beginning to analyse in depth, the 'global challenges surrounding slavery and environmental change [are] interconnected issues that continually shape one another and [demand that we] tackle these as part of holistic and integrated strategies' (Brown et al. 2019: 11). Ecological civil disobedience, then, must work to undo the 'complex and bi-directional relationship between environmental degradation and exploitative labour practices' in key fisheries, field, forests and factories alike (6). At the same time, we must be aware that situations of forced migration and human trafficking become more prevalent following natural disasters such as floods or famine: 'The use of informal and dangerous trafficking networks is likely to rise as the impacts of climate change become clearer, agrarian populations become increasingly desperate and nations in the Global North begin to increasingly fortify borders and limit inward migration' (Molinari 2017: 6, 7).

Thoreau's work does not, of course, anticipate the current geopolitical scenario of mass climate dissidence, mass climate migration or modern slavery. On its own, it cannot counter ecological degradation, neoliberal/neo-feudalist capitalism and the proliferation of modern slavery. But his scathing critique of his contemporaries' complicities in plantation slavery and its legal framework in his own time can provide a critical framework to understand better how our allegiances enable systemic injustice in our time. At the same time, Thoreau's philosophy of resistance can offer a form of resistance not only premised on the action of an individual rational and autonomous subject – the liberal subject of civil disobedience – but on interactive resistance based on a complex relational ontology of collective agencies. Collective agency does not mean diminished responsibility but quite the opposite: it calls for an ethics and a politics worthy of the complexities of relations that we shape and that shape us. In our own restless era of riots and protests, civil disobedience has again become a byword for resisting humanitarian and environmental devastation across the world. As Thoreau entreats us: 'It is not an era of repose. We have used up all our inherited freedom. If we would save our lives, we must fight for them' (Thoreau 1973: 108).

Works Cited

Arendt, Hannah (1972), *Crises of the Republic*, New York: Harcourt Brace and Company.

Augustine (2006), *Confessions of St Augustine*, 2nd ed., trans. F. J. Sheed, Indianapolis: Hackett Publishing Company, Inc..

Bennett, Jane (1994), *Thoreau's Nature: Ethics, Politics, and the Wild*, Thousand Oaks, London, New Delhi: Sage.

— (2010), *Vibrant Matter*, Durham, NC: Duke University Press.

— (2020), *Influx and Efflux: Writing Up with Walt Whitman*, Durham, NC: Duke University Press.

Braun, Bruce (2011), 'Book review: *Vibrant Matter: A Political Ecology of Things*', *Dialogues in Human Geography* 1(3): 390–3.

Brown, David, Doreen S. Boyd, Katherine Brickell, Christopher D. Ives, Nithya Natarajan and Laurie Parsons (2019), 'Modern Slavery, Environmental Degradation and Climate Change', *Environment and Planning E: Nature and Space*, <https://doi.org/10.1177/2514848619887156> (accessed 29 October 2021).

Colson, Daniel (2019), *A Little Philosophical Lexicon of Anarchism from Proudhon to Deleuze*, trans. Jesse Cohn, New York: Minor Compositions.

Deleuze, Gilles, and Félix Guattari (1987), *A Thousand Plateaus: Capitalism and Schizophrenia*, trans. Brian Massumi, Minneapolis: Minnesota University Press.

Ellis, Cristin (2018), *Antebellum Posthuman: Race and Materiality in the Mid-Nineteenth Century*, New York: Fordham.

Emerson, Ralph Waldo (1983), 'Politics', in *The Collected Works of Ralph Waldo Emerson, Volume III: Essays Second Series* (1983), ed. Robert Spiller et al., Cambridge, MA: Harvard University Press, 1971–.

Esposito, Roberto (2012), *Third Person*, trans. Zakiya Hanafi, Cambridge: Polity.

Finley, James (2013), '"Justice in the Land": Ecological Protest in Thoreau's Antislavery Essays', *The Concord Saunterer* (new series) 21: 1–35.

Gros, Frédéric (2020), *Disobey! The Philosophy of Resistance*, trans. David Fernbach, London: Verso.

Klein, Naomi (2009), 'The Seattle Activists' Coming of Age in Copenhagen Will Be Very Disobedient', *The Guardian*, 12 November 2009, <https://www.theguardian.com/commentisfree/cifamerica/2009/nov/12/seattle-coming-age-disobedient-copenhagen> (accessed 28 May 2021).

Lemke, Thomas (2018), 'An Alternative Model of Politics? Prospects and Problems of Jane Bennett's Vital Materialism', *Theory, Culture & Society* 35(6): 45.

Molinari, Nicole (2017), 'Intensifying Insecurities: The Impact of Climate Change on Vulnerability to Human Trafficking in the Indian Sundarbans', *Anti-Trafficking Review* 8: 50–69.

Richardson, Robert D. Jr (1986), *Henry Thoreau: A Life of the Mind*, Berkeley: University of California Press.

Thoreau, Henry David (1906), *The Journal of Henry David Thoreau*, vol. X, ed. Bradford Torrey and Francis Allen, Boston: Houghton Mifflin.

— (1972), *The Maine Woods*, ed. Joseph J. Moldenhauer, Princeton: Princeton University Press.

— (1973), *Reform Papers*, ed. Wendell Glick, Princeton: Princeton University Press.

— (2004), *Walden: Life in the Woods*, ed. Lyndon Shanley, Princeton: Princeton University Press.

Whitehead, Alfred North (1961), *Adventures of Ideas*, London: Cambridge University Press.

NOTES

1. See <https://www.theguardian.com/environment/2020/jul/29/record-212-land-and-environment-activists-killed-last-year> (accessed 29 October 2021).

2. In analysing Thoreau's civil disobedience, Hannah Arendt focuses not on the relationality that undergirds it, nor on the ecology of relations that constitute the essential facts of life, but on the individuality of conscience. In her own essay 'Civil Disobedience', Arendt urges us to go past Thoreau's discrete individual: 'we are no longer dealing with individuals, or a phenomenon whose criteria can be derived from Socrates or Thoreau' (Arendt 1972: 68). Indeed, the 'greatest fallacy' (which she holds Thoreau commits) in the discourse on civil disobedience is 'the assumption that we are dealing with individuals, who pit themselves subjectively and conscientiously against the laws and customs of the community' (98). She orients her argument against individual conscience to dissociate it from any form of antinomian enthusiasm, ideological mystification, or even a Transcendentalist 'higher law'. As such, it is impossible 'to keep civil disobedience from being a philosophy of subjectivity . . . intensely and exclusively personal, so that any individual, for whatever reason, can disobey' (55, 56–7). Civil disobedience, for Arendt, can only be a collective act premised on 'voluntary association', not an exceptional act of an exceptional individual based on the dictation of conscience (96, 76). Rather, civil disobedience is always already a group activity 'for the simple reason' that 'civil disobedience practiced by a single individual is unlikely to have much effect'; therefore, it implies the formation of a 'community of interest'. She thus takes Thoreau's understanding of conscience, because it is primarily self-interested and given to potential enthusiasm, to be 'unpolitical' (62). If Thoreau's resistance here is premised on the self-reliant thought that '[t]he only obligation I have a right to assume, is to do at any time what I think right', this can only be understood as a radical, communal responsibility to achieve justice.

3. Jane Bennett, following McKim Marriott, refers to our split condition in terms of our 'dividuality'. We exist as both singular but divided: 'to exist, dividual persons absorb heterogeneous material influences'; or in Whitmanic terms, dividuality connotes a 'magnanimous I' (Bennett 2020: xii–xiii).
4. Deleuze also uses the term 'dividual' in his 'Postscript on the Societies of Control'.
5. As Frédéric Gros articulates it, 'The civic dissident ends up giving away in the face of the intolerable he or she speaks because it has become impossible for them to keep silent. They scarcely even disobey; rather than attest to the impossibility of their continuing to obey . . . Civic dissidence is the inverted reflection of the initial concept of obedience. Submission was defined by the impossibility of disobeying. That was the only reason for obeying. The dissident, for their part, witnesses to the impossibility of continuing to obey' (Gros 2020: 142–3).

PART III

CHANCE ENCOUNTERS

8

MEXICO/BRITAIN: A HISTORY OF JULIA PASTRANA'S TEETH, 1860–2013

MARISSA LÓPEZ

'The most amazing thing about getting to tell a true story is that a true story is never *really* over.'

May Oskan performing *The Ape Woman:
A Rock Opera*, live at the Berkshire Fringe in 2014

In the Odontological Collection of the Hunterian Museum at the Royal College of Surgeons of London can be found a cast of Julia Pastrana's upper and lower teeth.[1] They reveal that Pastrana suffered from something called gingival hyperplasia, which caused an overgrowth of the gums, making her mouth appear unusually large. Gingival hyperplasia, Victorian dentists correctly suspected, is linked to congenital generalised hypertrichosis, with which Pastrana was also afflicted.[2] She was, in other words, hairy all over and her lips were quite puffy, but in her lifetime no medical explanation yet existed for her conditions.

Julia Pastrana, known variously as 'Ape Woman' and 'Bear Woman', was an Indigenous Mexican born in Sinaloa around 1834. She died in Moscow in 1860 a few days after giving birth to a child who lived only briefly. But why are her teeth in London? I focus on that central question here, and it is really four questions rolled into one: why did nineteenth-century spectators find Pastrana so compelling? Why is she still interesting in the twenty-first century? Why take a cast of her teeth? And, finally, why are those teeth in London, of all places? I approach these questions through the work of five contemporary artists – three from England, one from the US and one from Mexico – who take inspiration from Pastrana's story. Colonial histories of cultural appropriation weigh differently on each of these creators, and those differences help us if not unravel, then at least illuminate the tangle of transatlantic, trans-American, and transhistoric racial feeling that gathers around Julia Pastrana.

In her short life Pastrana travelled the world with her husband, Theodore Lent, who was also her manager, performing with carnival sideshows and as a solo attraction.[3] Doctors and sensation-seekers alike were keen to examine her in life and death. After her passing Lent exhibited her and their son's mummified remains. Pastrana's body continued to attract audiences, ending up eventually as a sideshow in a Norwegian carnival, and then in a warehouse when that carnival closed in the late 1970s. In 2013 Norway repatriated her remains to Mexico, and Pastrana was buried in Sinaloa.

During her lifetime, Pastrana was a global sensation (Fig. 8.1). A medical curiosity – was she human? An orangutan? A hybrid? – scientific articles concerning her abound in the 1850s and 1860s. She makes appearances in literary texts, and there is a tremendous amount of surviving ephemera documenting her many appearances in sideshows across the United States, Europe and Russia.[4] In death, Pastrana's popularity only increased (Fig. 8.2). Google's N-gram Viewer, which tracks n-gram frequencies in Google's digitised corpus of printed material from 1500 to 2008, shows a sharp spike in Pastrana references after 1860 when Lent began exhibiting her and their child's embalmed bodies.[5] According to the N-gram Viewer, interest declines moving into the twentieth century but remains steady right up until 2008, the last year for which data is available. Pastrana, evidently, remains on people's minds well into the twenty-first century thanks in part to books like Frederick Drimmer's *Very Special People: The Struggles, Loves, and Triumphs of Human Oddities* (1973), trade publications capitalising on people's enduring fascination with human difference.

Kept alive in the public imagination, Pastrana today inspires films, plays, poetry, music, visual art and performance from diverse artists.[6] In 1999 British actor and playwright Shaun Prendergast, influenced by Drimmer, premiered *The True History of the Tragic Life and Triumphant Death of Julia Pastrana, The Ugliest Woman in the World, performed in complete and absolute darkness* (Interview). Prendergast's play caused a sensation with its innovative use of sound and smell to present audiences with a story they were unable to see. It touched a nerve and continues to enjoy regular runs to this day. In 2003, Amphibian Stage Productions in New York invited the Mexican artist Laura Anderson Barbata to collaborate with them on a performance of *True History*, setting in motion a chain of events that would lead eventually to the repatriation of Pastrana's remains and a flurry of artistic production about Pastrana in the 20-teens, with which I am most interested here for what it can tell us about the long history of affective ties between Mexico, Britain and the United States.

Working on Amphibian's 2003 production of *True History*, Barbata became convinced that it was her 'duty as a Mexican artist, and as a woman, . . . to do everything possible to have Pastrana removed from the anatomy collection and returned to Mexico' (Barbata 2016: 132). Thus began a ten-year odyssey of public performance and political action ending with Pastrana's eventual burial in Sinaloa. Pastrana's internment was reported by major outlets around the world, including the *New York Times* (see Wilson 2013), inspiring a new generation of reflection on the politics of race, sensation and spectacle that Pastrana's story embodies.[7]

These works exemplify Pastrana's continued status as an object of artistic and intellectual inquiry, a status that has only increased since her repatriation and burial in 2013. Artists and other public intellectuals use Pastrana to trace genealogies of sexism and racism as well as to cultivate a presentism by virtue signalling their pity for her. Rosemarie Garland-Thomson, writing about Pastrana's nineteenth-century appeal, explains pity as a feeling that renders the person who pities superior to that which is pitied. 'Pastrana's presentation as semi-human', Garland-Thomson argues, 'legitimated the status of her onlookers as fully human and thus potential citizens in a democratic order' (Garland-Thomson 2017: 52). In other words, viewers who pitied Pastrana in the nineteenth century based their sense of self-worth on their difference from her; they created an idea of Pastrana that bolstered their belief in their own value as citizens of an expanding democracy.

This phenomenon unfolds in twenty-first-century reviews of Raúl Dorantes' bilingual play, 'The Inexplicable Pastrana', in Chicago's Spanish-language press. Gisela Orozco, for example, tells readers that Pastrana 'fue vendida a un circo como un objeto. Vendida varias veces para mostrarla en circos y ferias, primero en México y luego en EEUU, donde conoce a Theodore Lent, quien se casa con ella y, de esa manera, puede tener control sobre ella. Lent la expone. La explota' (n.p.).[8] White America might have controlled, exploited and displayed Pastrana, but Orozco's outraged pity implies that contemporary Latinxs are savvy and strong enough to escape such a fate.

Others, by contrast, use Pastrana to anchor ongoing oppression and injustice. For instance, when ABC cancelled the *Roseanne* reboot after its creator and star, Roseanne Barr, compared African American businessperson and political advisor Valerie Jarrett to an ape, DeNeen Brown explained in the *Washington Post* that comparing people of colour to animals has a long history in the US. Her opening example was Julia Pastrana, whose 'life was defined by the virulent racism of the 19th century', which, if Barr's behaviour is any indication, has not, according to Brown, dissipated (n.p.). Similarly, on the *Huffington Post*, The Lady Aye compared the body-shaming of contemporary actresses to Pastrana's othering. 'While critics were debating if Lena Dunham gets too naked too often', she wrote, 'or if Melissa McCarthy is too fat to be a movie star, Julia Pastrana's mummified remains were being collected from an Oslo medical facility and sent home to Mexico to be laid to rest' (n.p.). For The Lady Aye, Pastrana historicises the negative attention women like Dunham and McCarthy get for being plain and fat.

Reporting on Pastrana's repatriation for the *New York Times*, Charles Wilson splits the difference between pity and rage. He quotes Jonathan Fielding, who directed the production of *True History* that introduced Barbata to Pastrana: 'Her story has always had a bad ending. . . . The big difference is that now it has an appropriate ending' (n.p.). Twenty-first-century people, Fielding implies, are righting the wrongs of the nineteenth. Are they, though? In answering this question, I do not wish to succumb to what Robert Aguirre has described as a 'methodological bias towards synoptic overviews' plaguing both scholarly and popular analyses of nineteenth-century freakery (Aguirre 2005: 106). Instead, I focus on a small selection of works to figure out why that cast of Pastrana's teeth is at London's Royal College of Surgeons.

Pastrana appeared in London alive in 1857 together with her husband, Lent, and with her teeth firmly rooted in her mouth. Most of what is currently known about her life dates, according to Janet Browne and Sharon Messenger, from this time when Pastrana began attracting attention from the medical and popular press (Brown and Messenger 2003: 156). Google's N-gram Viewer, likewise, reveals that references to Pastrana in British publications far outpace those in US venues. Why? What do Julia Pastrana's teeth reveal about the historic and enduring triangulation of Britain, the United States and Mexico? After explaining the historical connections between the three countries, I examine a small sample of contemporary art and literature with the aim of uncovering the genealogies of racial feeling Pastrana illuminates into the present.

Step Right Up; Enjoy the Show

Pastrana was not the first hairy person to captivate international attention, and she certainly was not the last. By the nineteenth century, audiences had seen people similar to, though not exactly like, Pastrana.[9] Victorian England, however, that engine of empire, was particularly interested in display and adventure, notes playwright Shaun Prendergast. At a time when 'people were looking for post-Darwin answers within mysteries', Prendergast says, Lent was able to exploit Julia for profit (Interview). Nineteenth-century Americans, by slight contrast, explains Rosemarie Garland-Thomson, were extremely interested in appearances and the practices of looking as related technologies of policing the boundaries of democratic citizenship. 'The franchise and the rights it represented had been expanded in Jacksonian America, even as slavery forced a consideration of what constituted the human,' she writes (Garland-Thomson 2017: 35). Looking at Pastrana, in other words, codified increasingly flexible categories of the human to whom rights must be accorded in an expanding democracy. Competing, and often colluding, discourses of science and show-manship, moreover, struggled to define those categories in nineteenth-century Europe and the US. 'Human freak shows, quacks, and raucous displays of curi-osities and marvels' had always reliably supplied scientists with data (Browne and Messenger 2003: 156). Thus, as science, anthropology, ethnology and citizenship evolved in the nineteenth century, they did so in tandem with the carnival sideshow.

In her book *Extraordinary Bodies* (1997), Garland-Thomson situates Pas-trana at the crossroads of this uneasy alliance, asserting that her appeal relies on her ability to simultaneously shore up and dismantle the anthropocentric inequalities upon which emerging conceptions of citizenship in the US relied. Likewise, in Britain, Aguirre sees Pastrana exemplifying the Victorian appre-ciation for both displays of human difference and pre-Columbian relics. He explains how 'the British quest for and representation of pre-Columbian antiq-uity became a crucial cultural arm of the larger political and economic strategy historians call informal imperialism', the softer, subtler modes of economic and political control Britain employed in places where it was unable, or unwill-ing, to maintain outright colonial dominance (Aguirre 2005: xv).[10] For Agu-irre, Pastrana represents the confluence of race science and colonial dominance embodied by Victorian 'freak' shows. He focuses primarily on Máximo and Bartola, microencephalitics from El Salvador presented to Queen Victoria in 1853 as the last of a dying caste of Aztec priests. 'Freak' shows featuring the likes of them and Pastrana, Aguirre argues, shaped racial ideas of Mexicans and Latin Americans in the Victorian imagination and perpetuated stereotypes about inferiority through emerging scientific discourses of racial hybridity that upheld British superiority (126).

Physical difference generated a fascination, in Aguirre's analysis, not unlike pity, which, as Garland-Thomson explains, 'defines its object even as it depends upon that object for its enactment' (Garland-Thomson 2017: 53). Aguirre argues similarly that such shows generate a network of feelings grounding the belief that the looting and political control of Latin America are justified by the region's inferior population, which can neither appreciate nor manage itself. Ryan Alexander concurs with Aguirre, writing specifically of Pastrana that her performances 'served as exemplars of what nineteenth-century Europeans came to see as the racially inferior and sexually deviant peoples that populated far off lands' (Alexander 2014: 263). When British attention turned to Latin America, Pastrana emerged as the fascinating cynosure of American indigeneity that justified exploitation while fuelling scientific curiosity.

Historically, then, Pastrana can be understood as an icon of how nineteenth-century scientific discourse othered extraordinary bodies in the service of codify-ing raced, abled and gendered norms of citizenship, as Garland-Thomson argues of the US context. In Britain, as Aguirre shows, this becomes a mechanism of informal empire. But why does Pastrana still captivate in the twenty-first century? Of his play *True History*, Prendergast says, 'It's strange to me in a sense that something I wrote in four days has a life twenty years later' (Interview). Also strange is that someone who lived over a century ago is still so much a part of so many contemporary artists' creative lives.

Prendergast explains her allure along two parallel tracks: Pastrana's story speaks to current political struggles, but he also sees in it an inclusive appeal. *True History* is produced often around the world in part, Prendergast admits, because its lack of costumes and sets make it inexpensive, but also because 'there's a kind of zeitgeist political interpretation that happens' in each production. A recent staging in New Jersey cast primarily disabled performers; in Texas the play became – through marketing, reviews and audience response – 'very much the story of a Latin American woman being exploited by an American entrepreneur', and a director in the Philippines who wanted to make a statement about human trafficking decided to hood the audience rather than perform the play in darkness (Interview). Though much of Pastrana's story unfolds in England, Prendergast is reluctant to pin her down or historicise overmuch. 'I don't know if it's particularly British,' he says, 'or if it's just that her story is universal,' and therefore able to generate interest across time and space (Interview).

Most Pastrana think pieces from 2013 share Prendergast's investment in universality, extending it explicitly to concerns about humaneness and humanity. The Lady Aye, for example, observes how Prendergast's staging 'takes the emphasis off of Julia's looks and puts it back on her humanity' (n.p.). Garland-Thomson also relies on human pathos, taking the British medical journal *The Lancet* to task for publishing an autopsy of Pastrana that 'does not invoke a single trace of Pastrana's or her son's humanity' (Garland-Thomson 2017: 46). Such appeals to universality and turns to the human, however, elide Pastrana's particularity. Her story is not a universal one; it is a Mexican one. Orozco emphasises this in her coverage of Dorantes's play, but most coverage of Pastrana tends to shift attention from Mexico to more 'universal' concerns. 'Miss Pastrana's body', writes The Lady Aye, by way of illustration, 'served both as public spectacle and the receptacle of each generation's fears, expectations and controversies' (n.p.). From what, however, does this move to universality draw our attention away? What is driven to the margins when we foreground 'humanity'?

The push to universalise Pastrana is an attempt to undermine over a century of racial othering that her circulation makes visible. This global multicultural impulse, however, erases the power of her difference to create subterranean links between ostensibly separate times and places with Pastrana less as a reality than as a sort of virtual vector. The motor of this process is a redefinition of what constitutes the human, something that challenges the liberal humanist understanding of race. We lose this challenge when we elevate Pastrana's universality over her particularity.

To illustrate, a Norwegian newspaper describing Pastrana as 'half-human, half-animal' also alerted readers, 'You'll chill when you see her face' (Gylseth and Toverud 2004: 94). The 'universal' and the 'human' tamp down that 'chill', but it lingers in the air. Aguirre articulates that same chill when he notes that Britain's machinations in Latin America were largely a matter between elites. Wealthy and powerful Latin Americans, he asserts, 'did not passively await British influence but actively sought it out', colluding, over the course of the nineteenth century, to narrate and monetise America's pre-Columbian past (Aguirre 2005: xxi). Indigeneity thus emerges, in Aguirre's analysis, as a chilling sign of the colonial unconscious, haunting the galleries, museums, archives and literary histories that seek to contain it.

Through this lens Pastrana can be seen as a barometer of racial feeling indexing the contemporary manifestations of affective histories. It is easy to critique the sins of the past, in other words, but how might we still be experiencing Pastrana's chill in the twenty-first century? As Tim Stelloh writes in a *Buzzfeed* report on her interment, 'In life, Pastrana was a freak show celebrity. In death, she became a symbol of colonial-era exploitation and its aftermath. This is the story of her long journey home' (n.p.). Stelloh's phrasing suggests that the 'journey home' is something else, something other than exploitation. But what is it? What does contemporary attention to Julia Pastrana help us sense about the present, and what impact does that present sense have on our understanding of the past?

Answering that question requires keeping in mind that Pastrana both is and is not Mexican. She is a tool for imagining the Mexican triangulation of nineteenth-century British-US relations, but she is Indigenous. Upon discovering her and her mother, Christopher Gylseth and Lars Toverud remind readers, nomadic herders called her 'Julia Pastrana' since '[w]hatever Indian name she might have had was of no interest' (Gylseth and Toverud 2004: 4). Pastrana is 'Mexican' by fiat, her Native, Indigenous tongue replaced by the Spanish, French and English she spoke fluently. She hovers uneasily between national categories, her unmistakeable, incomprehensible appeal held at a distance, as Carol Birch dramatises in *Orphans at the Carnival*, a novelisation of Pastrana's life. Birch's rendition of Lent has him musing one evening about how 'he was no longer repelled' by Pastrana, how he 'could do everything with her but kiss her on the lips . . . in the dark she was a warm, shapely thing, a plush doll, easy to slip inside' (Birch 2016: 296). Pastrana enervates complicated networks of repulsion and desire at interpersonal and international registers.

These live wires are just as tangled and mysterious in the twenty-first century. Mexican and Mexican American labour drive economic activity in the southwestern US, and Mexico is one of the top US trading partners (US Census np). In 2016, however, Donald Trump was elected president of the US on a platform of vilifying Mexicans, building a physical barrier between the two countries and threatening to shut down US-Mexican trade. This contradiction finds its UK analogue in the curious case of Brexit, where immigration fears propelled the 2016 vote to leave the European Union (EU), a decision that, at the close of the 20-teens, threatens to push England into economic freefall (see Carl). One not-so-highly-publicised cost of leaving the EU for Britain would be its trading relationship with Mexico. This partnership has remained significant since the nineteenth century and has grown exponentially since the 2000 implementation of Mexico's Free Trade Agreement with the EU.[11] Should Britain remain in the EU its Mexico trade stands to increase substantially with the 2018 revisions to that agreement (see 'EU and Mexico reach new agreement on trade'). To this day, it would appear, Mexico finds itself the unwitting lynchpin of the global north's self-defeating hatred of its perceived racial others. There is, moreover, no clear consensus on who – or what – those others are; they remain a swarthy, animalistic amalgamation of desire, fear and greed.

It would be limiting, though, to see Mexico as merely an empty stage, or blank screen, on which England and the US might work through their racial angst. What agency, if any, does Mexico have in this triangulation? To historicise that question: how might we recover, or at least limn the shape of, all that was lost when Julia Pastrana was given her new name? Can we see beneath the surface of Latin American and British elite collaboration in the nineteenth century to the living, beating, haunting heart of American indigeneity?

Probably not. Aguirre argues, however, that we can get at *something* by thinking about performances like Pastrana's as acts of colonial subversion that invite critical reflection on our own observational practices. Máximo and Bartola were undeniably exploited, he concedes, but their enduring popularity suggests a savvy ability to find a niche in the colonial gaze and make it work to their benefit. There is nothing in the archive to indicate their feelings or motivations, but Aguirre speculates that Máximo and Bartola 'found ways to temper that subjection through the very vehicle of performance' (Aguirre 2005: 131). He bases this supposition on the contemporary work of Guillermo Gomez-Peña and Coco Fusco, whose durational performance piece 'The Couple in the Cage' saw the two posing, in a cage, as newly discovered Amerindians from the invented island of Guatinau. Viewers were not made aware that the piece was an ironic commentary on imperial practices of othering, and the resulting documentary covering its worldwide exhibition records audiences' alternating horror, apathy and casual racism. Gomez-Peña and Fusco's manipulation of colonial tropes helps us imagine what Máximo and Bartola might have been thinking as they performed for British audiences, and it demonstrates, according to Aguirre, 'the ongoing processes of subjectification that shape Latino/a identities in the present' (132). Gomez-Peña and Fusco give us, in other words, a way to feel Pastrana's chill by making us see her seeing us see her.

The ability to see ourselves seeing, that is – or the forced experience of the same – will help those of us in the global north move beyond the obvious in our analyses and do more than instrumentalise Mexico as that which is found when the US and England see through a glass darkly. Aguirre argues that understanding nineteenth-century displays of non-Anglo ethnicity as agentic performances 'reverses the gaze, upsetting the invisibility and neutrality that has been the presumed privilege of the dominant culture in its voyeuristic fantasies about the Other' (133). He also cautions, however, against reenacting these same othering processes in our critiques. 'It is all too easy to create intellectual capital by recycling racialized and sexualized images from the gallery of colonial atrocities in the name of critique,' he warns, and admonishes scholars that we are never entirely outside the structures we condemn (134). To grant Pastrana agency, to see contemporary Mexico as something other than a historical scrim, requires colonial critique to see itself seeing, to recognise its own coloniality.

Ryan Alexander attempts to do this in his work on Pastrana by focusing on that which is invisible and unknowable in the historical record. 'Pastrana', he writes, 'became swept up in a large matrix of political, historical, and scientific phenomena, but carved out her own place within it as well,' by donating a considerable portion of her earnings to charity and insisting upon making her own clothes (Alexander 2014: 265). Alexander warns that ignoring these documented facts does Pastrana a disservice and, moreover, that reading her marriage to Lent as an obvious sham disregards 'perhaps the only means by which scholars can piece together the ways in which Pastrana influenced relationships in which she was generally in a subordinate position' (276). Alexander thus attempts to recognise the coloniality of Pastrana scholarship, while other critics are less self-conscious.

Garland-Thomson, for example, has written brilliantly on Pastrana, but refers to her 'non-Western ethnicity' despite the fact that Sinaloa, Pastrana's birthplace, is on the west coast of the Western hemisphere (Garland-Thomson 1997: 72). Referring to Pastrana as a 'member of a Mexican Indian tribe' (72), moreover, evidences the continuing hold of the hierarchical structures of racialisation that surround Pastrana. Stelloh, by contrast, recognises the racial hierarchies of such generalisations and mocks his own desire to see Indians. 'At one point, after I ask about local indigenous groups, Rubio Valenzuela reaches for the sliding door of our van. With the vehicle still in motion, he throws it open and points at several ordinary-looking women trudging along the side of the road. "Look!" he shouts. "Indígenas!"' (n.p.). Stelloh ensures his readers see him seeing himself seeing, and he renders Mexico as coeval to the US by comparing a cluster of cow herders to the New York City mayor's caravan. As I shift now to consider contemporary, Pastrana-inspired artists, I am most interested in whether they, like Stelloh, are seeing themselves see Pastrana, or whether they are just looking at her teeth. I am interested, that is, in how their contemporary works explain why Pastrana's teeth are in London, in how their art either reasserts the colonial gaze or forces viewers to see themselves looking.

LOOKING AT PASTRANA

In Shaun Prendergast's *True History* audiences see nothing at all. Setting the play in total darkness thus forces a kind of existential consideration of 'sight' and how the things we 'see' are largely reflections of ourselves. As his Theodore Lent asserts, echoing Garland-Thomson on pity, audience empathy is just another way of thinking, 'Thank God she isn't me' (Prendergast 1999: 9). Exhibition and performance may create a hierarchical dynamic, but with both its staging and its closing lines, the play tries to equally distribute authority and control. At the very end, to Julia's ghost, which haunts him after her passing, Lent says, 'You were just a show. Well, show's over for this freak, folks. Give a dead man some rest' (45). The play undercuts Lent's dismissal by presenting Julia as a lingering presence. To Lent she is obviously more than just a show. By ambiguously folding himself into the category of 'freak', moreover, Lent stages the recognition that we are all always seeing and being seen, and the show will end for us all eventually.

On this levelled playing field, however, Julia has the nominal upper hand. She is the only character explicitly described as seeing. 'Look into my eyes, see yourself reflected there,' Lent exhorts. 'Look at your eyes, Julia' (11). She sees herself, the audience 'sees' her through her own descriptions, and that seeing is equated with agency and analytic skill. 'I have a sweet voice, great taste in music and dancing, and can speak three languages,' she says. 'I am very charitable, and give largely to local institutions from my earnings. Mr Lent invents wild tales about my past, but my true history is that I'm simply a hideously deformed young Mexican Indian woman' (10). Granted, Prendergast uses the flattening 'Mexican Indian', as Garland-Thomson does, but while the latter does not, in her published work, imagine Pastrana as anything other than abject and exploited, Prendergast's Julia makes her own financial decisions, critiques Lent's fabulations, is proud of her performance and takes the stage of her own free will. When the chorus tells Lent to 'make it sing', Lent replies 'Suppose she won't sing?' replacing 'it' with 'she', and making space for Julia's potential agency (10).

Carol Birch and Rosie Garland also take pains in their novels to depict their Pastrana-inspired characters as self-possessed actors motivated by free will. Birch's *Orphans of the Carnival* (2016) hews closely to Pastrana's known biography. Garland's *The Palace of Curiosities* (2013), by contrast, draws inspiration from Pastrana's life to tell the fictional story of Eve, a similarly afflicted woman in Victorian England, who finds lasting love with Abel, a modern-day Lazarus who heals miraculously from any injury and spends much of the novel piecing together the mystery of his former lives. Garland's Eve is a confident adventuress, and Birch's Julia is a similarly strong-willed advocate for herself.

Both novels, however, divest the historical Pastrana of actual agency and centre whiteness in ways that replicate the coloniality of the gaze. This centring is material and abstract, happening through deployments of race and theorisations of sight.

Both novels include descriptions of seeing that understand themselves as anti-colonial critiques of patriarchy, but devolve into refractions of whiteness. Birch, for example, describes an early-career performance during which Julia notices a little girl in the audience staring at her intently. Julia 'couldn't shake a funny feeling that she was also out there in the audience, staring at herself, [while the] monster, smiling, stared straight back at her' (Birch 2016: 103). The layers of vision and monstrosity are thick here: in seeing herself being seen, does Julia witness a monster or apprehend the monstrosity of whiteness? Similarly, after her husband Josiah gives her a mirror, Eve says she 'fell in love with [it]' because it showed her what she foolishly hoped to see: a woman Josiah could love (Garland 2013: 295). By the end of the novel, however, Eve has discovered an ability to 'see' people through touch; skin-to-skin contact gives her visions of people's inner lives, a sight the novel postulates as truer than that gleaned from the eyes. Whichever vision is more genuine, Eve only has access to the latter. Pressing her own palms to each other offers Eve 'no great insights' (237). Eve can only see herself through a mirror someone else has given her, and Julia's most profound vision of herself is through the eyes of a white girl. The reader may catch glimpses of Pastrana, but whiteness is the condition of her visibility for both Birch and Garland.

For Garland this is literally true as her Eve is white and blonde. Her hair is 'the color of combed flax' (19) and her face when she shaves is 'pale as a water biscuit' (130). This transformation is analogous to Rose's function in *Orphans of the Carnival* as the Anglo character who brings 'otherness' into view. Rose, a global consumer, lives in a flat decorated 'like an Arabian souk, all coloured hangings and cushions' (Birch 2016: 24), full of items 'she'd brought home from garbage bins and gutters and pavements, shelves full of stuff she felt sorry for . . . broken things, the teeming leavings of the world' (25). When Rose brings home what she thinks is a doll and the reader later learns is Pastrana's mummified baby, she sets it 'among her Indian cushions as if it were a cuddly toy' and mutters, 'Poor thing' (25). Such actions and descriptions posit Rose as a benevolent saviour seemingly unaware of the condescending – if informal – colonial objectification she performs.

Garland is similarly lured by the glow of racial proximity. Abel is 'dark [as a] Moghul' (Garland 2013: 153) with skin 'like . . . a Negro', even if he is not actually Black. Eve, likewise, is aligned with Blackness through her admiration of Olaudah Equiano (313).[12] This claiming of racial otherness finds a formal analogue in how each writer imagines a historical elasticity that allows stories to talk to each other over vast swathes of difference. To illustrate, 'There are no better days,' says Lent in Birch's novel to a man who tells him he looks as if he has seen better, 'they're all one' (Birch 2016: 311). If all time is the same time then Rose's struggles in 1983 can be read against and through Pastrana's in the 1850s. Garland also, by presenting dreamlike snippets of Abel's past lives in multiple historical periods and places, signals a temporal homogeny that echoes Eve's imaginary friend Donkey-Skin's pronouncement that 'Beauty is truly skin deep. We are all horrors under the skin' (22).

On the one hand, emphasising similarity over difference is a novelistic strategy of keeping Pastrana's story alive; on the other hand, it can be read as the (predominantly) white privilege of the global north to see itself everywhere. It is to write a novel, as Birch does, in which a white, European woman asserts her ghostly presence in the Americas and puts Indigenous Mexicans in their place: at the novel's end Rose has died in a fire and her ex-boyfriend, Adam, takes Pastrana's mummified son to Mexico City's Isla de las Muñecas (Birch 2016: 333).[13] It is also, as Garland does, to appropriate Black cultural production while subjecting Black characters to gruesome, lethal acts of violence: Eve may be inspired by Equiano to write her own autobiography, but the only actual Black people in the novel are eaten alive by attack dogs while white onlookers place bets on which dog will finish their victims first (Garland 2013: 274). For an author to depict a character claiming autobiographic desire while wresting the power of life writing from real historical figures presents an ethical dilemma to the critic: how to make sense of these resonances of colonial violence?

SEEING OURSELVES SEEING

Birch's and Garland's calls to see Julia stir up a hornet's nest of racialised conflict that Prendergast manages to avoid by refusing sight altogether. Laura Barbata and Mari Hernandez, by contrast, contemporary artists from Mexico and the United States, respectively, tackle these conflicts head on. Birch and Garland appreciate Pastrana in relation to normative standards of beauty and the human, eliding difference in ways that elide the power of whiteness and legacies of colonial violence. Barbata and Hernandez, on the other hand, imagine Pastrana in relation to differential, decentred networks of power that undermine the ability of whiteness to condition contemporary imaginings of Pastrana's legacy.[14] Barbata illustrates this approach in 'Sin lo uno no hay lo otro' (Without the one there is no other), a TedX talk she gave in Mexico City, offering art as a vehicle for change in a world of disasters. Discussing a series of her own nature-based photographs and installations, Barbata offers a theory of art as a *semilla* (seed) that sprouts and takes root in people, opening them to the world and connecting them with each other. Such connections comprise, she avers, a meaningful intervention in the social world that is aesthetically and politically significant in its avoidance of direct resistance to centres of power.

In 2005, shortly after learning about Pastrana, Barbata undertook a government-funded residency in Oslo, during which she executed several happenings around Pastrana's story that function as such *semillas*. These events, organised with help from Norway's Office of Contemporary Art, drew crowds as well as press attention. They 'touched many people on a deep level and confused others', says Barbata (Barbata 2017: 135). They also led to Pastrana's eventual repatriation six years later, a feat Barbata was able to achieve through an artistic practice that catalyses awareness and cultivates networks of feeling and connection. Barbata's 'Julia Pastrana. Su vuelta y sus raíces' (Her return and her roots), a short, stop-motion animation film, plants similar, catalysing seeds.

Rafael Esquer directed the film, which depicts Pastrana's story in a series of connected *papel picado* vignettes during which Pastrana, represented in abstract, geometric shapes, morphs into flocks of birds, boots and an underground network of roots.[15] The film ends with black string on a pink background, forming '1834' (the year of Pastrana's birth), spooling towards the right forming '1860' (the year she died), then a dashed line forming '2013' (the year she was repatriated from Norway and buried in Mexico), followed by a period. These threaded years are filmed moving off screen to the left with the final period turning into an ellipsis, signalling to the viewer that the story will continue.

'Su vuelta y sus raíces' conveys Pastrana's travels, her *mexicanidad*, and, with the threaded years, the sense that her story can pull together people across time and space. The movie also suggests the interconnection of the more than human. The birds, the roots, the animated thread and paper indicate Pastrana's story as materialising an American affect that runs through multiple forms of American life. 'I knew', writes Barbata, 'there were simple things I could do publicly to immediately acknowledge Pastrana's humanity' (Barbata 2017: 134). Barbata emphasises humanity and rights, but equally significant are the ways Pastrana exceeds the human. Everything about her is excessive: too much hair, too much gingival tissue, too much animality. 'Human' does not fully describe her; Barbata's Pastrana projects work not by making Pastrana legible as human, but by depicting the ways in which she exceeds the category. Pastrana's story and Barbata's art make visible the permeability, rootedness and connective, excessive tissue between the human and the non.

Mari Hernandez, a San Antonio, Texas-based photographer specialising in imaginative self-portraits, illuminates Pastrana's transhistorical, transcorporeal connecting energy in a series of images taken for 'Ruda Phat', a 2013 exhibition at the Institute of Texan Cultures exploring body image. Hernandez, who learned about Pastrana from Wilson's article in the *New York Times*, says she felt an 'immediate connection' with Pastrana through her own struggles with unwanted body hair (Interview). Pastrana's story also resonated politically with Hernandez, who understands her as a flashpoint in a longer history of the commoditisation and oppression of women of colour in the Americas. 'Our bodies are always politicised, and people always try to take them over or say that they have a right to them in some way,' Hernandez argues, connecting Pastrana's life and death to contemporary struggles around educational and economic opportunities for women, in addition to reproductive health and political freedom.

The fact that even after Pastrana's death 'people continued to view her body as some sort of object' is a point of 'deeper connection' for Hernandez, one she manifests in a series of images showing herself as Pastrana, dressed in intimate apparel in a boudoir setting (Figs 3–5). In contrast to the majority of extant photos of the historical Pastrana, Hernandez gazes directly into the camera and appears more often than not in motion, rather than posed. Her Pastrana is active, agential and unabashed, transforming the viewer's understanding of, even as Hernandez transforms herself into, Pastrana. She achieves this metamorphosis, in part, by using facial prostheses, as in her current work featuring imagined characters with 'some sort of unnatural appearance' who embody raw emotion.[16] These 'not-quite-human' figures gesture towards something Hernandez also explores with Pastrana: 'how brown women, indigenous women [are] not considered within our society, [are] still considered as less than something, [as] not fully human' (Interview). People like Pastrana have always been seen as 'disposable', notes Hernandez, who insists, with her images, on visceral truths which cannot be so easily discarded (Interview).

By recording the physical transformation of her body into another, by reading Pastrana as contemporary analogue rather than historical anecdote, Hernandez pushes past the conceptual confines of liberal humanism into the more than human. By this I mean that her Pastrana-inspired art makes visible the forces that still condition bodies around the world but are often occluded when subjectivity and the human are foregrounded. Significantly, neither Hernandez nor Barbata is interested in representing Pastrana so much as they seek to cultivate a public sensitivity around her. Neither offers Pastrana as an object upon which a disconnected observer might reflect; they deploy her as a thing with the power to transmute hierarchies of gender, race and nation into tools for building a more equitable future.

Barbata and Hernandez generate a sensorium of oppression; Birch and Garland, on the other hand, enact the forces catalysing global inequality. Their novels are the literary equivalent of that cast of Pastrana's teeth at London's Royal College of Surgeons: objects of curiosity, radiating colonial racism masked as social scientific truth, that tell the observer what they already think they know. Those teeth, however, are just a trace, a lingering impression. They are not the real thing, if such a thing could even be said to exist. The difference between the teeth in Pastrana's mouth and their imprint in London is the difference between Barbata's and Hernandez's art and that of Birch and Garland. It is a difference that brings forth enduring truths about the legacies of both formal and informal empire, the perniciousness of liberal multiculturalism, and how both Mexico and the global circulation of Mexican bodies can get us closer to understanding and dismantling power.

Works Cited

Aguirre, Robert D. (2005), *Informal Empire: Mexico and Central America in Victorian Culture*, Minneapolis: University of Minnesota Press.

Alexander, Ryan M. (2014), 'Mexico's "Misnomered Bear Woman": Science and Spectacle in the Sideshows of Nineteenth-Century Europe', *The Journal of Popular Culture* 47(2): 262–83.

Angier, Natalie (1995), 'Modern "Wolfmen" May Have Inherited Ancient Gene', *New York Times*, 31 May.

Ass Ponys, 'Julia Pastrana', *YouTube*, <https://youtu.be/NDND3Sz_ASU> (accessed 29 October 2021).

Barbata, Laura Anderson (n.d.), 'Sin Lo Uno No Hay Lo Otro', *YouTube*, <https://www.youtube.com/watch?v=zRzYfaUCCXI> (accessed 29 October 2021).

— (2017), 'The Repatriation Pilgrimage of Julia Pastrana', in Donna Wingate and Laura Anderson Barbata (eds), *The Eye of the Beholder: Julia Pastrana's Long Journey Home*, Seattle: Lucia|Marquand, pp. 131–46.

Birch, Carol (2016), *Orphans of the Carnival*, New York: Anchor Books.

Brown, DeNeen (2018), '"The Bear Woman": The Brief, Sad Life of Julia Pastrana', *Washington Post*, 3 June, <https://www.washingtonpost.com/news/retropolis/wp/2018/06/03/the-bear-woman-julia-pastranas-humiliation-150-years-before-rose-annes-racist-tweet/> (accessed 25 September 2018).

Browne, Janet, and Sharon Messenger (2003), 'Victorian Spectacle: Julia Pastrana, the Bearded and Hairy Female', *Endeavour* 27(4): 155–9.

Calzada, Billy (n.d.), *Self-Portrait Artist*, <http://www.marihernandez.com/about.html> (accessed 2 July 2019).

Carl, Noah (2018), 'Leavers Have a Better Understanding of Remainers' Motivations Than Vice Versa', *London School of Economics: BREXIT*, 4 May, <https://blogs.lse.ac.uk/brexit/2018/05/04/leavers-have-a-better-understanding-of-remainers-motivations-than-vice-versa/> (accessed 29 October 2021).

Drimmer, Frederick (1973), *Very Special People: The Struggles, Loves, and Triumphs of Human Oddities*, New York: Amjon Publishers.

Esquer, Rafael (2013), 'Julia Pastrana. Su Vuelta y Sus Raíces', *YouTube*, <https://www.youtube.com/watch?v=UtnOlQXlNdc&feature=youtu.be> (accessed 27 March 2019).

'EU and Mexico Reach New Agreement on Trade' (2018), *Trade – European Commission*, 21 April, <http://trade.ec.europa.eu/doclib/press/index.cfm?id=1830> (accessed 22 April 2019).

Farias, Larissa (n.d.), 'The Bearded Lady', *YouTube*, <https://www.youtube.com/watch?v=LHLQ8hhCFQU> (accessed 24 January 2019).

Garland, Rosie (2013), *The Palace of Curiosities*, London: Harper Collins.

Garland-Thomson, Rosemarie (1997), *Extraordinary Bodies: Figuring Physical Disability in American Culture and Literature*, New York: Columbia University Press.

— (2017), 'Julia Pastrana, the "Extraordinary Lady"', in Donna Wingate and Laura Anderson Barbata (eds), *The Eye of the Beholder: Julia Pastrana's Long Journey Home*, Seattle: Lucia|Marquand, pp. 31–60.

Gylseth, Christopher, and Lars Toverud (2004), *Julia Pastrana: The Tragic Story of the Victorian Ape Woman*, trans. Donald Tumasonis, Stroud: Sutton Publishing.

Hong, Grace Kyungwon, and Roderick A. Ferguson, eds (2011), *Strange Affinities: The Gender and Sexual Politics of Comparative Racialization*, Durham, NC: Duke University Press.

Hussey, Kristin (2014), 'Casts of the Teeth of Julia Pastrana (1834–1860), the Nondescript', *Morbid Anatomy*, <http://morbidanatomy.blogspot.com/2014/01/casts-of-teeth-of-julia-pastrana-1834.html> (accessed 29 October 2021).

The Lady Aye (2013), 'Beauty Is an Impediment: Julia Pastrana and the Modern-Day Politics of Being Seen', *HuffPost: The Blog*, 7 August, <http://www.huffingtonpost.com/the-lady-aye/beauty-is-an-impediment-j_b_3541617.html> (accessed 11 July 2014).

López, Marissa (2019a), interview with Shaun Prendergast, 25 January.

— (2019b), interview with Mari Hernandez, 22 February.

Orozco, Gisela (2013), 'Julia Pastrana: Su triste, inexplicable y maravillosa historia', *Hoy*, 31 October, <https://www.chicagotribune.com/hoy/ct-hoy-8373863-julia-pastrana-su-triste-inexplicable-y-maravillosa-historia-story.html> (accessed 24 January 2019).

Oskan, May (2013), *The Ape Woman*, <https://theapewoman.com/> (accessed 24 January 2019).

Prendergast, Shaun (1999), *The True History of the Tragic Life and Triumphant Death of Julia Pastrana, The Ugliest Woman in the World*, TS.

Rose, Wendy (1985), *The Halfbreed Chronicles and Other Poems*, New York: West End Press.

SIAVI – Sistema de Información Comercial Via Internet (n.d.), <http://www.economia-snci.gob.mx/> (accessed 23 April 2019).

Stelloh, Tim (2013), 'Behold! The Heartbreaking, Hair-Raising Tale of Freak Show Star Julia Pastrana, Mexico's Monkey Woman', *BuzzFeed*, 13 December, <https://www.buzzfeed.com/timstelloh/behold-the-heartbreaking-hair-raising-tale-of-julia-pastrana> (accessed 25 September 2018).

Wilson, Charles (2013), 'Julia Pastrana, Who Died in 1860, to Be Buried in Mexico', *New York Times*, 11 February, <https://www.nytimes.com/2013/02/12/arts/design/julia-pastrana-who-died-in-1860-to-be-buried-in-mexico.html> (accessed 29 October 2021).

Figure 8.1 Poster advertising appearances by Julia Pastrana at the Regent Gallery, London, singing romantic songs and performing 'fancy dances'. Image courtesy of the Wellcome Library.

136   THE PENNY ILLUSTRATED PAPER.   [March 1, 1862.

Figure 8.2 'Miss Julia Pastrana, the embalmed nondescript: exhibiting at 191, Piccadilly.' Image courtesy of the Wellcome Library.

Figure 8.3 Mari Hernandez as Julia Pastrana. Image courtesy of Mari Hernandez.

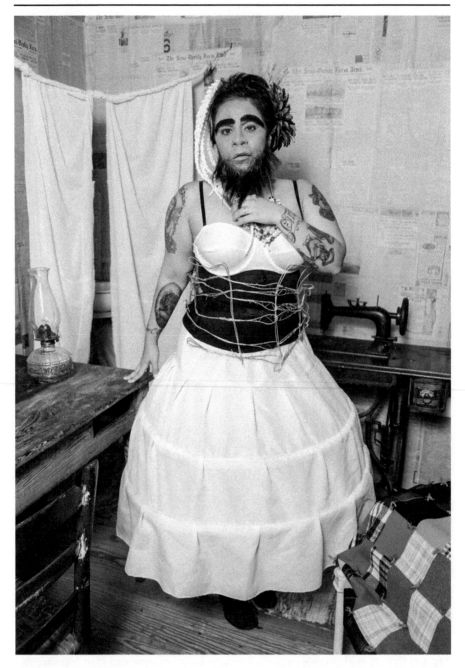

Figure 8.4 Mari Hernandez as Julia Pastrana. Image courtesy of Mari Hernandez.

Figure 8.5 Mari Hernandez as Julia Pastrana. Image courtesy of Mari Hernandez.

Notes

1. It is not clear how these casts came into the museum's possession. Hussey reports that the museum acquired them in the mid-nineteenth century, possibly as part of the founding collection from the College of Dentistry. Several different doctors are reported to have presented these casts from 1859 on, suggesting that the museum once held several sets, of which only one now survives (n.p.).

2. There is, actually, as Janet Browne and Sharon Messenger note, still debate among experts over whether Pastrana suffered from congenital hypertrichosis lanuginose or hypertrichosis terminalis. In the former, foetal hair is retained after birth; in the latter, which is usually accompanied by facial deformity, fetal hair is replaced by adult hair (158).

3. Christopher Gylseth and Lars Toverud acknowledge the difficulty in determining the details of Pastrana's early life especially. Most extant information comes from pamphlets publicising her appearances, and these were more focused on sensationalising rather than accurately reporting (140). Stelloh offers an overview of existing versions of her story, including contemporary oral lore he collected during a 2013 visit to Sinaloa (n.p.).

4. See Gylseth and Toverud (20–33) for an overview of nineteenth-century scientific studies of Pastrana. Gylseth and Toverud also, as do many who write about Pastrana, discuss Arthur Munby's 1909 poem 'Pastrana', which recounts his viewing of her in 1857. Pastrana references, however, can be found in a diverse range of nineteenth-century literature, including Leo Tolstoy's 1863 story of domestic labour, *Polikushka*, British writer Charles Reade's 1871 novel *A Terrible Temptation*, and many more. London's Wellcome Collection library of health, medicine and medical history houses a large collection of Pastrana ephemera that demonstrates just how popular and visible she was both in life and death.

5. 'N-gram' is the term computational linguistics uses to describe a sequence of items such as phonemes, syllables, letters or words from a sample text.

6. The Hopi-Miwok poet Wendy Rose included 'Julia', a lyric meditation in Pastrana's voice, in her collection *The Halfbreed Chronicles* (1992). Cincinnati indie rockers the Ass Ponys tell her story in 'Julia Pastrana' from their album *Grim* (1993).

7. In *The Ape Woman: A Rock Opera* (2014), for example, May Oskan uses Pastrana to meditate on the artistic exploitation of women's bodies, as does Larissa Farias in her one-woman play *The Bearded Lady* (2015). British novelist Carol Birch's *Orphans at the Carnival* (2016) uses Pastrana's life to illuminate the struggles of a frustrated artist in contemporary Britain, while the British musician Rosie Garland's much-awaited first novel, *The Palace of Curiosities* (2013), claims Pastrana as inspiration for a steampunk, Victorian fantasy of carnival freaks and sexual knife play. Colectivo el Pozo, a Chicago-based theatre ensemble dedicated to creating opportunities for Latinx actors, dwell on Pastrana's *mexicanidad* in their 2013 bilingual production of Raúl Dorantes's play *The Inexplicable Pastrana*, using her as an occasion to meditate on contemporary migration.

8. '. . . was sold to a circus like an object. She was sold multiple times for display at circuses and carnivals, first in Mexico then in the US, where she met Theodore Lent,

who married her and, in this way, was able to control her. Lent displayed her. He exploited her' (my translation).

9. In the seventeenth century, the German-born Barbara Urslerin suffered from hypertrichosis while entertaining crowds across Europe on her harpsichord. A century before that, young, hirsute Petrus Gonzales was taken from the Canary Islands for presentation at the Parisian court, where he was pampered, educated and well married, producing several similarly afflicted children whose lives and travels were well documented in scientific literature and the visual arts. See Angier on late twentieth-century cases of congenital generalised hypertrichosis documented in Mexico.

10. Aguirre looks from 1821 to 1898, during which time Latin America was Britain's second largest export market, behind India, receiving 10 per cent of all British international trade. At the same time, he writes, England 'witnessed an extraordinary burst of representations that occurred between the first European museum exhibit of Aztec antiquities (mounted in London) and the absorption of pre-Columbian materials into the British novel' (xiv).

11. Mexico's Secretaría de Economía makes such data available online (see SIAVI).

12. Equiano, a former slave living in Britain and known during his lifetime as Gustavas Vassa, published a memoir, *The Interesting Narrative of the Life of Olaudah Equiano*, in 1789.

13. The Island of Dolls is a tourist attraction in Parque Ecológico de Xochimilco where the trees and bushes are filled with old, discarded dolls and doll parts. Legend has it that one day the island's caretaker found a young girl drowned; shortly after that he found a doll, which he believed contained the girl's spirit. He placed the doll in a tree and began collecting more. Aided by tourists, the collection has grown substantially over the years and now fills the island.

14. The artists' strategy recalls Grace Hong and Rod Ferguson's discussion of woman of colour feminism and queer of colour critique in their introduction to *Strange Affinities*. Comparative methods of racial analysis seeking commonality across difference, they argue, historically centre the whiteness of European modernity, methodologically masking the workings of race and colonial power. Comparative methods centring difference, by contrast, enable coalitions across race and class while making visible the structures of power that condition the lived experience of bodies and subjects that deviate from heteronormative, bourgeois whiteness.

15. Paper cut-outs; a traditional Mexican folk art.

16. See, for example, 'Self-Portrait Artist', a video on Hernandez's website which shows her transforming into one of these nameless characters.

9

MATANZAS, CUBA/KESWICK, ENGLAND: MARIA GOWEN BROOKS VISITS ROBERT SOUTHEY, 1831

ERIN C. SINGER

After the death of a husband thirty years her senior, and fresh from a sojourn at her brother's coffee plantation in Matanzas, Cuba, Maria Gowen Brooks arrives in Keswick, England. It is the spring of 1831. She brings with her a poetry manuscript titled *Zóphiël*, which is to be her magnum opus, as well as a new name: 'Maria del Occidente'. She has already published *Zóphiël*'s first canto in Boston in 1825, but under the name 'Mrs Brooks'. Brooks writes that the full version of *Zóphiël*, all six cantos complete with notes, was composed across a wide geography: 'some in Cuba, some in Canada, some at Hanover, United States, some at Paris, and the last at Keswick, England, under the kind encouragement of Robert Southey, Esq.' (Brooks 1833: 251).

Robert Southey, the Poet Laureate, helps Maria Brooks publish *Zóphiël* in England under the name Maria del Occidente. Brooks aligns herself with the English high Romantic literary tradition through association with Southey and through the genre, formal and thematic choices in her poetry. At the same time, she also begins to make a name for herself in the literary tradition of the American Renaissance or American Romanticism. While the term 'American Renaissance' is contested as historically exclusionary,[1] in order to understand Brooks's significance to American literary history it is helpful to read her work along with that of her canonical contemporaries such as William Cullen Bryant and Henry Wadsworth Longfellow.

The reception history of *Zóphiël*, as well as the historical descriptions of Brooks herself preserved in Southey's letters, shows that nineteenth-century critics on both sides of the Atlantic struggled to categorise this poetic work, as well as the woman who produced it. Charles Lamb famously quipped, 'Southey says it is by some Yankee woman: as if there had ever been a woman capable of anything so great!' (quoted in Gustafson 1879: 250).

Well into the twentieth century, scholars still grappled with how to understand Brooks. Her own refusal of geographic fixity contributed to her indeterminate legacy. Kirsten Silva Gruesz explains how Brooks defies a narrow sense of borders – not only of genre and of nineteenth-century womanhood, but also of American geography:

> Like Cuba itself, Brooks alternately courted and resisted alliance with England and the United States during this period, as first Robert Southey (in the 1830s) and then Rufus Griswold (in the 1840s) championed her work to their respective countrymen . . . . To make a rough analogy, both the poet and her island have been treated as exceptional cases (Gruesz 2008b: 39).

Perhaps Brooks's most difficult contradiction to reconcile well into the twenty-first century is her problematic ideological and material relationships to slavery (Gruesz 2008b: 47). Her financial independence and leisure time for literary production was achieved by the labour of the enslaved people on her coffee plantation. We must foreground the fact that Brooks's ability to challenge gender roles in her life and her poems was due to her whiteness and her wealth.

Maria Gowen Brooks – or Maria del Occidente – has been described from the nineteenth century to the present as masculine and feminine; romantic and sentimental; and American, English and Cuban, among other contrasting concepts. This indeterminacy may be why her work has not been more central to nineteenth-century literary studies. Brooks's person and poetic style both refuse geographic and genre categories. It is precisely because she is so innovative in her poetics that for almost two centuries, many have missed her tremendous contributions to the modern epic poem. She both feminised and hemispherised a genre of male, Anglo-American epic poetry, and her formal innovations have been misrecognised. What seems to be an almost-forgotten poem with limited critical reception in her own era is in fact an important source that engages with questions of transnationalism, multivocality and gender in the context of the early nineteenth century, earlier than several canonical writers.

In attempting to situate Brooks's poetry within an existing critical context, I studied her biography, her correspondence with Southey[2] and the reception history of *Zóphiël*. I found myself with two significant problems: first, the difficulty of separating the author from her work; second, that her work defies a singular or even dual critical framework. As regards authorial performance and biographical myth, it is helpful to compare Brooks to other poets of her era whose personas are sometimes foregrounded over their literary production (Walt Whitman and Edgar Allan Poe come to mind). For example, Brooks herself, and much of Brooks scholarship, puts Robert Southey in the position of her mentor. Yet in examining the written record of their letters, my research shows that Southey's actual influence in Brooks' life was minor. Rather, he was a name Brooks used to gain access to the English Romantic tradition, as well a thematic inspiration for her poetry.

Concerning the difficulty of placing Brooks within a critical framework, it is precisely this difficulty that argues for Brooks's poetics as her most significant contribution. Her poetry hybridises existing critical and geographic categories, as her person (and performative persona) move among them. I have been unable to fix her as a poetess or a high Romantic poet; nor as a US American, transatlantic or Caribbean writer. Ultimately, Brooks's poetry offers readers a critical framework that is indefinite and multifarious.

What is missing from several earlier studies of Maria Gowen Brooks (with the exception of Greusz's work) is close reading of Brooks's poems. *Zóphiël* in particular needs consideration as an epic poem, and should be brought to light as an essential link in the grand narrative of American poetry. It seems to me that Brooks's work has been mostly treated as a historical object. What this chapter adds to the conversation is an attention to it as a literary text. The American nineteenth-century epic does not emerge suddenly in 1855 with Walt Whitman's *Leaves of Grass* or Longfellow's *The Song of Hiawatha*. I argue in this chapter that we must read *Zóphiël* and other works like it to more fully understand the development of American Romantic poetry.

In this chapter I will closely analyse a few sections of *Zóphiël*, focusing on the poem's formal qualities to show how Brooks innovates within the epic form in order to argue for a feminine, transnational alternative to the American or English national epic. Though I disagree with some of Mikhail Bakhtin's theory of the epic (I believe it is equally, if not more capacious, than the novel), his contrast between monologic and dialogic ethoi are particularly useful in understanding Brooks's poetic innovations (see Bakhtin 2004). I ultimately find that her work in *Zóphiël* argues for a dialogic poetics (see Ramazani 2013). Maria Gowen Brooks reminds us that the epic, often seen as a closed form, is in fact a discursive, dynamic and flexible poetic form.

In terms of genre, Brooks competes for fame on the same ground as the Romantics. Both the first and second generations of British Romantics all wrote at least one epic poem. Examples include Wordsworth's *The Prelude*, Blake's *Milton*, Southey's *Madoc* and Keats's attempted *Hyperion*; as well as poems that are what we might call epic-adjacent, such as Coleridge's 'Rime of the Ancient Mariner' and Shelley's *Queen Mab*. Southey even credits his own work for what he calls the 'epomania' of the era (quoted in Beshero-Bondar

2011: 17). Given that Southey feels himself responsible for reinvigorating the epic genre for the Romantics, it would make sense that Brooks would position herself as his poetic heir.

Kirsten Silva Gruesz, who provides the most robust twentieth-century scholarship on Maria Gowen Brooks, highlights how Brooks's work is situated at the crossroads of both genre and gender. Brooks is neither the high Romantic male poet nor the sentimental poetess. The high Romantic male poet can be broadly defined by his work (consider the examples of England's poets laureate in the nineteenth century: Robert Southey, William Wordsworth and Alfred, Lord Tennyson). The poetess, by contrast, is defined by her person. Tricia Lootens explains the poetess as:

> A mythic, composite presence defined by 'acceptance' of the 'doctrine of separate spheres' . . . that Poetess thrives in a realm of shifting literary (and, of course, political) open secrets, easily located between the unspeakable and the all-too familiar. She emerges, most famously, within the poems, introductions, and interstices . . . . Within the nineteenth century, for an actual writer to take – or, for that matter, be aggressively assigned – this title was, by definition, to step forth as heir or counterpart to a whole range of [tragic] figures. (Lootens 2016: 3)

Though named as a poetess by Robert Southey – he writes that Brooks was 'the most impassioned and most imaginative of all poetesses' (Southey 1836: 222) – Brooks mostly manages to avoid the label. I must note that almost everyone who studies women poets of the nineteenth century agrees that the category of poetess is an empty container (see Gruesz 2008a; Jackson and Prins 1999; Richards 2004; Looten 2016). Further, an attempt to understand the poetess tradition as a proto-feminist tradition also ignores how these writers saw themselves and their work (see Ezell 1996).

And yet, whatever it means to be a poetess, I present the concept as having some critical utility: as one end point on the spectrum of poetics in the nineteenth century. Laura Mandell's catalogue of formal poetic techniques provides a framework for considering where along the spectrum Brooks's work falls between the poetics of Romantics and poetesses, which I put to use later in this chapter (Mandell 2003). Brooks is in the interesting position of being called a poetess in reviews, but produces work that eschews poetess style.

Though her work primarily focuses on the late Romantics, Mandell provides a framework of the formal qualities of Romantic poetics and poetess poetics. Her work details the different ways Romantics and poetesses use meter, audience, rhetorical moment, diction, subjectivity and ideological orientation. Using Mandell's taxonomy, I found commonalities among (1) Romantic aesthetics (2) epic conventions and (3) Brooks's own epic poem.[3] The epic genre allows Brooks to position herself as a Romantic poet rather than a poetess. Her choice of both genre and form are inextricably tied to her own writerly ambitions. As a poet who wrote to avoid the poetess label, and an epic poet, Brooks constructed the poem as a future historical object and wrote to fellow highly educated, multilingual readers.

In other words, the poetess does not write epic poems, but the Romantic poet does. Brooks clearly sides with Romantic forms of poetry, but refuses fixity there as well. She forms her own poetics, blending high Romanticism and a feminised style. Moreover, she adds a hemispheric, transnational perspective to the thematic space of the Americas as an epic subject. The grounds for this kind of thematic focus are there (Robert Southey's *Madoc* was, after all, set in North America), but Brooks exceeds previous iterations of the American epic.

Before I proceed with formal analysis, I will provide some background information on Maria Gowen Brooks's epic poem. The full edition of *Zóphiël* published in 1833 contains six cantos, each with its own argument and explanatory notes. The book also contains a few poems at the end. I argue that the inclusion of these poems is a claim that Brooks's work fits the category of poet, rather than poetess. The additional poems showcase Brooks's mastery of multiple genres: not only epic, but more lyric modes such as ode and song.

The plot of *Zóphiël* derives from the apocryphal Book of Tobit. In the original, a demon interferes with Sarah's wedding nights, killing her husbands before they can consummate the marriage. It ends when God has the angel Raphael kill the demon so that Sarah can finally marry Tobias (son of Tobit). Maria Gowen Brooks turns her attention to the tale of Tobias's wife, Sarah. In Brooks's version, the fallen angel Zóphiël falls in love with Egla (a Sarah figure), and indeed kills her husbands. However, in Brooks's poem, Egla has no desire to marry these men. She has had a premonition of her future husband, named Helon (a Tobias figure), whom she ultimately successfully marries. Thus Zóphiël, for his own reasons, helps Egla arrive at her destiny still a virgin before he is thwarted by God (with quite a few adventures in between). Yet in Brooks's retelling, Zóphiël evokes some sympathy. It is easy to read Brooks's focus on Egla as a proto-feminist move that repositions a woman at the centre of scripture and myth. However, this move was not new for Brooks, whose first book of poems focused on the apocryphal and Biblical stories of Judith and Esther.

Formally, Brooks was a master of meter, inventing her own riff on the Spenserian stanza 'with six lines rhymed ABCCBA (two pentameter lines, two trimeter lines, and a final couplet formed of one pentameter line and one alexandrine)' (Gruesz 2008a: 98). Yet what she chooses for *Zóphiël* is the relatively no-frills *ABAB* stanza (followed by *CDCD*, *EFEF*, etc.) in rhymed iambic pentameter. While in light of Brooks's considerable talent, her use of four-line stanzas with alternating rhyme written in iambic pentameter might seem a mundane choice, it is still worlds away from the poetry of the poetess, which relies on 'highly imitable' poetic forms of the less wealthy and less classically educated (Mandell 2013). Mandell writes:

> The metrics, iambic tetrameters and trimeters, make for sing-song poetry, but they are much closer to common ballad forms with which those of the laboring classes would be most familiar: they are not iambic pentameters and alexandrines that one has to acquire through learning Latin and Greek, reading expensive and time-consuming texts by Spenser and Milton, and/ or through reading continental Latinate languages. (Mandell 2013)

Her use of iambic pentameter is another way for Brooks to elevate her work to the level of national epic, both in terms of the Western classics and the English tradition. Decasyllabic verse evokes Western epics such as Virgil's *Aeneid*, which was first translated into English in decasyllables. The meter also evokes the work of John Milton, though he, like Brooks's contemporaries Wordsworth and Coleridge, preferred blank verse to the rhymed version of the meter.

However, Brooks strategically departs from iambic pentameter at several moments throughout *Zóphïël*. She shows her virtuosity by including, for example, a poetess poem within her high Romantic epic. She complicates the genre of epic in a strikingly modern way, emphasising the epic's multivocal, multigenre possibilities. This is an important point, because it is usually proto-modernist or modernist poets such as Walt Whitman or T. S. Eliot who are credited with incorporating collage and juxtaposition into their poems (see Miller 2010; Perloff 1998). Yet poets such as Brooks, writing before the mid-nineteenth century, experiment in ways that prefigure the evolution of multivocal poetry through the next century.

One such section in Brooks's epic appears in Canto VI, 'Bride of Helon', which poet and biographer Zadel Barnes Gustafson indicated was some of Brooks's best work (Gustafson 1879: 257). In this section, the poem changes both genre and meter to include Egla's song:

> VII. SONG.
> Day, in melting purple dying,
> Blossoms, all around me sighing,
> Fragrance, from the lilies straying,
> Zephyr, with my ringlets playing,
> Ye but waken my distress:
> I am sick of loneliness. (Brooks 1833: lines 45–50)

While Brooks has kept to five full cantos of the same style (rhymed iambic pentameter in form *ABAB*), this example changes rhyme and meter in order to change the speaker. It is Egla speaking, not Brooks's poetic persona as narrator. Specifically, it is Egla singing, which necessarily would sound different from the epic poem in which she is embedded. The song here is in the form of six-line stanzas, composed of four rhymed lines of trochaic tetrameter, followed by a rhyming couplet (rhyme scheme AAAA BB). The couplet is written in a trimeter composed primarily of trochees, varied from a perfect trochaic trimeter by the inclusion of one iamb ('distress' in line 49) and one dactyl ('loneliness' in line 50).

Egla's song continues:

> Thou to whom I love to hearken,
> Come, ere night around me darken;
> Though thy softness but deceive me,
> Say thou'rt true and I'll believe thee,
> Veil, if ill, thy soul's intent,
> Let me think it innocent!
> Save thy toiling, spare thy treasure:
> All I ask is friendship's pleasure:
> Let the shining ore lie darkling,
> Bring no gem in lustre sparkling;
> Gifts and gold are nought to me;
> I would only look on thee!
> Tell to thee the high-wrought feeling,
> Ecstasy but in revealing;
> Paint to thee the deep sensation,
> Rapture in participation,
> Yet but torture, if comprest
> In a lone unfriended breast.
> Absent still? Ah! Come and bless me!
> Let these eyes again caress thee;
> Once, in caution, I could fly thee;
> Now, I nothing could deny thee:
> In a look if death there be,
> Come and I will gaze on thee! (lines 51–74)

The trochaic tetrameter of the first four lines of each stanza of Egla's song pays homage to poetess poets such as Felicia Hemans. Brooks's use of this meter also prefigures later uses of trochaic octameter such as in Edgar Allan Poe's *The Raven* (1845). Poe uses this meter to imbue his poem with an otherworldly tone by juxtaposing its regularity and sing-song quality with a macabre theme. Brooks deserves equal credit for doing the same thing more than a decade before Poe, only in half the metrical feet. Egla's song is one of despair, and is a haunting melody that can affect even the angels. Maria Gowen Brooks moves beyond merely borrowing from poetess poetics to remaking them by combining their same metrical techniques with new themes, and positioning them in a different context.

The manner in which Brooks emphasises the epic's multivocal qualities while simultaneously feminising the genre through her use of metrical variation appears again at the conclusion of *Zóphiël*. In the final section (LXIV) of the final canto (Canto VI), which takes the form of a single stanza, Brooks plays with the contrast between iambic and trochaic meter.

> The fiercest pains of death had been relief,
> And yet his quenchless being might not end.
> Hark! Raphael's voice breaks sweetly on his grief:
> 'Hope, Zophiël! hope! hope! hope! – thou has a friend!' (lines 375–8)

The first two lines are in iambic pentameter, while the third begins a shift towards falling meter using trochees and anapaests. The fourth and final line of this stanza is dominated by stressed syllables: a stress ('Hope,'), then dactyl ('Zophiël!'),[4] then three stresses that I think of as a super-spondee ('hope! hope! hope!'), then a caesura, and finally ending with two iambs ('thou has a friend!').

Brooks accomplishes several things simultaneously with her trochaic finale to the final canto. First, she differentiates Raphael's voice from the voices of the other speakers in the poem. The use of stressed syllables and spondees imbues his tone with divine authority. Second, she uses this declarative tone and departure from the rest of the poem's regular meter to emphasise this ending's singularity, both in form and theme. Just as Brooks uses Egla's song to show mastery of poetess forms, I argue that Brooks changes her meter at the end to refuse the limitations of Romantic English epic meter. Southey, for example, ends his *Madoc* with iambic pentameter all the way through the final lines. Wordsworth's *The Prelude* maintains its iambic meter throughout, and even Blake's syllabic experiments in *Milton* lean iambic at the conclusion. In this context, Brooks's metrical variation seems particularly significant: it is a chance for her to remake the rules of the decasyllabic line into her own adaptation of the form.

These are just a few examples of Maria Gowen Brooks's use of meter to create a feminine high Romantic epic. The notes to *Zóphiël* show another side of Brooks as poetic innovator, whereby she globalises the epic by incorporating a multitude of voices into her poem. Brooks appends between four and sixteen notes to each of her six cantos, totalling seventy-three explanatory notes. Their content is fascinating, and contains, just to name a few examples: Brooks's musings on the difference between body and soul, citing Plato, Bonaventure, the

Quran and Robert Southey; naturalist descriptions of the caves of Virginia and Cuba; French translations of Tertullian alongside the original Latin descriptions of women's make-up practices in the third century CE (both the French and Latin untranslated into English). This last example of Tertullian from the second canto notes gives a good sense of Brooks as a researcher:

> The above extract is from a French translation, or rather compendium, of Tertullian, which was sent to me by Monsieur Van Praët, from the Biblioteque du Roi at Paris. But as many of the most curious passages were entirely omitted, the same gentleman was so obliging as to look for the Latin folio, containing that very amusing article of Tertullian, entitled *De Habitu Muliebri*; from which I had intended to have given, in this note, a longer extract, written out for me by Baron Joseph de Palm; from whose very beautiful German verses two inadequate translations will appear in this volume. The extract, however, was accidentally left at Paris; and Zóphiël being reviewed and arranged for the last time at Keswick (England) I fear it may not reach me soon enough to be inserted. (Brooks 1833: 97)

Here is a poet writing in Cuba, corresponding with a French librarian about translations of an African Christian gnostic (presumably, Brooks is able to translate between Latin, French and English). She compares the published French translations of the Latin original source to the handwritten French translations made by a German (or possibly, the German translations of the Latin original instead). All of these materials are in transit by mail between Cuba, France and England as Brooks awaits her book's publication.

In her acts of writing, reading, corresponding, translating and travelling, Maria Gowen Brooks remakes American literature into a world constellation (see Habermas 2001). She maps (see Casanova 2007; Moretti 2003) ways of poetic composition that not only exceed national boundaries, but reimagine or recycle them (see Dimock 2013). In other words, Brooks reveals that the category of an American poem is an artificial one; examining her work reveals how globally, linguistically and generically complex nineteenth-century literature has always been.

Brooks globalises the epic through challenging the linguistic primacy of English. She leaves French and Latin untranslated in her notes, which accomplishes three purposes: (1) showcasing her education, allowing her to compete for poetic achievement on the same grounds as her male Romantic counterparts; (2) confirming that multilingualism is essential to the epic form; and (3) highlighting the practice of translation as a method of poetic composition. Although the text of her poem is in English, the notes underlying it are far more linguistically complex. To elaborate, Brooks's translation practice as composition practice, differentiates her from other Romantics. In the first canto, for example, Brooks writes a note about the following couplet from section eighty-seven:

> And o'er her sense, as when the fond night-bird,
> Woos the full rose, o'erpowering fragrance stole. (lines 671–2)

The images of the nightingale and the rose are hardly new to English or American literature (Shakespeare, Milton and Keats all come to mind as examples). What is new are the sources Brooks cites, ranging from seventh-century BCE Greece through fourteenth-century Persia and finally ending with eighteenth-century English writers colonising Turkey and India for the British empire.[5] Though exhibiting Orientalism in her note (a problem), Brooks does something beyond participating in a long tradition of Western poets exoticising Eastern writers. She also de-anglicises these symbols and repositions them in their proper place as far more global, and far older, than either English or American writers.

Given all these innovations, why is Maria del Occidente missing from the larger story of American poetry? In 1879, Zadel Barnes Gustafson writes in *Harper's* magazine that perhaps America was not yet ready for a poet like Brooks: 'A country with a young civilization and a young literature, we did not expect and were not prepared to meet a revelation of American genius ranking with the great poets of the world' (Gustafson 1879: 258). Perhaps Gustafson is correct, and Maria Gowen Brooks was a poet ahead of her time. Another possibility lies precisely in Brooks's current appeal as a transnational figure who refuses the expected literary gender roles. She may not fit neatly into the story of nineteenth-century American literature precisely because she was a transatlantic, hemispheric poet; one whose work defied not only expectations of place, but also of genre and gender. Yet these reasons for Brooks's lack of enduring fame in her own era serve as a call for us to reconsider her work today, as we attempt to better understand what literary history can tell us about the present.

WORKS CITED

Bakhtin, Mikhail (2004), *The Dialogic Imagination: Four Essays*, ed. Michael Holquist, Austin: University of Texas Press.

Beshero-Bondar, Elisa (2011), *Women, Epic, and Transition in British Romanticism*, Newark: University of Delaware Press.

Brooks, Maria Gowen (1833), *Zóphiël; Or, The Bride of Seven*, London: R. J. Kennett.

Casanova, Pascale (2007), *The World Republic of Letters*, trans. Malcolm DeBevoise, Cambridge, MA: Harvard University Press.

Dimock, Wai Chi (2013), 'Recycling the Epic: *Gilgamesh* on Three Continents', *English Language Notes* 51(1): 19–33.

Ezell, Margaret (1996), *Writing Women's Literary History*, 2nd ed., Baltimore: Johns Hopkins University Press.

Gruesz, Kirsten Silva (2008a), 'Maria Gowen Brooks, In and Out of the Poe Circle', *ESQ: A Journal of Nineteenth-Century American Literature and Culture* 54(1–4): 75–110.

— (2008b), 'The Cafetal of María del Occidente and the Anglo-American Race for Cuba', in Meredith L. McGill (ed.), *The Traffic in Poems: Nineteenth-Century Poetry and Transatlantic Exchange*, Rutgers, NJ: Rutgers University Press, pp. 37–62.

Gustafson, Zadel Barnes (1879), 'Maria del Occidente', *Harper's New Monthly Magazine* 58: 249–61.

Habermas, Jürgen (2001), *The Postnational Constellation: Political Essays*, trans. and ed. Max Pensky, Cambridge, MA: MIT Press.

Jackson, Virginia and Yopie Prins (1999), 'Lyrical Studies', *Victorian Literature and Culture* 27(2): 521–30.

Kennett, R. J. (1838), 'Works Lately Published', *The Publisher's Circular* 1: 108.

Lootens, Tricia (2016), *The Political Poetess: Victorian Femininity, Race, and the Legacy of Separate Spheres*, Princeton: Princeton University.

Mandell, Laura (2013), 'Introduction: The Poetess Tradition', *Romanticism on the Net*, 29–30, <https://doi.org/10.7202/007712ar> (accessed 29 October 2021).

Miller, Matt (2010), *Collage of Myself: Walt Whitman and the Making of Leaves of Grass*, Lincoln: University of Nebraska Press.

Moretti, Franco (2005), *Graphs, Maps, Trees: Abstract Models for Literary History*, New York: Verso.

Perloff, Marjorie (1998), 'Collage and Poetry', in Michael Kelly (ed.), *Encyclopedia of Aesthetics*, vol. 1, New York: Oxford University Press, pp. 384–7.

Ramazani, Jahan (2013), *Poetry and Its Others: News, Prayer, Song, and the Dialogue of Genres*, Chicago: University of Chicago Press.

Richards, Eliza (2004), *Gender and the Poetics of Reception in Poe's Circle*, Cambridge: Cambridge University Press.

Southey, Robert (1836), *The Doctor, &c.*, New York: Harper & Brothers.

NOTES

1. The term 'American renaissance' was coined by F. O. Matthiessen in the 1940s and refers mostly to a collection of white men writers in the New England area, thus leaving out women writers, writers of colour and southern writers, to name but a few.

2. The letters that I relied on most for this study were Southey's 'Letter to Caroline Bowles; March 8, 1831', 'Letter to Caroline Bowles; October 12, 1833', and Caroline Bowles's 'Letter to Robert Southey; February 14, 1834'. All three of these are located in *The Correspondence of Robert Southey with Caroline Bowles*. I also found useful Southey's 'Letter to Lord Mahon; Keswick; May 12, 1834' in *The Life & Correspondence of the Late Robert Southey*, as well as Ruth Grannis Shephard's transcription of letters in *An American Friend of Southey*.

3. I have rewritten Laura Mandell's framework in table format:

	Romantic	*Poetess*
Meter	Iambic pentameter and alexandrine	Iambic trimeter and tetrameter
Audience	Highly educated readers of canonical poems	A large community of readers
Rhetorical moment	Writing towards an imagined future; constructing a monument for posterity	Writing for a specific moment in the present
Diction	Defamiliarised and experimental	Conventional poetic diction
Subjectivity	Consolidated; the poet gives a strong sense of him- or herself even when describing seemingly objective scenes	Diffuse; the poet does not unpack cultural constructs, nor elevate him- or herself to a place in a grand history of poetry
Ideological orientation	Critique	Conformity

4. Although the name Zóphiël is not produced with an accent in the text of the poem, it is clearly accented in the title of the epic, and thus takes the form of a dactyl (one stressed followed by two unstressed syllables). Further evidence that this name is dactylic meter is that it likely matches the rhythm of the name Raphael used just above it in the third line, at least in English. I will note that in Spanish and Italian the name Raphael, like Zóphiël, would be in anapestic meter (two unstressed syllables followed by a stressed one). Given Brooks's fluency in both English and several romance languages, she likely made an intentional choice for the word Zóphiël to have the English pronunciation, and inserted the acute accent to clarify that for the reader.

5. In note ten of Canto I, Brooks lists the following sources for her thinking of the nightingale and the rose: *Fable of the Gardener and Nightingale* (likely references to 600–500 BCE Greek writers Hesiod or Aesop); Lady Mary Wortley Montagu (eighteenth-century English poet, married to the British ambassador to Constantinople, known for her descriptions of the Ottoman empire); Hafiz (fourteenth-century Persian poet); Sir William Jones (eighteenth-century English linguist and Supreme Court judge in British-occupied Calcutta), Gelaleddin Ruzbehar (could be Gelalo'ddin Ruzbehar, or another name variation; likely another Persian poet, mentioned in Jones's translations) and Pliny the Elder (first-century CE Roman historian) (Brooks 1833: 47).

10

ENGLAND/NEW ENGLAND: A BRITISH QUAKER AND A FUGITIVE FROM SLAVERY ENCOUNTER EACH OTHER ON A TRAIN, 1850

BRIDGET BENNETT

On the morning of Monday, 15 July 1850, two strangers briefly entered each other's orbit.[1] They were both travelling in a train going the short distance from Lynn to Boston. One of them, Wilson Armistead, was a Leeds-based Quaker merchant and abolitionist who was on a short visit to the United States combining business interests with family visits and meetings with New England abolitionists. The other, Thomas H. Jones, was a self-emancipated fugitive from Wilmington, North Carolina, who had escaped to New York the previous September and subsequently relocated to New England. Their unlikely meeting would later be described by Armistead in an unsigned series, 'Reminiscences of a Visit to the United States, in the Summer of 1850', which appeared sporadically in a Quaker journal, *The British Friend*, from November 1850 to December 1852. Details of their brief moment of crossing are sparse; Armistead affords it just ten lines, writing,

> In the carriage in which I was seated were three coloured people, one of whom I found to be a fugitive from the horrors of slavery, which he had endured in North Carolina for forty-three years. He furnished me with a few particulars of his history, as [*sic*] also of the providential escape of his family (a wife and three children), whom he succeeded in aiding away previously. Having preserved this account, I purpose transcribing it briefly in time for your next number. ('Reminiscences', July 1851: 151)

Embedded deep within Armistead's text are the 'few particulars' with which Jones 'furnished' him. They comprise the first and only UK publication of *The Experience of Thomas Jones, who was a Slave for Forty-Three Years*. Its existence has been completely unsuspected until now. I came across it by chance, while undertaking research on Armistead's abolitionist activism in nineteenth-century Leeds. I was not looking for, or expecting to find, a previously unknown edition of a self-emancipated fugitive. My research on Armistead, a quiet Quaker merchant and devoted abolitionist, has also produced other surprises. Eight months after meeting Jones, and seven months before writing about it, he was involved in a piece of activism centring on the UK census of 1851. The fugitives Ellen and William Craft stayed with Armistead and his family in their house in Leeds on the night of the census, and Armistead made sure they were each recorded as a 'Fugitive Slave'. He did this to draw attention to the politics of US enslavement in a state document that at surface level had no connection with slavery.[2] His principled opportunism would be repeated in a different way when he included Jones's narrative in his 'Reminiscences'. He did this in order to bring attention to the fact that what to a British audience might seem like an extraordinary meeting with a fugitive was more ordinary within the context of New England. Yet in textual terms, the juxtaposition of the mundane nature of a chance encounter with its remarkable outcome makes their meeting especially important. Indeed, the inclusion of Jones's narrative in Armistead's work is a really striking moment in what otherwise is a relatively conventional travelogue.

Though William Wells Brown wrote that 'Few English gentlemen have done more to hasten the day of the slave's liberation than Wilson Armistead' (Brown 1855: 148), Armistead has had limited scholarly attention. Yet he was an important activist whose 1848 work *A Tribute for the Negro* had already attracted significant interest by the time he met Jones. George Shepperson argues that his work was critical for African nationalists, arguing that 'it may . . . be safely said that Wilson Armistead's *A Tribute for the Negro* was one of the most outstanding – if not the most outstanding – ideological influence from the Abolitionist Epoch on African political thought' (Shepperson 1964: 24). My ongoing research continues to reveal new details about this internationalism, particularly his influence on African intellectual and political thought. Once he returned from the US he would go on to become the librarian for the Leeds Antislavery Association, which he helped to found in 1853, and would produce many books in support of abolition and on the lives of eminent Quakers including the Philadelphian abolitionist and teacher Anthony Benezet.

The identity of Jones's companions may never be known. However, we do know quite a lot about Jones himself, thanks to recent archivally-led recovery work. He was born into enslavement in North Carolina, one of six children born to enslaved parents. John Hawes, who held Jones in slavery, sold him to a Wilmington shopkeeper when he was nine years old. After an unhappy period, he was put to work in the shop. He taught himself to read and write in secret and he became a Christian, eventually preaching to large groups. He was allowed to revisit his former home when he was twenty-two, and found that his father and siblings had all been sold and only his mother remained. In early versions of his narrative (including the Armistead edition), this is the only point at which Jones describes seeing his family after their early separation. But the 1885 edition recounts a meeting with his father about three years after they were parted, as well as considerable further details of their lives.[3] In 1829 Jones was purchased by an attorney named Owen Holmes. He worked as a stevedore and was allowed largely to manage his own time and money. Hiring his time for $150 per year, he rented a house from Dr E. J. Desert, saved some of his earnings, and ministered to Black and white communities. He also entered into a common-law marriage with an enslaved woman, Lucilla Smith, whose enslaver was a Mrs Moore. They went on to have three children. But when Moore moved to New Bern she took Smith and their three children, Annie, Lizzie and Charlie. Jones only saw them just once again, for a single night when Moore moved to Tuscaloosa and stayed overnight in Wilmington. In later editions he gives more detail about their separation and his unsuccessful attempts to find them after the end of the war.[4] Armistead faithfully reproduces Jones's devastation. After several years he entered into a second marriage to Mary Moore. They had a son, Edward, before Jones was able to purchase Mary's freedom for $350. The couple then had three further children.

In the winter of 1848–9 Jones was warned that the liberty of his wife and children was under threat. He showed great perspicacity, first consulting a local lawyer, who tried to secure their emancipation, and when that was unsuccessful, suggesting that they escape as soon as possible. He purchased tickets for them on a vessel leaving for New York and they fled to Brooklyn, where they stayed with 'a true-hearted friend', Robert H. Cousins, who was also sheltering Jones's sister. Meanwhile Jones and Edward, who were both enslaved, remained in Wilmington. He had purchased three modest properties, using a white proxy to overcome prohibitions placed on enslaved individuals owning property. After his wife's departure he spent three months trying to get what was rightfully his and send rent money to Mary. Having been cheated by an apparent friend, he took advantage of his enslaver's sudden illness to escape by sea. He travelled up the eastern seaboard on the brig *Bell*, leaving Wilmington on 11 September 1849. Though he persuaded the steward to allow him to stow away, he became ill with turpentine fumes and was eventually discovered by the captain, who threatened to return him to captivity. Eventually he escaped overboard after constructing a makeshift raft. He was picked up by friendly sailors, who assisted him and gave him money and clothing. The Armistead edition ends with the point at which the reunited family moved to Boston. Shortly after this, the two men met each other.

The existence of the Armistead edition has been entirely forgotten until now. Though I came across it by chance, it was a serendipitous archival encounter that exemplifies the themes of chance and mobility amplified below. The Armistead edition gives researchers, teachers, students and general readers unique new material to work with because the larger 'Reminiscences' (themselves never republished) contain both Jones's narrative and a first-person account of the moment the men met. The way Armistead describes the process of the preservation and subsequent transcription of Jones's text is revealing about his practice as an editor-activist, developed over several years of experience, and subsequently further revised in consequence of his reading of Jones's work. He shaped Jones's narrative to fit both publication and audience. In addition, he crafted it in ways that are revealed only when it is compared with the original pamphlet. He had to contend with the implications of serial publication (including how to make transitions between journal issues); limitations of space and length; and, critically, how to incorporate a slave narrative into his own autobiographically driven piece. These elements contributed to shaping the form of Jones's narrative when it appeared serially within Armistead's 'Reminiscences'.

Since the publishing history of Jones's work has not yet been securely established, the Armistead edition extends our knowledge in important ways. I situate my reading with reference to new ways of interpreting African American testimony and the circulation of transatlantic print culture. Uncovering this story of crossing involves exciting discoveries – including this entirely new edition – and frustrating dead ends, due to silences and inaccuracies in the historical record. The meeting is a vivid example of the role chance can play in building allegiances and networks that cross boundaries such as the nation-state. It calls for interpretive strategies to help develop models for understanding the events leading up to the physical and textual encounter and its aftermath. The first extant edition of the text was published in Boston by the African American printer Daniel J. Laing. Its appearance was announced in *The Liberator* on 1 March, four months before Jones and Armistead met.[5] The texts of the Laing and Armistead editions bear a close relation to each other, suggesting that the Laing edition was most probably the basis for the Armistead edition.[6] However, it is worth speculating about the disputed existence of an even earlier edition, of which no trace has yet been found, believed to have been published in Worcester in 1849 (Davis in Andrews et al. (eds) 2003: 200–1).[7] Its possible existence speaks to the way Black experience both is, and is not, archived in the nineteenth century and reminds us how much work remains to be done in order to have the fullest picture of it. Since in addition to the Armistead edition I have also located another previously unknown edition, published in St John, Canada in 1853, continuing to look for the 'missing' Worcester edition is worthwhile labour.

Two pieces of evidence are particularly of note to help with this task. The first comes from the prefatory page of the 1850 Laing edition, dated 25 November 1849 and containing two testimonials, one signed jointly by E. A. Stockman, pastor of the Wesleyan Church in Boston and Daniel Foster, pastor of the Free Evangelical Church in North Danvers, and the other by A. B. Flanders, the pastor of the Wesleyan Methodist Church in Exeter. They attest to Jones's identity, stating that he had already spoken at their churches. Stockman and Foster call his narrative 'one of thrilling interest, calculated to secure the attention of any audience, and to benefit the sympathising hearts of all who will make themselves acquainted with the present condition and past experience of a true-hearted brother' (Jones 1850: 3). This is obviously designed to create an audience for Jones, though not necessarily a reading audience for his text. Soon after his escape from enslavement he started to give testimony in churches in the North. He was certainly living a hand-to-mouth existence while supporting his family. Evidence reveals that he was financially astute and kept detailed accounts, though Armistead leaves out the careful detail Jones gives of the amount of money he earned through lecturing. Yet Jones's precision reveals his determination to be independent and self-sufficient. He was shaping himself as a citizen. Jones notes that a lecture at Stockman's church raised $3.33, while one at Flanders's church resulted in 'a generous contribution of nearly ten dollars' (Jones 1850: 47), just under the $10 he was given at Foster's church. On the reverse side of the page is a direct undated address by Jones, stating,

> A suffering brother would affectionately present this simple story of deep personal wrongs to the earnest friends of the Slave. He asks you to buy and read it, for, in so doing, you will help one who needs your sympathy and aid, and you will receive, in the perusal of this simple narrative, a more fervent conviction of the necessity and blessedness of toiling for the desolate members of the one great brotherhood who now suffer and die, ignorant and despairing, in the vast prison land of the South. 'Whatsoever ye would that men should do unto you, do ye also unto then [sic].' (Jones 1850: 4)

His words explicitly prompt sympathisers to purchase the narrative. None of this provides definitive evidence of a date of composition or publication, though it does show how quickly Jones built connections with abolitionist networks, something Armistead was also successful in doing.[8] He would go on to publish multiple editions of his narrative, in Canada and in the United States, right up until 1888, when the Boston firm A. T. Bliss and Company produced the last known edition to be published before his death on 6 June 1890.[9] This textual project was a significant feature of his life once he left Wilmington, revealing an ongoing desire to archive his life and experiences.

A second piece of evidence certainly suggests that some kind of written text was produced within a short time of his escape. Towards the end of the 1850 narrative, Jones notes that the following day is Thanksgiving. Though this only became an official national holiday in 1863, in 1849 it was celebrated on Thursday, 22 November. It is reasonable to assume that he was creating this part of his narrative (whether as written notes for a lecture or as the text for a printed narrative) on 21 November 1849. He had left Wilmington on 11 September, joining his family in New York and then rapidly moving alone to Hartford and Springfield before arriving at Boston on 7 October. He gave three lectures in Boston, earning $8.44 in total. He was also lent $5 by an unnamed 'generous friend' (Jones 1850: 47) and was able to reunite his family in Boston. Since he describes himself as being penniless and needing funds, it is highly probable that he would have needed to put together a narrative as quickly as possible so that he could sell it to continue to support his family. He had been accustomed to hiring out his time in the last period of time in which he was enslaved (see below) and was clearly desirous of having the dignity of financial independence. In one of the most vivid passages in his narrative, he describes the slow period of saving the $350 needed to purchase his wife's freedom:

> we made a box, and, through a hole in the top we put in every piece of money, from five cents up to a dollar, that we could save from our hard earnings. This object nerved us for unceasing toil, for twenty months, or about that time. What hopes and fears best us as those months wore away. I have been compelled to hide that box in a hole, dug for it, when I knew the patrollers were coming to search my cabin . . . . How often have I started and turned in sudden and terrible alarm, as I have dropped a piece of money into my box, and heard its loud ring upon the coin below, lest some prowling enemy should hear it, and steal from me my hoarded treasure. (Jones 1850: 34)

He had learned how to make and save money in very difficult circumstances, as this extraordinarily evocative language reveals. He clearly understood the relationship between saving money, secrecy and freedom; the sound of a coin dropping onto the others he had already saved renders this audibly. The lesson would remain with him throughout his life. Later still, he would sell copies of his narrative to collect sufficient funds to redeem his son Edward, who remained enslaved.[10] All of this suggests that Jones would have been inclined to publish his story as quickly as he was able. There is not yet definitive evidence one way or the other for an 1849 narrative, but the fact that the narrative was probably completed around 21 November, and the testimonials were written on 25 November, suggests that an edition may have been produced in late November 1849.

I will now turn back to the moment at which the paths of both men crossed. The fact that they met by chance on a train seems a detail better suited to nineteenth-century fiction than real life. Nathaniel Hawthorne made a meeting between strangers on a New England train a key moment in *The House of the Seven Gables* (1851). The crossing of Armistead and Jones was, paradoxically, both improbable and likely. Both were in transit, meaning that they were only in each other's geographical orbit very briefly. Any such encounter would have been much less likely only a few years earlier. The Eastern Railroad had operated the practice of segregation from its opening in 1836 until it was forced to change its policy in 1843 after a lengthy campaign by opponents.[11] By 1850 the line had been desegregated for some time and was frequently used by abolitionists. Further, it is likely that Armistead wore Quaker clothing.[12] The strategic use of dress codes was advocated in an unsigned article in *The British Friend* in July 1853. A 'Convinced Friend' (meaning someone not born a Quaker) argued that,

> It is quite a mistake to suppose the 'peculiarity' of simple dress is of no use in modern times . . . . See yon panting fugitive escaping from slavery! the blood-hounds are on his track! O! to see a white person in whom he can confide! 'tis a question of life or death with him! Ask of him the value of the Friend's coat, the broad brim, the quiet cap. He can tell! (*The British Friend*, July 1853: 175)

If Armistead did wear simple dress it would have signalled abolitionist sympathies to Jones, increasing the probability of conversation between them. Jones would of course have known of the importance of members of the Society of Friends in the Underground Railroad and was familiar with the activities and beliefs of the Society of Friends. He had spent three years receiving religious instruction from a Quaker while still enslaved in Wilmington, something omitted from the Armistead edition.[13] Had they not encountered each other on a train, they might have done so in the abolitionist circles in which they were both active. Yet given the brevity of Armistead's visit, this seems unlikely.

Armistead had to mediate his meeting with Jones for a British Quaker audience who would have already been familiar with first-person accounts of the self-emancipated formerly enslaved individuals who were on well-publicised lecture tours in Ireland and Great Britain. Since while writing about his meeting with Jones he was leading abolitionist activism in Leeds, he was sensitive about how he imagined him. He presents Jones as a human with complex agency, not as an individual wholly circumscribed within a dramatic story of enslavement and escape. His ethical care can be seen in the way he treats the narrative. The description of their encounter ends the July instalment and is taken up once again in the next instalment, in October. He opens this with an introduction to what will follow:

> The touching circumstances connected with the life of the fugitive slave with whom I fell in on my journey from Lynn to Boston cannot be better related than in nearly his own words; for although deprived of moral and mental cultivation, during the 43 years of slavery he had endured, he was able to relate his history with such perfect clearness as to leave the most vivid impressions, and to arouse a renewed feeling of sympathy towards the vast numbers of the one great brotherhood who daily suffer and die, ignorant and despairing, in the prison-land of slavery from which Thomas Jones – for such was his name – had happily escaped. ('Reminiscences', October 1851: 229)

The phrase 'nearly his own words' indicates that Armistead had already decided upon some revisions and abbreviations to Jones's text. Significantly, he omits an exchange of letters between Mary Jones and her husband, placed just before the end of the pamphlet. In two letters which were dictated to an amanuensis Mary describes her concern and distress about their son Edward, her separation from Jones and her financial difficulties. So although the Armistead edition brings Jones's voice to life for its readers, it simultaneously silences Mary, unlike all the other editions of Jones's narrative. While this was probably due to a desire to focus attention on his experience of enslavement and escape in a manner corresponding to the way formerly enslaved lecturers were performing in public, its effect is to make Mary's connection to the text secondary. In fact her letters bear important testimony to the female Black experience and to what it meant to be the mother of enslaved children. A fuller expression of this would be made by a few years later by Harriet Jacobs, who lived in Edenton, about 150 miles north of Wilmington.

Jones's narrative goes on to dominate the next four instalments of the 'Reminiscences'. Armistead obviously struggled to abridge his gripping and poignant testimony. It abruptly stops in January 1852, when Armistead writes that 'it has extended far beyond my intention when I first put pen to paper' ('Reminiscences', January 1852: 6). During his visit to the United States he met larger numbers of African Americans than he had ever previously encountered, especially in the days leading up to the train journey. Until that time he had chiefly met African American abolitionists who were lecturing in England, including Frederick Douglass. His first day in Boston was spent with the lawyers Robert Morris, Macon B. Allen and George B. Vashon and the newspaper editor and Congregational minister Samuel Ringgold Ward. He used his 'Reminiscences' to inform his British readers of the existence of a Black professional class they may not have otherwise imagined. He would return to depictions of these men in his 1854 work *God's Image in Ebony*.

Although Jones's work is enclosed – even hidden – within the larger text that frames it, the fact that almost the entire pamphlet is reproduced shows the huge impact it had on Armistead. The intertwined nature of both men's texts suggests the manner in which Armistead's editorial practice seems designed to respect the integrity of Jones's testimony and to recognise the textual and political power of the first-person voice. Each extract is surrounded by inverted commas: he does not attempt to pass off Jones's words as if they were his own. This corresponds to the quite extensive use he makes of other sources from which he quotes, such as Charles Dickens's *American Notes* (1842) and Joseph Sturges's *A Visit to the United States in 1841* (1842). The 1885 edition gives considerably more detail of Jones's life than earlier editions (including the names of his children and several others as well as a quite positive description of his last enslaver, Owen Holmes).[14]

When Armistead wrote the 'Reminiscences' he was highly conscious that Jones's situation remained precarious. The Fugitive Slave Law was passed on 18 September 1850 and Armistead ends his edition by the erroneous speculation that Jones 'is probably long ere this, under the fiendish workings of the odious Fugitive Slave Law, dragged back to the endurance of chains and slavery to the end of his days' ('Reminiscences', January 1852: 6). However, Jones remained free, though some details of his life remain unclear. Chief of these is the question of whether or not he visited England. This tantalising possibility is raised in a number of letters, the earliest of which is a letter of introduction written by William Lloyd Garrison on 29 March 1851:

> In consequence of the passage of the Fugitive Slave Law, at the last session of Congress, a general flight from the country of all fugitive slaves in the Northern States has become necessary as a matter of personal safety. Among the number thus compelled to leave is the bearer of this, Thomas H. Jones . . . [who] must flee to England to prevent being again reduced to the condition of a beast! May the God of the oppressed raise him up many friends abroad. (Andrews et al. (eds) 2003: 270–1)

Garrison's letter is only evidence of intention in the broadest sense. Jones certainly moved to British territory – to Canada – in 1850 after the passing of the Fugitive Slave Law, not permanently returning to the United States until 1854, though he visited on a number of occasions.[15] What isn't yet established is whether he visited England at some point in 1851, and whether his meeting with Armistead might have encouraged him to consider the trip in the months that followed. He first mentions a planned visit in a letter of 5 May 1851 to the abolitionist and minister Daniel Foster. Foster supported Jones personally and financially from 1849 until his own premature death in 1864 in the Battle of Chaffin's Farm, Virginia. He arranged for the publication of the letter in *The Liberator*, along with another dated the following day. In this letter Jones writes from Canada in powerfully visceral language of bodily reclamation, 'I know it will be a source of pleasure to you to be informed of my safe arrival here on British ground. Quite free from terror, I now feel that my bones are a property bequeathed to me for my own use, and not for the service of the white man, in that gloomy and sultry region, where the hue of the skin has left my race in thraldom and misery for ages' (*The Liberator*, 30 May 1851: 88). He writes admiringly of the people of St John, where he is staying, stating that 'only that my mission calls me beyond the seas' and he would be happy to remain. Finally, he adds: 'In a few days, I proceed to Halifax, and thence to England, as soon as circumstances will permit.' This is an unequivocal statement of intent, yet so far I have been unable to find more solid evidence. Perhaps 'circumstances' did not 'permit'. Certainly, scholars have unequivocally contended that the trip did not happen, yet after Foster's death in September 1864, a grieving Jones was quoted in *The Liberator* as saying that he 'sent me to England with his own money when he was very poor, to save me from the slave-hunter' ('An Earnest Abolitionist Fallen', *The Liberator*, 25 November 1864: 191). In summary, then, since it is clear that Jones planned to visit England in 1851 and states that he had visited England by 1864, more work needs to be done. Yet equally the lack of evidence paradoxically reveals the success of his plan to evade slave hunters, to travel in relative obscurity and to avoid being an object of curiosity or novelty.[16]

While it is difficult to ascertain precisely when a visit to England might have taken place, we can assume that it must have been between those two dates. Working on that assumption, I'll turn to the existing evidence. A number of testimonials were published at the end of the later editions of Jones's narrative, two of which are addressed to London ministers. The first, dated June 1851, is from R. Irvin, a Presbyterian minister, and addressed to Rev. J. C. Gallaway. The latter had previously lived in St John, and had preached in the pulpit from which Jones would also preach. In the 1885 edition, Jones writes that he met Gallaway in Canada, noting that 'He invited me to England, and promised if I would do so to introduce me to the public there' (Andrews et al. (eds) 2003: 264). Irvin tells Gallaway that Jones 'is on his way to Great Britain' suggesting the fulfilment of an invitation (Andrews et al. (eds) 2003: 272). The second letter, written in St John on 9 June 1851, is a letter of introduction to Jones written by J. D. Caswell and addressed to 'Rev. Dr. Hoby, or Howard Hinton, London'. Hoby, a British Baptist minister, had written *The Baptists in America* (1836) following a visit to Canada and the United States in the 1830s. John Howard Hinton, also a Baptist minister and abolitionist, had attended the World's Anti-Slavery Convention in 1840. Caswell's introductions were undoubtedly intended to bring Jones to the attention of men who participated in London's abolitionist circles.

I have not yet been able to find details of Jones's activities in England, but other evidence is helpful in working out when he might have visited. Correspondence suggests he may well have left St John for Halifax in June 1851, visited England and then returned to Halifax in the autumn (*The Liberator*, 13 August 1852: 132.)[17] Finally, a London primary school, the Thomas Jones School in Notting Hill, believes that it is named after him.[18] In pursuing these intriguing possibilities my research is indebted to recent critical work that represents field-changing paradigms. A number of issues in particular are raised regarding the kinds of challenge of archival discovery and critical interpretation posed by my discovery of the Armistead edition. These include questions of inclusion, interpretation and methodology which themselves lead to field adjustments. Ellen Gruber Garvey has probed the limitations of the current shape of the archive (Gruber Garvey 2012) and Sandra Gustafson has raised issues about interpreting our archives (cited in Gikandi 2015: 81–2). Jared Hickman has called for a historicisation offering ways of reorienting the discipline (Hickman 2012). Increasing self-reflexivity in the discipline is evidenced by models of critical investigation, including postcolonial studies; Black Atlantic studies (Gilroy 1993); transatlantic literary and cultural studies (Giles 2001; Manning and Taylor 2007); hemispheric and oceanic studies (Blum 2013; Levander and Levine 2008; Pisarz-Ramirez and Heide 2016). It has become commonplace to speak of the way that the transnational turn marked a decisive shift away from earlier, exceptionalist, paradigms (Fluck et al. 2011) to develop a more 'worlded' American Studies. Scholarship with a transatlantic focus has long exemplified such models. Indeed, work on slavery and abolition by UK-based scholars has pioneered such research (for instance Murray 2020; Rice 2003; Sweeney 2007, and Sweeney and Rice 2012; and the web-based scholarship of Murray and Newman et al.).

In order for American Studies scholarship to correspond to its transnational ambitions, it needs to continue to develop more effective methods. One important possibility is for scholars to examine some potentially transformative yet under-researched areas. These include archives located outside of the United States, including local history collections (often located in regional libraries) and less well-known depositories. The highly focused expertise of local and regional historians, librarians and archivists is especially useful for scholars whose training is often with larger sources and transnational or even national models. However, it is important that the discovered material should not be simply taken into a reshaped yet fundamentally unchanged field imaginary.

This story of crossing has implications for an American Studies that might further open itself up to the significance of some knowledge repositories (in the widest sense of meaning), especially those located outside of the nation. It calls for a more generative and generous discipline, fully attuned to the politics of the discipline and of the twenty-first-century academy. Doubtless there is more to be done in understanding not just Jones's life but the lives of many formerly enslaved women and men who became highly mobile in consequence of self-emancipation. Multiple crossings coalesce in this brief encounter between strangers on a train. They include the passage from slavery to freedom; transatlantic travel; a conviviality allowing for trans-racial and homosocial sympathy; and the complex transformation of African American testimony into print culture. The story that unfolds involves questions of agency and recovery and exemplifies the kinds of questions raised in a 'post-crossings' critical age. Interpreting it requires us to reflect upon textuality and materiality, including the practices of nineteenth-century print culture; to probe where and what are our archives; to ask how we expand our conversations and research methodologies to recover neglected and important figures like Armistead and Jones; and finally, to acknowledge the impact of temporality and probability and their roles in crossings.

WORKS CITED

'A Convinced Friend' (1853), *The British Friend*, July, p. 175.

'A False Charge Corrected' (1854), *The Liberator*, 29 September, p. 3.

'An Earnest Abolitionist Fallen' (1864), *The Liberator*, 25 November, p. 191.

'By a Leeds Man' (n.d. [1868]), in *Memoirs of Eminent Men of Leeds, with Sixteen Photographic Portraits, and Views of the Old and New Infirmary*, London: G. J. Berger; Leeds: D. Green and Sons.

'Caution' (1850), *The Liberator*, 8 March, p. 39.

'Letter from a Fugitive Slave' (1852), *The Liberator*, 13 August, p. 132.

'New Publications' (1850), *The Liberator*, 1 March, p. 35.

'Remarkable Return in the Census. Disgrace to America' (1851), *The British Friend*, May, pp. 106–7.

'Rev. Thomas H. Jones' (1854), *The Liberator*, 18 August, p. 3.

'Thomas H. Jones' (1851), *The Liberator*, 30, p. 88.

Andrews, William L., ed. (2003), *North Carolina Slave Narratives: The Lives of Moses Roper, Lunsford Lane, Moses Grandy, and Thomas H. Jones*, Chapel Hill: The University of North Carolina Press.

Armistead, Wilson (1850–2), 'Reminiscences of a Visit to the United States, in the Summer of 1850', *The British Friend*, November–December.

— (1859), *Anthony Benezet*, London: A.W. Bennett; Philadelphia: Lippincott & Co., 1859.

Augst, Thomas, ed. (2001), 'The Library as an Agency of Culture', *American Studies* 42(3).

Augst, Thomas, and Kenneth Carpenter, eds (2007), *Institutions of Reading: The Social Life of Libraries in the United States*, Amherst and Boston: University of Massachusetts Press.

Bennett, Bridget (2020), 'Guerrilla Inscription: Transatlantic Abolition in the 1851 Census', *Atlantic Studies: Global Currents* 17(3): 375–98.

Blum, Hester, ed. (2013), 'Special Focus Issue: Oceanic Studies', *Atlantic Studies* 10(2): 151–227.

Brown, William Wells (1855), *The American Fugitive in Europe: Sketches of Places and People Abroad*, Boston: John P. Jewett.

Davies, David (2003), 'Introduction', in William L. Andrews (ed.), *North Carolina Slave Narratives: The Lives of Moses Roper, Lunsford Lane, Moses Grandy, and Thomas H. Jones*, Chapel Hill: The University of North Carolina Press, pp. 189–202.

Fluck, Winfried, Donald E. Pease and John Carlos Rowe, eds (2011), *Re-framing the Transnational Turn in American Studies*, Hanover: Dartmouth College Press.

Gikandi, Simon (2015), 'Rethinking the Archive of Enslavement', *Early American Literature* 50(1): 81–102.

Giles, Paul (2001), *Transatlantic Insurrections: British Culture and the Formation of American Culture, 1730–1860*, Philadelphia: University of Pennsylvania Press.

Gilroy, Paul (1993), *The Black Atlantic: Modernity and Double Consciousness*, London: Verso.

Gruber Garvey, Ellen (2012), *Writing with Scissors: American Scrapbooks from the Civil War to the Harlem Renaissance*, New York: Oxford University Press.

Hickman, Jared (2012), 'On the Redundancy of "Transnational American Studies"', in Russ Castronovo (ed.), *The Oxford Handbook of Nineteenth-Century American Literature*, Oxford: Oxford University Press, pp. 267–88.

Huzzey, Richard (2012), *Freedom Burning: Anti-Slavery and Empire in Victorian Britain*, Ithaca: Cornell University Press.

Jones, Thomas H. (1850), *The Experience of Thomas Jones, who was a Slave for Forty-Three Years*, Boston: Daniel Laing Jr.

— (1854), letter to William Lloyd Garrison, 16 February, <https://www.digitalcommonwealth.org/search/commonwealth:5h740b180> (accessed 29 October 2021).

Levander, Caroline F. and Robert S. Levine, eds (2008), *Hemispheric American Studies*, New Brunswick: Rutgers University Press.

Manning, Susan, and Andrew Taylor, eds (2007), *Transatlantic Literary Studies: A Reader*, Baltimore: Johns Hopkins University Press.

McCarthy, B. Eugene, and Thomas L. Doughton, eds (2007), *From Bondage to Belonging: the Worcester Slave Narratives*, Amherst: University of Massachusetts Press.

McHenry, Elizabeth (2002), *Recovering the Lost History of African American Literary Societies*, Durham, NC: Duke University Press.

Moore, Sean D. (2019), *Slavery and the Making of Early American Libraries: British Literature, Political Thought, and the Transatlantic Book Trade, 1731–1814*, Oxford: Oxford University Press.

Murray, Hannah-Rose (2020), '"I shall speak out against this and other evils": African American Activism in the British Isles 1865–1903', *Slavery & Abolition* 41(1): 79–92, <http://frederickdouglassinbritain.com/> (accessed 29 October 2021).

Newman, Simon et al. (n.d.), *Runaway Slaves in Britain*, <https://www.runaways.gla.ac.uk/> (accessed 29 October 2021).

Pisarz-Ramirez, Gabriele, and Markus Heide, eds (2016), *Hemispheric Encounters: The Early United States in a Transnational Perspective*, Frankfurt: Peter Lang.

Rice, Alan (2003), *Radical Narratives of the Black Atlantic*, New York: Continuum.

Ruchames, Louis (1956), 'Jim Crow Railroads in Massachusetts', *American Quarterly* 8(1): 61–75.

Shepperson, George (1964), 'Abolitionism and African Political Thought', *Transition*, January–February, pp. 22–26.

Spires, Derrick R. (2019), *The Practice of Citizenship: Black Politics and Print Culture in the Early United States*, Philadelphia: University of Pennsylvania Press.

Sweeney, Fionnghuala (2007), *Frederick Douglass and the Atlantic World*, Liverpool: Liverpool University Press.

Sweeney, Fionnghuala, and Alan Rice (2012), 'Liberating Sojourns? African Americans and Transatlantic Abolition 1845–1865', *Slavery & Abolition* 33(2): 181–9.

Van Vranken, Sadie, 'Thomas H. Jones', <https://www.americanantiquarian.org/blackpublishing/thomas-h-jones> (accessed 29 October 2021).

Notes

1. Armistead does not specify the date. However, evidence from the 'Reminiscences' allows us to piece together his journey. He left Liverpool on 29 June and arrived at Boston on Friday 12 July. He then departed Boston for Lynn on the afternoon of Saturday 13 July. He spent two nights there, staying with David Ellis, before returning to Boston by rail on Monday morning.

2. This extraordinary piece of well-publicised activism deliberately drew attention to the politics of slavery and the possibilities of subverting state records. See 'Remarkable Return in the Census. Disgrace to America', *The British Friend*, May 1851: 106–7, and my discussion of it in Bennett 2020.

3. Anna Jones, who had purchased Jones, invited his father to visit his son whenever he was able. Eventually Jones redeemed both his parents from slavery and they lived with him until their deaths. See Andrews et al. (eds) 2003: 266–70.

4. See Andrews et al. (eds) 2003: 244–7.

5. 'Just received, and for sale at the Anti-Slavery Office, 21 Cornhill – The Experience of Thomas Jones, who was a Slave for forty-three years. Written by a friend, as given him by the victim. This is an affecting and authentic narrative. Price 12 1–2 cents' ('New Publications', *The Liberator*, 1 March 1850, p. 35). A letter from Samuel May dated 22 February 1850 warns of a fugitive called William Jones who was fraudulently collecting money and notes that he was not the Thomas Jones who had 'recently published a brief Narrative of his experience' ('Caution', *The Liberator*, 8 March 1850, p. 39).

6. Undoubtedly the Laing edition had been through the hands of a white amanuensis well-versed in working with African American testimony. Evidence for this is on the title page. Immediately under the title are the words 'Written by a friend, as given to him by Brother Jones'. The word 'given' implies oral testimony. By the 1862 edition the attribution was subtly altered to 'related'.

7. In a short essay published in the American Antiquarian Society's *Black Self-Publishing* project, Sadie Van Vranken argues that the Laing edition is the first edition of Jones's narrative. She writes, 'The American Antiquarian Society's copy of this undated Howland printing was initially cataloged as 1849 (based on the copyright date), and later revised to read "not before 1859." Whether the AAS record originated the misidentified 1849 publication date is unclear, but the error remains in other library records and scholarship.' See <https://www.americanantiquarian.org/blackpublishing/thomas-h-jones> (accessed 29 October 2021).

8. A year later, a letter of introduction from William Lloyd Garrison dated 29 March 1851 describes Jones as 'a Wesleyan preacher, and pastor of a colored church in the neighboring city of Salem, who carries with him a narrative of his life for sale'. Garrison's letter was published in *The Liberator* and was subsequently used to preface the 1862 edition.

9. This was based on the 1885 revised edition published by E. A. Anthony and Sons, which considerably extended earlier versions of his narrative.

10. In a letter published in *The Liberator*, Daniel Foster notes that Jones had been 'soliciting for aid for the redemption of his son' but has been attacked in a Worcester paper claiming that he is a fraud ('Rev. Thomas H. Jones', *The Liberator*, 18 August 1854, p. 3). A refutation of all charges against Jones, made by George H. Washington – the man who had made them – and written on 28 August 1854 was published in *The Liberator* the following month ('A False Charge Corrected', *The Liberator*, 29 September 1854, p. 3).

11. In 1838, the activist barber Henry Scott wrote an impassioned piece to his 'fellow citizens' of Worcester (where Thomas Jones would later settle with his family) protesting against segregation and the treatment of African Americans who wished to travel on the line (McCarthy and Doughton eds 2007: xl). Scott was clearly enacting or practising his citizenship in the manner Derrick Spires draws attention to (Spires 2019). Anti-segregation activism was taking place on other lines too. On 6 July 1841 David Ruggles, another self-emancipated activist, who was travelling the New Bedford and Taunton line from New Bedford to Boston, was ordered to move from his seat to a segregated carriage. When he refused, he was forcibly removed. He later (unsuccessfully) took out a suit against those who had forced him off the train. Subsequently (and more famously), Frederick Douglass's protests against similar treatment on the same line helped to create a climate in which the practice was discontinued (Ruchames 1956).

12. The only known image of him from an 1868 publication is too small for this to be clear, though he does have a distinctive Quaker beard. See 'By a Leeds Man', *Memoirs of Eminent Men of Leeds, with Sixteen Photographic Portraits, and Views of the Old and New Infirmary*, London: G. J. Berger; Leeds: D. Green and Sons, n.d. (1868).

13. Jones writes: 'At the expiration of six months, I was received into the church in full fellowship, Quaker Davis's class. I remained there three years' (Jones 1850: 26).

14. See David A. Davis's interpretation in Andrews et al. (eds) 2003: 196. The brief account of Jones's life which I include in this article uses details from the 1885 edition.

15. Davis in Andrews et al. (eds) 2003: 199. He is mentioned a number of times in *The Liberator* as an active abolitionist and speaker. A letter to William Lloyd Garrison sent from New Haven and dated 16 February 1854 states that he has settled his children into school and 'is still in this land of oppression'. He expresses anxiety about allowing his whereabouts to become known, but states that he will travel via Boston to Canada in April (Jones 1854).

16. This was not always the case. An article from 19 August 1853 reveals that he was refused a berth on the steamer *Eastern City* during a journey from St John to Boston, and had his coat torn by the boat clerk (*The Liberator*, 19 August 1853, p. 131).

17. His attendance at a meeting of the 'colored citizens of Windsor' (*The Liberator*, 15 October 1852, p. 3) on 27 September 1852 enables us to trace him as living in Canada at that date. He notes that after recently speaking at the Anti-Slavery Convention for Western Massachusetts he visited Daniel Foster, who 'has been to me more than a brother' ('Letter from Rev. Thomas H. Jones', *The Liberator*, 2 September 1853, p. 1). This might intimate that Foster had extended him particular generosity, such as helping him to fund a trip to England.

18. Emma Jones, personal correspondence, 28 June 2019. The school's 2009 Ofsted report states: 'It is believed that the school is named after Thomas Jones, born in North Carolina in 1806. A passionate critic of slavery, Thomas Jones obtained a rudimentary education, and used his skills to emancipate his own children' (<https://files.ofsted.gov.uk/v1/file/916109>, accessed 29 October 2021).

PART IV

IMPOSSIBLE SYSTEMS

11

SLAVE LABOUR/WAGE LABOUR: READING BARTLEBY'S REFUSALS, 1850

TOMOS HUGHES

In his 1854 pro-slavery treatise *A Sociology for the South*, George Fitzhugh adopts an idiosyncratic version of a prominent figure in nineteenth-century Atlantic thought: the wage slave. In the US, this politically promiscuous metaphor brought together disparate pro-slavery and pro-labour critiques of industrialisation around a sense that the wage undermined patriarchal ties of the household economy central to republican notions of freedom in the North and popular representations of chattel slavery in the South.[1] Its political flexibility is rooted in a series of racialised identifications and disavowals that structure familiar narratives about the crossings between slavery and capitalism in mid-nineteenth-century America; or better, that explain repeated failures, past and present, to imagine connections between these systems as they map geographies of freedom and dependence. Departing from conventional usage, this essay considers an errant and less stably metaphorical version of the wage slave, which repurposed the staging of a hybrid social subject to make available unfamiliar speculations about capitalism and slavery's spatial and temporal dynamics. Beginning with Fitzhugh, who envisions slavery's universal trajectory beyond the South as a progressive form of political economy, I trace the emergence after 1850 of the wage slave on strike as a contradictory subject. Through this figure, a diverse group of thinkers – including Herman Melville, Fredrick Douglass and Karl Marx – at once envisioned slavery's mobility across borders and placed a crisis at the centre of imaginary renderings of slavery's dynamic, modern character. This contradictory subject requires us to rethink the stakes involved in employing crossing as the cultural metaphor for connections between nineteenth-century America's dominant social systems and their representative collective subjects.

Without conflating the disparate politics coalescing around wage slavery, the discourse notoriously structured critiques of capitalism along spatially, temporally and racially segregated lines, drawing together two systems of exploitation, and two differently 'enslaved' subjects, only to disavow their connection. Making wage slavery representative of the 'failure of free society', Fitzhugh utilises an established pro-slavery argument that distinguished slavery from industrial capitalism by depicting urban proletarians as subject to a diabolical mastery, lacking the 'never-failing protective, care-taking and supporting feature of slavery' apparently characteristic of the South's master-slave relationship (Fitzhugh 1854: 68). In turn, when urban radicals attacked the destitution of wage workers by comparison with chattel slaves, they often employed nostalgic conceptions of American slavery as a patriarchal institution, confined to the South's peculiar social and racial conditions. Orestes Brownson, for instance, saw Northern hirelings as 'virtual slaves' (Brownson 1840: 13). Imagined by Brownson in grotesque analogue to a temporally, spatially and racially distinct system, labour under capitalism posed a threat to the vaunted independence of northern white workers; but, by its very anachronism, 'virtual slavery' confirmed freedom (and mastery) as the white worker's republican birthright. Despite experience to the contrary, the independent white mechanic could remain the nineteenth century's political subject because chattel slavery's dependencies were confined to a peripheral South, and (in theory) to the past. As Brownson put it, 'our business is to emancipate the proletaries as the past has emancipated the slaves' (13).

These metaphorical displacements shadow a series of scholarly narratives about nineteenth-century literature and political culture. Wage slavery suggests a missed identification between an emergent working class and the abolitionist movement: ultimately a racialised (mis)idenitification through which working-class culture grafted itself to whiteness by the 1840s (Du Bois [1935] 1992: 17–22, 700–1; Roediger 1999: 80–7; Lott 1993: 197–201). The metaphor also infused a new sectionalist discourse which made a premodern, monolithic 'Slave South' the periphery against which to imagine northern capitalism as national freedom (Greeson 2010: 119–21). Finally, the breakdown of the metaphor's ambivalent coherence into outright fantasies of racial panic and Western escapism, by 1850, encapsulates the collapsed Jacksonian innocence of the Renaissance generation, pivoting on the shift between an 'American 1848' and a New World Brumaire, embodied by the 1850 Compromise and its reinforced Fugitive Slave Law (Rogin 1983: 103–6).[2]

If wage slavery's ambivalent investments map sectional, temporal and racial coordinates that were entrenched by 1850, this moment also marks a different understanding of the metaphor and of slavery's time-space. I called Fitzhugh's seemingly routine opposition between slavery and industrial capitalism idiosyncratic because his version of wage slavery is much less stably metaphorical, portending a breakdown of conventional distinctions. Rather than an exceptional and regionally contained institution, Fitzhugh treats slavery as a universal principle of human sociality, of socialism even. Moving past normative distinctions between forms of dependence, North and South, he imagines proletarianisation as a positive move towards slavery beyond the South, rendering slavery the progressive tendency of modern world history. Fitzhugh gives flesh to his famously tendentious claim that 'socialism is the science of slavery' by arguing that across the US and Western Europe, industrial workers were striking in a bid to become slaves (Fitzhugh 1854: 61):

> The poor themselves are all practical Socialists, and in some degree proslavery men. They unite in strikes and trades unions, and thus exchange a part of their liberties in order to secure high and uniform wages. The exchange is a prudent and sensible one; but they who have bartered off liberty, are fast verging towards slavery . . . and towards slavery the North and all Western Europe are unconsciously marching. (45)

Fitzhugh employs a conservative commonplace: that slavery was merely one iteration of the dependence inherent in labour. But unlike traditional defenders of the South's peculiar institution, he argues that the social conflicts generated by the wage will generalise slavery beyond the South. Making slavery's abstract universality in the pro-slavery defence concrete, Fitzhugh exemplifies slaveholding conservatism's shift towards speculative ideologies of imperial expansion, from the 1850s (Johnson 2013: 398–9; Wyatt-Brown 1982: 36–8; Bonner 2009: 267). What interests me is the imaginative language he employs, indeed strains at, to combine the concrete and the abstract. For Fitzhugh, slavery is not a pejorative condition forced on putatively 'free' labourers. He renders the negative critique of urban wage slavery positive by making the striking worker a willing slave. 'Verging towards' real slavery, the historical tendency of the wage – embodied in workers' collective desire to become slaves – encapsulates the peculiar institution's mobility across time, space and even social forms. By literalising the metaphor of the wage slave, he materialises the crossover of social systems that sectional ideology opposed.[3]

Fitzhugh's is a metaphor for transition rather than separation. However, the strike is a figure of fracture and cessation (not to mention rebellion) that complicates his fantasy of slavery's mobility. As a manifestation of unfreedom's dynamism beyond the South's master-slave relation, the voluntary free association of the strike bursts the boundaries of a 'prudent and sensible' exchange of freedom for dependence (or even a dispute over wages) to threaten the particularity of chattel slavery itself. As Fitzhugh argued, 'society must be ruled, not by mere abstractions but by men of flesh and blood' (Fitzhugh 1854: 70): free society's universalisation of slavery through the wage lacked the master's individual sovereignty, generalising the threat of servile rebellion explicit in the strike. His appeal to personal sovereignty notwithstanding, to realise his claim that 'slavery will everywhere be abolished, or everywhere be re-instituted', Fitzhugh has to devise a mechanism for its spread beyond the South as a hegemonic social form which is more than mere metaphor: he has to socialise the master-slave relationship (94). The result is a contradictory subject who materialises the abstract and apparently impossible sovereign-less slavery of the wage system: a conscious actor who embodies a society 'unconsciously marching' towards slavery. Torn between chattel slavery's worldmaking force, once liberated from the boundaries of the plantation South, and its dissolution as a universal system, he alights on a collective subject who is a figure for crisis: the waged, and striking, slave.

Fitzhugh's pained explication of the wage slave on strike is more than a quirk of his unusual political imagination. By using the strike to give unstable flesh to the abstraction of wage slavery, Fitzhugh joins an ideologically disparate group of thinkers who confronted the problem of reinventing the era's political subject following slavery's seeming liberation from the bounds of sectional space after 1850. The fragile metaphoricity of the figure (literally) embodies a crisis in the attempt to think slavery in non-sectional terms. As Neil Roberts argues, 'the metaphor of slavery is a trope in the Western imagination that overextends itself, the metaphorical eclipsing the experiences of the real' (Roberts 2015: 28). But, in the discourse I trace, overextension is the point. The figure of the waged and striking slave made thinkable alternative temporal and spatial paradigms for understanding chattel bondage at midcentury, even as it mined a certain impossibility or contradiction implicit in imagining slavery's progressive, expansive future.

These tensions animate nineteenth-century literature's most enigmatic wage slave on strike: Melville's Bartleby. Fitzhugh's striking slaves seem an odd counterpart to Bartleby's refusals. But the attempt to imagine the peculiar institution's liberation from sectional time-space after 1850 lends a revealing context to a story first published a year prior to Fitzhugh's book, and set in 'the Mississippi of Broadway' (Melville [1856] 1984: 652). Melville's narrative turns on the bonds of affection, conflicts and schemes of 'masterly management' pursued by an employer faced with the 'strange willfulness' of a striking worker who, by withdrawing his labour, impossibly becomes a slave (658, 647). Read as an attempt to embody a subject who bridges the worlds of slavery and waged capitalism, the story's ambiguity – the stubborn sense that it should yield an allegorical double in the era's labour struggles, alongside its enigmatic resistance to allegory – gains new meaning (Foley 2000; Kuebrich 1996). 'Bartleby' stages an account of political subjectivity which does not allegorise a collective subject.

For Melville, as well as for Frederick Douglass and Karl Marx, the unstable metaphoricity of the wage slave was not an ideological blind spot, but a tool to think with. Absent a coherent collective subject, 'Bartleby' is part of a broader 'production of meaning' which takes place when the conditions shaping such a subject overspill the boundaries of pre-existing models (Rancière 2011: 27). The language of wage slavery gained new meaning after 1850, when imagining the era's political subject meant confronting the crisis of time-spaces that shaped existing discourses of freedom and slavery. These tensions also raise important qualifications for modern scholarly attempts to map slavery's cosmopolitan and transnational cultural reach 'across a more opaque and amorphous sphere' than the nation-state and its sectional history (Giles 2019: 113).

An Illiberal Archive

The 1850 Compromise stands at an important nexus, here. Central to narratives of antebellum sectionalism, the Compromise also altered slavery's spatial coordinates otherwise. The crisis over the Fugitive Slave Law blurred the divide between free and unfree space, even as it fuelled sectional conflict. The demarcation between northern freedom and southern slavery already rested on precariously maintained cultural, legal and political distinctions that obscured the messy valences of unfreedom in antebellum America. These distinctions were to an important degree 'a regional fiction of abolitionism', which flattened mutual dependencies and kinships that slaves carried across jurisdictions into a legally cognisable concept of freedom based on the individual contracting subject and apportioned according to state boundaries (Wong 2009: 93–100). As a juridical-spatial fix, the Compromise built on a long legal and print-cultural struggle to resolve the putative universality of American liberalism with the 'territorialization of freedom in the Atlantic world' (Wong 2009: 16; De Lombard 2007: 58). However, 1850 solidified the unambiguously national character of American slave law, ushering in a more troubling proposition: the replacement of a precariously territorialised freedom with a de-territorialised slavery (Fehrenbacher 2001: 227–44). According to Douglass, federal requisition of runaways meant that 'slavery has been nationalised in its most horrible and revolting form', so that 'Mason and Dixon's line has been obliterated; New York has become as Virginia; and the power to hold, hunt, and sell men, women, and children as slaves, remains no longer a mere state institution, but is now an institution of the whole United States' (Douglass 1855: 448–9). For Douglass, a nationalised Slave Power disturbingly heralds the dissolution of spatial limits altogether, layering New York onto Virginia and by extension turning the nation-state into the harbinger of a transnational pro-slavery future: 'the power is co-extensive with the star-spangled banner and American Christianity. Where these go, may also go the merciless slave-hunter' (449).

From the opposite perspective, pro-slavery thinkers mapped a progressive future defined by chattel slavery's imbrication with spaces beyond the South, arguing, as did journalist Edward Pollard, that 'the manifest destiny of the South' – and with it 'the world's progress' – lay in the peculiar institution's liberation from (and dissolution of) sectional space (Pollard 1859: 107, 109; Hutchison 2012: 28–9, 55–62). The slippage between section, nation and world-mission conveys that pro-slavery conservatives in the decade before the Civil War were 'culturally hybrid philosophers of chattel bondage', attempting to shape the intellectual culture of a 'pan-American master-class' that took in Central America and the Caribbean (Guterl 2008: 6, 9; Johnson 2013: 413). Such a reading chimes with a transnational turn which defamiliarises nation-bound accounts of the history and culture of slavery by uncovering what Lisa Lowe calls the 'intimacies' between national history – along with the bourgeois subject at its centre – and histories of unfreedom premised on supranational connections effaced by 'the economy of affirmation and forgetting that structures and formalises the archives of liberalism, and liberal ways of understanding' (Lowe 2015: 3, 18). This formulation frames the cultural critic as engaged in a fraught recovery of forms of unfree subaltern consciousness resistant to limits fixed onto our histories of slavery by liberalism and 'its attendant discourse of Man' (Hartman 2008: 12; Wong 2015: 125).

In the discourse I am tracing, the difficulty of imagining slavery's cosmopolitanism poses a different question, resting on a more literal reading of (political) economy than Lowe suggests. Viewed from the horizon of liberalism, the intimacy between slavery and capitalism's social subjects is a repressed or spectral presence: an 'unspeakable unspoken' by which the American canon 'distinguishes itself as a coherent entity' (Morrison 1989: 14; Morrison 1992: 6).[4] But, what if we shift the object of study from the effacements of liberalism to cultural forms generated by modes of capitalist expansion and management that are not hegemonically liberal? Coming at the fragmented cultural treatment of slavery's connections to capitalism through pro-slavery political economy – a genre of conservative writing that reinvented slavery, mastery and racial domination as institutions with worldmaking capacities, and which celebrated slavery's centrality to modernity – focuses attention on different kinds of spatial and temporal limits. These limits emerge from attempts to confront the crossover between slavery and capitalism's social subjects that 'liberal ways of understanding' efface. In particular, such contradictions characterise attempts to reimagine capital's cosmopolitanism through slavery's peculiar fusion of the political and the economic, after 1850.

Shifting the lens as I have suggested also provides a new perspective on some of the strange figures that populate nineteenth-century writing, both imaginative and political. The emergence of a new and not quite metaphorical version of the wage slave presents us with manifestations of subjectivity that are premised on contradictions that a gothic understanding of slavery's presence in nineteenth-century literature has seen American writers as evading. Nevertheless, I am proposing that the recognition, as opposed to the disavowal, of slavery's cosmopolitan tendencies does not manifest in a coherent hybrid subject who links the worlds of slavery and waged capitalism. Such a model of subjecthood may be an alluring possibility, given the need to overcome the spatial and racial boundaries that governed nineteenth-century American political thought and shaped the subsequent formation of the literary canon. However, these disciplinary and ideological boundaries cannot be corrected by adopting an expanded lens alone. Writing which entertains the speculative possibility that the historical tendency of the nineteenth century was moving towards the conjunction (rather than the separation) of slavery and liberal capitalism is populated instead by impossible subjects. The second half of this essay traces some variations on this speculative theme to outline the stakes involved more specifically, and to highlight struggles with the difficulty of imagining slavery and capitalism together that did not emerge from the blind spots of liberalism. Outlining the politically various reformulations of an impossible subject which populated the imaginative life of mid-nineteenth-century critiques of liberal political economy allows us to pinpoint the conjuncture that shaped attempts to map slavery's expanded trajectories.

This is where, for Fitzhugh and others, the wage slave comes in. To craft a pro-slavery argument appropriate for an emergent world-market, advocates of a new positive-good defence asserted not only slavery's moral superiority over wage labour, but also its capacity to perfect political economy's vision of the wage as key to a dynamic, self-perpetuating system of production and circulation. Space precludes a full account of pro-slavery's ambivalent embrace of political economy, but a key feature is the strange animism embedded in its 'pessimistic Malthusianism' (Hodgson 2009: 748). Pro-slavery thinkers argued that by severing production from direct reproduction of the labour force, waged capitalism leveraged its progressive capacity on its creation of an abject surplus population which it condemned to destitution. In an ironic inversion of capital's supposed liberation of labour, the wage alienated the vitality of the master-slave relation, which united production and reproduction in the master's 'one directing mind and one controlling will' (Ruffin 1857: 8). By sucking mastery's life-force, however, the wage renders capital, in Henry Hughes's words, 'a live murder-machine' (Hughes 1854: 145). Like Fitzhugh, Hughes – a keen advocate for reopening the international slave trade – refuses to dispense with capital's alienated life-giving force in favour of a parochial defence of slavery. Rooting slavery's cosmopolitanism in its ability to reunite circuits of production and reproduction that the wage liberated from the master's control, he models a hybrid system on a fantasy of the slave trade's limitless expansion beyond the South. In his 1854 *Treatise on Sociology*, he models this system on the literal wage slave.

Before developing on Hughes's use of metaphors of wage slavery and the slave market to model pro-slavery's ambivalent cosmopolitanism, it helps to expand on a more familiar example of a similar metaphor as it appears in a very different critique of political economy: Marx's *Capital*, Volume 1. Tracing the figurative work of Marx's treatment of the ambiguously metaphorical wage slave reveals how it helped to de-abstract the links between slavery and capitalism and to shape a critique of political economy in which slavery was not an unthought term but a central premise. In a key turn in chapter 25 of *Capital*, 'The General Law of Capitalist Accumulation', Marx develops explicitly on an ambiguity present throughout the book: alongside using wage slavery as a metaphor for the exploitative nature of capitalist production, he shifts the emphasis towards the arguably more important metaphor of the reproduction of the labour market as a slave trade. Through this doubling, he foregrounds capital's peculiar combination of production and reproduction of the labour force, which bourgeois political economy separates; the ambiguity in the figure of the wage slave introduces a temporal long view of capitalism's systemic tendencies and allows Marx to represent a crisis in what Frederic Jameson dubs the 'autotelic' capacities of capital's 'infernal machine' (Jameson 2011: 87).[5]

When Marx argues that capital 'constantly "sets free" a part of the working class', creating a mass of unemployed workers that 'belongs to capital just as absolutely as if the latter had bred it at its own cost', he theorises capitalism's dependence on a 'general law' pertaining both to production and population (Marx [1867] 1990: 786, 784). Crucially, his account of capitalist crisis hinges on the precarious metaphoricity of the 'as if'. This instability emphasises the contradictory nature of capital's expansionist synthesis of production and reproduction. Because, over time, increased productivity turns the 'industrial reserve army' emancipated by capital into a 'relative surplus population' that capital neither owns nor controls in fact, the abstracted breeding of a 'free' labour force 'as if' it were enslaved foreshadows a crisis: capital's thirst for labour that it sheds at an exponential rate comes 'at its own cost' in the sense that capital is fatally reliant on valorising labour power that it can neither fully assimilate through future production, nor dispense with completely (798–9). The full implications of Marx's rewriting of the master-slave relationship as 'the despotism of capital' comes from imagining workers enslaved not just by production but by being cast from production into 'enforced idleness' (793, 789).[6] The jarring metaphor of a class of slaves 'rivet[ed] . . . to capital' by worklessness rather than work enables Marx to embody a system simultaneously in expansive motion across time and space, and locked into the horizon of a totalising crisis modelled on a contradiction in the master's fantasy of seamless reproduction of his slaves (799). Writing in 1867, as chattel slavery experienced terminal crisis in the US, Marx imagines capital's own reproductive crisis through the slaveholder's nightmare of being bonded to a constantly expanding class of workless slaves.[7]

By contrast, in the midst of post-1850 expansionist fervour, Hughes envisions slavery as the pristine realisation of capital's autotelic capacities. Nevertheless, embodying this through the literal wage slave, he frames his own crisis. In Hughes's view, the South's was a peculiar institution indeed: one that had been 'miscalled slavery' so as to sever it from modernity (Hughes 1854: 82). In what he insisted was a 'warrantee', or 'liberty labour' system, there were apparently no slaves, 'property in man . . . [being] a fiction of law for convenience of alienation', so that 'what is owned is the labour-obligation, not the oblige' (106, 167). Reimagining slavery as the voluntary contract by which a class of 'simple-laborers' bond themselves to the state, Hughes argues that human capital is collectively rather than individually owned (104). This means that 'the master is a magistrate' who manages and circulates labour power in the economic interests of the state (106). Hughes's magical rewriting of chattel bondage as collective freedom simultaneously liberates slavery from the confines of the South's personal (and parochial) master-slave relationship and embodies the abstract labour market in the image of personal mastery. By modelling the whole economy on a sovereignty he argued did not exist at an individual level, Hughes unites capital's drive to expand across time and space by commodifying labour power, with the apparently limitless self-reproductive capacities of a market in human property: as both free waged subjects and chattel, 'the laboring class . . . become self-circulating; for labor is capital, and capital circulates itself' (106).

Hughes' systematising outstrips Fitzhugh. Nevertheless, both imagine wage dependency as a transition to, rather than analogue of, slavery and both personify this transition in the literal wage slave. As Hughes argued, 'the system of Free-labor must . . . progress into a system of liberty-labor [and] of such a progress, the Trades-Unions of Free-Labour systems, supply the elements' (187). For Hughes, the trade union is 'the body economic or economic state' (189). However, the seemingly impossible agency of the wage slave, manifest in the strike, shadows a crisis in slaveholding cosmopolitanism. By making slavery universal and abstract, Hughes, like Fitzhugh, risks negating racialised chattel slavery as the cornerstone of the plantation economy and the concrete form of slavery's world-historic expansion.[8] The impossible (a)volition of the collective subject, who embodies the unity of reproduction and production (the political and the economic) central to mastery's expansion, concretises slavery's abstract universalism with devastating repercussions. In Hughes's system workers cannot strike; like fugitive slaves, they 'abscond' (111). The subjectivity of a subject simultaneously controlled by the master and abstractly enslaved through the 'body economic' manifests in a collective will not to work which transcends wage bargaining. When the strike creeps into Hughes's system it is all the more totalising because he has collapsed the distinctions on which liberal political economy relies: 'a strike in warranteeism is a revolt. It is a rebellion against the state' (110). If chattel slavery can be generalised, and the master-slave relation made to underpin all social relations, then all that survives of actually existing slavery is that all social disorder is slave rebellion.

This illiberal archive reveals contradictions in the attempt to imagine slavery across borders that do not result from liberalism's disavowals. Instead, they suggest a moment in which slavery's expansionist tendencies made the separation of the political and the economic central to bourgeois orthodoxy particularly untenable. The waged and striking slave made thinkable the limits of a cosmopolitanism that embraced connections which liberalism effaced: none more so than that between capital and crisis. This focus on crisis comes to the fore when the disavowals of liberalism are transcended and the historical tendency that has come to define nineteenth-century understandings of modernity is reversed, so that history moves from liberal capitalism, or so-called 'free' labour, to universal slavery. Tracing this temporal and spatial arc through the figure of the wage slave is important because it allows us to see an unexpected trajectory that goes against the grain of the stories we tell about slavery and capitalism in the nineteenth century. More than this, though, that the waged and striking slave was an explicitly contradictory subject suggests the added significance that the recognition and projection of slavery's modernity is not a seamless process (a simple corrective or reversal of liberal historicism). Exploring the fantasy life of this contradictory subject beyond the genre of political economy, in works by Herman Melville and Frederick Douglass, helps to clarify how it conditioned the imagination of social struggles at midcentury. When the 'master is a magistrate', it seems that the wage slave becomes both a necessary and a necessarily impossible subject. Enter Bartleby.

The Mississippi of Broadway

In Melville's story 'the master is a magistrate', specifically a 'Master in Chancery' who, true to the values of his legal office, attempts to imbue his literal office with paternal bonds disappearing from the industrialising north-east (Melville [1856] 1984: 636). The narrator's need to section off his office and workers so that 'privacy and society were conjoined' (642) is the desire of a man, in Michael T. Gilmore's words, 'divided between two economic perspectives': an employer seeking to resolve the logic of the market with ties of sociality it eroded (Gilmore 1985: 135). However, in reconstructing bonds of affection and clientage, he is confronted with a disturbing vision of those relations as popularly understood in the American 1850s: as a chattel principle. The story's strangeness lies in Melville's fragile literalisation of the wage slave. Bartleby is impossibly bonded to the narrator as chattel by his refusal to work. By foregrounding allusions to slavery as they manifest through (rather than in comparison with) a wage worker on strike, I am not suggesting that 'Bartleby' is an allegory for either form of labour. The restaging of the wage slave, post-1850, recontextualises the totalising nature of Bartleby's refusals and their resistance to allegorical reading, revealing Melville to be one amongst several thinkers producing strange new meaning from the ruins of an old metaphor.

Reading Bartleby as on strike is not new. Less often noticed is that Bartleby's 'strange wilfulness' – the expression of a preference which indicates an absence of will – renders him oddly slave-like (Dayan 2015). Bartleby, though, is a disconcertingly literal wage slave, as indicated by the narrator's initial unease, which emerges not from Bartleby's refusals but his overwork. The narrator 'should have been quite delighted with [Bartleby's] application, had he been cheerfully industrious. But he wrote on silently, palely, mechanically' (Melville [1856] 1984: 642). His mechanised labour, specifically his unexpected whiteness in conducting it, thrusts an exploitative scene of wage slavery into the personal rhythms of affection and consent (of humanity) that structure the office. And yet, it is precisely the industrialised character of Bartleby's labour that prevents the lawyer from treating him like a proletarian: 'had there been any thing ordinarily human about him', the narrator explains, 'doubtless I should have violently dismissed him from the premises' (643). Because he looks like a wage slave, even down to his disconcerting whiteness constituting a compromised humanity, the narrator cannot treat him like one: he cannot do what pro-slavery and pro-labour advocates believed was creating conditions akin to slavery in northern cities, and fire him.[9] Both the narrator's disgust and affection stem from attempting to sentimentalise a figure who is not 'ordinarily human' but is instead a curiously living mechanism, who 'seemed to gorge himself on my documents' (642). To achieve his desired conjunction of privacy and society, the narrator humanises Bartleby *as* chattel.

If Bartleby were 'ordinarily human', he would be a 'virtual slave', but his disruption of human-object relations prevents his slavery from being metaphorical, as labour advocates such as Brownson understood it. The lawyer repeatedly struggles to articulate his relationship with Bartleby by cycling between terms of contract and bondage. He asks himself, 'was there any other thing in which I could procure myself to be ignominiously repulsed by this lean, penniless wight? – my hired clerk?' (648). With clear racial overtones, he does not expect such insolence from (nor to be repulsed by) a white man. He is forced to remind himself that the dependant from whom he expects obedience, and with whom he imagines personal connection, is a *hired* clerk. 'Procur[ing]' his own repulsion, the narrator purchases the privilege of being bonded to a recalcitrant slave. Something has gone wrong, both in the relationship of hiring and Bartleby's figurative status. Lean, penniless and white, he looks like a contracted labourer; yet his ghostliness suggests both a white man acting Black, and an employer paradoxically paying to subject himself to a repulsive dependence. This suspension drives the narrator's incomprehension at Bartleby's intransigence, not least when he asks:

'will you not do anything at all to give a colouring to your refusal to depart the premises?' (661). When Bartleby prefers not to, in the narrator's eyes he willingly becomes a slave by going on strike; as willing master, the narrator reciprocates by reimagining slavery as voluntary contract. However, rather than redeeming the distinction between bondage and freedom or affirming the benevolent character of dependence in opposition to alienated labour, the narrator's attempted mastery produces an impossible figure. 'If you do not go away from these premises before night', he tells Bartleby, 'I shall feel bound – indeed I am bound – to – to – to quit the premises myself' (667). His reasoning falters over the word 'bound', collapsing completely when he reimagines bondage as voluntary contract: the right to 'quit' which Bartleby confounds.

This suspension also characterises Bartleby's (non-)demands. By collapsing distinctions, his strike escapes the logic of the wage: no offer of better terms suffices. The narrator faces a dependence that extends not from work (as in Hegel's dialectic of lordship and bondage) but a worklessness – indeed, an absence of any action – that totalises his relationship to Bartleby. A conflict that seems to relate to labour forces the narrator to face the intrusion of all Bartleby's reproductive processes – his eating, sleeping, hygiene and ultimately their cessation along with his work – into the workplace. In this, Melville's waged slave who will not work shares something with Marx, Hughes and Fitzhugh's varying reformulations of wage slavery: imagining slavery beyond the South's plantation regime requires a figure in whom production and reproduction are at once inseparable and at the same time impossible to conceive as such without a crisis of existing ideologies of slavery and wage labour. Accordingly, Bartleby's refusals also push to absurdity the logic of the master-slave relationship as a means of resolving production and reproduction. The narrator's resigned declaration to Bartleby that 'the predestined purpose of my life . . . is to furnish you with office-room for such period as you may see fit to remain' parodies defences of masterly responsibility, because Bartleby's comic refusal to do anything but 'remain' encapsulates mastery's failure to structure dependence in 'the Mississippi of Broadway' (662).

Colin Dayan argues that Melville's 'spectacle of servitude and possession' tracks the law's 'transubstantiation' of various unfree subjects into civilly dead objects in antebellum America, exposing via a gothic logic 'the abstractions of a democracy that promises equality but masks oppression' (Dayan 2015: 1, 3, 15). I would suggest the relationship between metaphorical and literal unfreedom works differently, plotting a temporal and spatial shift from former to latter. Through Bartleby, a popular metaphor for unfreedom in general becomes literal and specific; the narrator's accounts of affiliation collapse into (and collapse) chattel slavery's violent logic. The narrator identifies this pattern as his 'doctrine of assumptions' (Melville [1856] 1984: 660). Considering Bartleby an extension of his will, he assumes the scrivener's compliance. However, what enrages him is that the bond between sovereign and retainer proves useless without a violent conflict that threatens his self-image. Crucially, Bartleby never quite refuses. Instead, his ambiguous words initiate what Deleuze calls a 'formula', whose tendency to run a logic to its devastating limit-point is laced with pro-slavery assumptions (Deleuze 1998: 68–70): by preferring not to, Bartleby invites the lawyer to force him; 'burn[ing] to be rebelled against', the lawyer wills Bartleby to refuse; appropriately for one without will, Bartleby reminds the narrator that a preference, as opposed to a refusal, invites negation by compulsion ('You *will* not?' the lawyer asks, 'I *prefer* not,' Bartleby corrects); finally, the narrator becomes enraged, checks himself and approaches Bartleby with a new strategy of 'masterly management', renewing the sequence (Melville [1856] 1984: 648). The narrator's flawed 'doctrine' apes Thomas Ruffin's famously pained legal dictum, in *State v. Mann*, that 'the power of the master must be absolute to render the submission of the slave perfect' (*State v. Mann* 1829). 'I assumed the ground that depart he must; and upon that assumption built all I had to say,' the narrator conjectures. Melville mimics Ruffin's deductive syntax, stressing the subjunctive conditionality of a verb that acknowledges absolute mastery to be a 'beautiful thought', but one which fails to grasp the real precarity of a sovereignty that is mediated and reliant on violence (Melville [1856] 1984: 658).

Crucially, Ruffin's ruling adjudicates property rights when a slave is mistreated in the act of being hired out; its bald explication of the master-slave relationship as a legal fiction that masks a violent struggle (in which mastery is divided and precarious) addresses a moment, like that in 'Bartleby', when slaves are manifestly both human capital and commodified labour power: a moment in which slaves are, however indirectly, waged (Martin 2004: 12). The personal clash of wills between slave and master opens onto a more totalising problem: a crisis implicit in imagining the socialisation of mastery as the basis for all social relations across a market economy. Locating slavery in the symbolic heart of a national marketplace, Bartleby's curious strike similarly reverberates across all aspects of his and the narrator's relationship: destroying distinctions between political and economic sovereignty, shattering the narrator's patriarchal 'doctrine of assumptions' and calling forth state violence. It is only through imprisonment and death at the hands of the state that 'fears . . . of a mob' are subdued and Bartleby is made to sleep 'with Kings and Counsellors' (Melville [1856] 1984: 666, 671) where, as Job specifies, 'the servant *is* free from his master' (*King James Bible*, Job 3.19).

Melville's impossible wage slave responds to tensions in new speculative mappings of slavery after 1850. Ultimately, he does not envision a coherent hybrid collective subject, but a crisis in previous ways of imagining one. Bartleby's totalising refusals suggest the breakdown of competing logics which ambivalently plotted the unity of the political and the economic: both mastery and wage slavery. Like the other figures explored here, Melville makes the precarious overlap between the spaces of slavery and wage labour (rather than their unity or separation) central to imagining freedom and dependence at midcentury. While not a politics, this contradictory crossing contains the basis for an emancipatory thought. By way of demonstrating this, and moving to conclusion, it is worth recalling Frederick Douglass's account of his literal experience as a waged, and fleetingly striking, slave, hired out in Baltimore's shipyards. When Douglass's master prevents him from hiring his time, Douglass retaliates by 'spend[ing] the whole week without the performance of a single stroke of work' (Douglass 1855: 331). Faced with the practical 'folly' of this position for an individual slave, his actions nevertheless respond to a combination of indirect exploitation and direct domination that 'kept the nature and character of slavery constantly before me' (325); his strike opens up a radicalising contradiction that leads to his decision to escape at all costs. Withdrawing from waged slavery as a delusive partial liberty, Douglass comes to see freedom in totalising, zero-sum terms: complete self-emancipation or death.

This moment is treated briefly in Douglass's first autobiography. But tellingly, in *My Bondage and My Freedom* (1855), responding to the crisis of pro-slavery expansionism, he extends it into a more complete (and collective) theorisation of the crossover between waged and slave labour, 'a phase of slavery destined to become an important element in the overthrow of the slave system' (309). He does this by juxtaposing two versions of the wage slave on strike. In Baltimore, Douglass first experiences the strike as racial violence, when he is brutalised by white workers who refuse to work alongside slaves. By turning his subsequent strike into a parable of partial freedom rejected, he holds (in the face of personal experience) to an emancipatory horizon for the imbrication of slavery and the wage, in which white workers realise that 'the difference between the white slave, and the black slave, is this: the latter belongs to one slaveholder, and the former belongs to all the slaveholders, collectively' (310). By restaging his radicalising strike as a sequel to one that enforces the wages of whiteness – and positioning each as parables for 'the overthrow of the slave system' – Douglass implies that an increasingly literal wage slavery necessitates an understanding of abolition as the collective escape from both domination and exploitation. These two strikes sit in productive tension, with no explicit transition between them. In this silence, Douglass shares with Melville an attempt to imagine the structural knitting together of slavery and the wage as a crisis in the political language of wage slavery that makes thinkable other trajectories for understanding freedom.

The versions of wage slavery traced here all understand crossing as crisis. In them, we witness thinkers making imaginative use of the alternative trajectory of nineteenth-century history I have plotted, which runs from liberal capitalism towards universalised slavery. More importantly, their speculations turn on, and in various ways render theoretically productive, contradictions involved in imagining slavery as capitalism. These contradictions pose useful questions about present theorisations of border-crossing as the sign of slavery's modernity. The latter impulse has demonstrated the cultural processes through which the liberal nation-state accommodated, harmonised with and drew upon forms of bondage it helped to spread transnationally. However, as we move from an era in which the liberal nation-state has been the hegemonic form of capital and empire, to one in which a crisis of US hegemony foregrounds increasingly manifest contradictory relationships between capital's transnational imperatives and ethnonationalist modes of political management, a cultural theory premised on repressed 'intimacies' between liberalism and slavery answers less directly to the problems of our moment. If such connections are increasingly not repressed (as in the rightward political shift across the over-developed world), our way of understanding the time-spaces that slavery bequeathed to the present require rethinking.[10] Attention might usefully be paid to ways of knowing slavery that explicitly foreground its contradictory temporal and spatial mobility, and which use its self-limiting expansionist dynamics to rethink previous conjunctions between freedom and dependence. In addition, as the present transcends the recent past's models of the collective subject, the reformulations of such a subject explored here provide an imaginative archive of crisis theory useful for our times.

Works Cited

Anderson, Kevin (2010), *Marx at the Margins: On Nationalism, Ethnicity, and Non-Western Societies*, Chicago: University of Chicago Press.

Arrighi, Giovanni (2010), *The Long Twentieth Century: Money, Power, and the Origins of Our Times*, new and updated ed., London: Verso.

Baucom, Ian (2005), *Spectres of the Atlantic: Finance Capital, Slavery and the Philosophy of History*, Durham, NC: Duke University Press.

The Bible: Authorized King James Version (2008), Oxford: Oxford University Press.

Bonner, Robert E. (2009), 'Proslavery Extremism Goes to War: The Counterrevolutionary Confederacy and Reactionary Militarism', *Modern Intellectual History* 6(2): 261–85.

Brownson, Orestes (1840), *The Laboring Classes, An Article from the Boston Quarterly Review*, Boston: Benjamin H. Greene.

Clover, Joshua (2011), 'Autumn of the System: Poetry and Financial Capital', *Journal of Narrative Theory* 41(1): 34–52.

Cunliffe, Marcus (1979), *Chattel Slavery and Wage Slavery: The Anglo-American Context, 1830–1860*, Athens: University of Georgia Press.

Dayan, Colin (2015), 'Bartleby's Screen', *Leviathan: A Journal of Melville Studies* 17(2): 1–17.

Deleuze, Gilles (1998), *Essays Critical and Clinical*, trans. Daniel W. Smith and Michael A. Greco, London: Verso.

DeLombard, Jeannine (2007), *Slavery on Trial: Law, Abolitionism, and Print Culture*, Chapel Hill: University of North Carolina Press.

Douglass, Frederick (1855), *My Bondage and My Freedom*, New York: Miller, Orton and Mulligan.

Du Bois, W. E. B. [1935] (1992), *Black Reconstruction in America, 1860–1880*, New York: The Free Press.

Fehrenbacher, Don E. (2001), *The Slaveholding Republic: An Account of the United States Government's Relations to Slavery*, Oxford: Oxford University Press.

Fitzhugh, George (1854), *Sociology for the South, or the Failure of Free Society*, Richmond, VA: A. Morris.

Foley, Barbara (2000), 'From Wall Street to Astor Place: Historicizing Melville's "Bartleby"', *American Literature* 72(1): 87–116.

Genovese, Eugene (1970), *The World the Slaveholders Made: Two Essays in Interpretation*, London: Penguin.

Giles, Paul (2019), *American World Literature: An Introduction*, Chichester: Wiley.

Gilmore, Michael T. (1985), *American Romanticism and the Marketplace*, Chicago: University of Chicago Press.

Greeson, Jennifer Rae (2010), *Our South: Geographic Fantasy and the Rise of National Literature*, Cambridge, MA: Harvard University Press.

Guterl, Matthew Pratt (2008), *American Mediterranean: Southern Slaveholders in the Age of Emancipation*, Cambridge, MA: Harvard University Press.

Hartman, Saidiya (2008), 'Venus in Two Acts', *Small Axe: A Caribbean Journal of Criticism* 12(2): 1–14.

Hodgson, Dennis (2009), 'Malthus' Essay on Population and the American Debate over Slavery', *Comparative Studies in Society and History* 51(4): 742–70.

Hughes, Henry (1854), *Treatise on Sociology: Theoretical and Practical*, Philadelphia: Lippincott, Grambo and Co.

Hutchison, Coleman (2012), *Apples and Ashes: Literature, Nationalism, and the Confederate States of America*, Athens: University of Georgia Press.

Jameson, Fredric (2011), *Representing Capital: A Commentary on Volume One*, London: Verso.

Johnson, Walter (2013), *River of Dark Dreams: Slavery and Empire in the Cotton Kingdom*, Cambridge, MA: Harvard University Press.

Kuebrich, David (1996), 'Melville's Doctrine of Assumptions: The Hidden Ideology of Capitalist Production in "Bartleby"', *The New England Quarterly* 69(3): 381–405.

Lott, Eric (1993), *Love and Theft: Blackface Minstrelsy and the American Working Class*, Oxford: Oxford University Press.

Lowe, Lisa (2015), *The Intimacies of Four Continents*, Durham, NC: Duke University Press.

Martin, Jonathan D. (2004), *Divided Mastery: Slave Hiring in the American South*, Cambridge, MA: Harvard University Press.

Marx, Karl [1867] (1990), *Capital, Volume 1*, trans. Ben Fowkes, London: Penguin.

Melville, Herman [1856] (1984), *Pierre, Israel Potter, The Piazza Tales, The Confidence-Man, Billy Budd, Uncollected Prose*, New York: Library of America.

'Misery and Debt', *Endnotes* 2, <https://endnotes.org.uk/issues/2/en/endnotes-misery-and-debt> (accessed 29 October 2021).

Morrison, Toni (1989), 'Unspeakable Things Unspoken: The Afro-American Presence in American Literature', *Michigan Quarterly Review* 28(1): 1–34.

— (1992), *Playing in the Dark: Whiteness and the Literary Imagination*, Cambridge, MA: Harvard University Press.

Pollard, Edward (1859), *Black Diamonds Gathered in the Darky Homes of the South*, New York: Pudney and Russel.

Rancière, Jacques (2011), *Staging the People: The Proletarian and His Double*, trans. David Fernbach, London: Verso.

Roberts, Neil (2015), *Freedom as Marronage*, Chicago: Chicago University Press.

Roberts, William Clare (2017), *Marx's Inferno: The Political Theory of Capital*, Princeton: Princeton University Press.

Roediger, David (1999), *The Wages of Whiteness: Race and the Making of the American Working Class*, rev. ed., London: Verso.

Rogin, Michael Paul (1983), *Subversive Genealogy: The Politics and Art of Herman Melville*, New York: Knopf.

Ruffin, Edmund (1857), *The Political Economy of Slavery*, Washington, DC: Lemuel Towers.

State v. Mann (1829), 13 N.C. 263.

Sugden, Edward (2018), *Emergent Worlds: Alternative States in Nineteenth-Century America*, New York: New York University Press.

Sundquist, Eric (1985), 'Slavery, Revolution and the American Renaissance', in Walter Benn Michaels and Donald E. Pease (eds), *The American Renaissance Reconsidered*, Baltimore: Johns Hopkins University Press, pp. 1–35.

Thompson, Graham (2012), '"Through Consumptive Pallors of This Blank, Raggy Life": Melville's Not Quite White Working Bodies', *Leviathan: A Journal of Melville Studies* 14(2): 25–43.

Wong, Edlie L. (2009), *Neither Fugitive Nor Free: Atlantic Slavery, Freedom Suits and the Legal Culture of Travel*, New York: NYU Press.

— (2015), 'Storytelling and the Comparative Study of Atlantic Slavery and Freedom', *Social Text* 33(4): 109–30.

Wyatt-Brown, Bertram (1982), 'Modernizing Southern Slavery: The Proslavery Argument Reinterpreted', in J. Morgan Kousser and James M. McPherson (eds), *Region, Race and Reconstruction: Essays in Honor of C. Vann Woodward*, pp. 27–49.

Zimmerman, Andrew (2017), 'Introduction', in Karl Marx and Friedrich Engels, *The Civil War in the United States*, New York: International Publishers.

Notes

1. On the metaphor's transatlantic origins, see Cunliffe.
2. A similar shift animates Eric Sundquist's account of Renaissance writers' ambivalent navigation between slavery and 'the meaning of the revolutionary tradition in America' (28).
3. This opposition characterises Eugene Genovese's canonisation of Fitzhugh as pro-slavery's archetypal anti- (and pre-)capitalist thinker (Genovese 130–57: 217).
4. For slavery's spectrality and liberal capitalism, see Baucom.

5. On the introduction of time into Marx's theory in Part 7 of *Capital*, see William Clare Roberts, 184.
6. My reading draws on Endnotes.
7. On Marx and US emancipation, see Anderson (82–9); Zimmerman.
8. Fitzhugh railed against the economic dependence implicit in plantation monoculture. Nevertheless, he rooted 'national' greatness in the South's racialised chattel slavery, arguing it to be a model for the global management of non-white populations (94–5). His combination of cosmopolitanism and southern nationalism cannot imagine social organisation beyond the plantation. Similarly, Hughes ends his sociological tract about the diversification of slavery with a utopian fantasy of society as a federation of 'leagued plantations', embodying 'the rhapsody of a progress epic in its grandeur' (292).
9. On Bartleby's off-whiteness, see Thompson (38–9).
10. On the territorial contradictions of US hegemony crisis, see Arrighi (70–85; 378–86); on periodising nineteenth-century American literature after US empire, Sugden (189); on imperial decline and literary periodisation, Clover.

12

ANTIQUITY/MODERNITY: AN ISSUE OF *PUCK* MAGAZINE, 1889

MARK STOREY

Consider one particular issue of *Puck* magazine – the satirical periodical that appeared weekly between the 1870s and 1918 – published on Wednesday, 17 July 1889. There is nothing exceptional about it in terms of the magazine's output, and from a cultural or print-history perspective there are many things one could pick up on: the caricatured realism of its numerous illustrations and cartoons; the insight it now offers into the historical contingency of humour; its advertisements (one for the first Kodak camera, just over a year on the market by this point); its irreverent distillation of all the vanities, worries and cant of middle-class American life in the late nineteenth century. Such would be the typical frames and contexts that a reconstruction of this issue's historical ecology might rest on. But two elements of this particular issue of *Puck*, the cartoon on the front cover and a story inside by Charles Chesnutt, are the subject of this essay; or, rather, the subject will be how the constellation of historical relations that exist within and between these two elements ask us in turn to address the problem of how we read them 'in context'. The point will be to take a perhaps counterintuitive perspective on the relationship between history and our ways of reading, and the forms of historical time we have to encounter when the nineteenth century no longer seems a feasible container for the object in our sights.

The issue in question carried on its front cover (Fig. 12.1), as usual, a satirical cartoon. It was drawn by Joseph Keppler, an Austrian immigrant who founded the magazine in 1871 and as a regular contributor came to characterise its house style;

MASTER AND SLAVE.

Figure 12.1 Front Cover of *Puck*, 17 July 1889.

his ceaseless critiques of American politics and his adeptness with historical – especially classical – allusions still mark him out as the one of the era's great satirists. This particular image, once you decode it, lampoons the newly elected Benjamin Harrison's Republican Party and their commitment to trade tariffs, an issue that had dominated the recent presidential campaigns. It's a characteristically pointed bit of mockery for the pro-Democrat magazine: the bloated Sultan of Monopoly (with his sword of money, or 'boodle', and the hookah pipe of aromatic 'war tariffs' still in place after the Civil War) is flattered by the music of trade protectionism from a feminised Republican Party administration. It is, as Keppler's cartoons for *Puck* often were, densely topical in its references and biting (if situational) in its humour. I will have more to say about its caption in a moment, but read as a metaphorisation of the cartoon's satiric target the 'Master and Slave' analogy being evoked wears its meaning in plain sight. As Marc-William Palen has demonstrated, not only was the Republican Party's advocacy of tariffs connected with their imperial desire to break open foreign markets for US advantage, but they were often posed through the 'master-slave' metaphor as a way of caricaturing the position of US trade within the rapidly globalising economy of the 1880s: 'free trade and equal access to the world's markets would free the "enslaved" working class', American Cobdenites claimed, 'an argument that struck a chord with some among the burgeoning American labor movement' (Palen 2016: 121). Like many of Keppler's cartoons, if we want to historicise it according to our usual hermeneutical protocols and replace it in its moment of time, a quite detailed degree of contextual knowledge is required to allow us, now, to read it.

Turning from the front cover that morning in July 1889, readers would also find inside the same issue, between illustrations and cartoons, the latest story from Charles Chesnutt: a sketch, barely half a page long, called 'A Roman Antique'. Written during a period of prolific creativity for Chesnutt,[1] its plot is just a single comic scene: a narrator sits on a bench in New York's Washington Square and an 'old, white-haired Negro' walks up to him, claiming that he is from Rome and that he is 'nineteen hund'ed' years old; he was, he says, 'Mars Julius Cæsar's fav'rite body-sarven'. The old man continues his story, saying that following Caesar's assassination there were 'directions in his will fer me ter be gradu'lly 'mancipated'. He also had a quarter that Caesar had given him, but he's spent it now, 'en I needs ernudder fer ter git some liniment fer my rheumatiz'. A short, tall tale, but it suitably bewitches the white man on the bench, our narrator: 'A vision of imperial Rome rose up before me, with all its glory and magnificence and power. In a fit of abstraction I handed the old man a twenty-dollar gold piece.' The men part; the story ends.

If we need to know about the 1888 presidential election and the role of tariffs in American free trade imperialism to 'get' Keppler's cartoon, what frame of knowledge – what granular historical details – does Chesnutt's story demand? Like the cartoon, it also mutates its literal slave into a metaphorical one, asking to be read not as the historical figure it appears to be (Keppler's orientalised musician; Chesnutt's ancient manservant) but as a comic cipher for the moment of contemporary life into which it has anachronistically erupted. Chesnutt's Roman slave can in this way be understood as a literate bit of classical allusion borne out of his own extensive historical learning,[2] something he put to use in several of his other stories. He had in fact taken an extended trip to Washington, DC in 1879 as an impressionable twenty-one-year-old, a time when he marvelled at the neoclassical architecture and flourishing of nationalist art but noted also how these spectacular displays of imperial inevitability elided the history that felt most painfully close to his own life: American slavery.[3] Biographically conditioned like this, the satire of 'A Roman Antique' therefore turns on its setting, Washington Square, which had taken on a strikingly neoclassical air in this same summer of 1889 – a temporary neo-Roman triumphal arch had been erected there, part of the city's centennial celebrations of Washington's presidential inauguration. (Stanford White's permanent marble structure would replace it a few years later.) The appeals to classical imperial iconography in the Washington celebrations felt to the historically literate Chesnutt like the latest iteration of the civic invisibility of Black history, something made visible in 'A Roman Antique' by that other and rather different vestige of ancient Rome, the slave. As John Levi Barnard says in his exemplary reading of the story, read in this light – in this context – the story brilliantly inverts one of the conventional analogies of the nation's founding, 'the struggle of Roman republicans against the tyranny of Caesar', by 'link[ing] Washington to ancient imperial rulers through the institution of slavery' (Barnard 2017: 114, 115). The ancient Black slave and the tale he tells set Chesnutt's satiric point within the paraliterary form of the comic sketch, which through the evocation of Caesar at the site of Washingtonian hagiography asserts, as Barnard compellingly argues, 'a skeptical view of the idea of historical progress itself' (117).

This is all to say that from one perspective both Keppler's cartoon and Chesnutt's sketch are locatable in the particular coordinates of a moment in time. They become meaningful to us when we take that reassuring calendrical signifier of their place in history – 17 July 1889 – and use it to anchor the biographical, political and cultural conditions that render them legible. They are, after all, satires, that most contextually indebted of all narrative forms. Context – or at least a particular historiographical conception of context – becomes the privileged way for us to allegorically decode them: Chesnutt's Roman slave is *really* a cipher for the triumphalist classicism going on in Washington Square; Keppler's lyre-playing attendant is not *about* Ottoman culture, but a 'comical' (and racialised) embodiment of Harrison's Republicans. 'Master and Slave' is not there to signify real masters and real slaves, but a hyperbolic metaphor for the uneven and exploitative political economy of the 1880s. Antiquity is only a way to storify modernity.

The point here is not to nullify or repudiate these responses. The form of historicist critique that this approach to reading has underpinned is still valuable, even vital. But by insisting on a less contextually circumscribed historicism to bring these texts into focus, we can suggest that even here, in these time-bound forms in this time-bound periodical, we might better grasp the temporally dispersed constellation of points that constitute each artefact of American literary culture. That metaphor, the 'constellation', will be the key, provoking some of the historical connections that this issue of *Puck* generates. It also takes us to a critic who has continued to deeply influence the refigurations of historical time that recent American Studies have developed. 'Ideas are to objects as constellations are to stars' (Benjamin [1928] 1998: 34), Walter Benjamin aphoristically says in the prologue to his study of German tragic drama. Later, in *The Arcades Project*, this has become a more explicit reckoning with history's shape and topology: it is 'not that what is past casts its light on what is present, or what is present its light on what is past', he says, but that what-has-been comes 'together in a flash with the now to form a constellation' (Benjamin 1999: 462). By the time of his final and one of his most enduring essays, 'On the Concept of History' (1940), the Benjaminian constellation is the counter to the arid forms of historicism that his own historical materialism evinces – the historian 'who stops telling the sequence of events like the beads of a rosary' and, instead, 'grasps the constellation which his own era has formed with a definite earlier one' (Benjamin [1940] 2003: 263). It is this refusal of developmentalist and sequential accounts of historical time, and instead an emphasis on the temporal alignment of past and present – moments of time not otherwise connected – that has given Benjamin's deployment of the constellation much of its subsequent conceptual utility. It has proven to be a remarkably generative epistemological method – or if not a method, as such, then what Andrea Krauss calls an 'interpretive procedure' (Krauss 2011: 439). The analogy with star-gazing that 'constellation' evokes becomes a way to render cultural and literary relations newly legible, an assertion that 'puzzlingly structured "surfaces" . . . only coalesce into recognisable astral images when an "external" knowledge intrudes into the domain of dispersed points of light' (Krauss 2011: 439). Constellations, Krauss goes on to explain, therefore not only offer an opportunity for new knowledge formation, but do so by designating it as 'a problem of object-*formation*' that – unlike our usual historicist print-cultural frames – do not privilege 'connections of literary-historical influence, biographically documented networks, or contexts of transmission' (440). Borrowing the constellation here, we can ask not so much what the 'meaning' of the cartoon and the sketch are in the context of July 1889, but more what assemblage of knowledges constitute them as an object – an object only insufficiently graspable through that date on the front cover. Constellating across the history that these texts produce will make antiquity not only an allegorical device for contemporary satire, but wrest past and present, antiquity and modernity, into something less sequential than that, less indebted to lineages of classical 'reception' and modernity's apparent supercession of the past – something more like a dialectical image, in fact, which instantiates not historical distance but historical coevality.

To pose it as a question: can we see this issue of *Puck*, and the two parts of it I have already highlighted, as requiring from us a more constellated way of reading? Keppler's front cover certainly opens us out to its possibilities. Its simple caption – 'Master and Slave' – can, as I've suggested above, be read satirically: a comment about the new Republican government, analogised with an 'Oriental' past that in the process brackets off the US's own master-slave dynamic with an appeal to an ostensibly timeless relationship of enslavement. Yet the caption's stark simplicity and the associations it trails surely also infer something less topical and more politically materialised than that, neither contained by 17 July 1889 nor timelessly untethered from history. This is a little over thirty years since slaves were emancipated in the US, a decade or so since the end of Reconstruction. For *Puck*'s readers, slavery was still a dominant part of their cultural memory and its ongoing, often escalating violences were an everyday reality of their social and legal worlds. 'Master and Slave', however much the cartoon is posing it as an image of an obsolete and caricatured past, must have felt uncomfortably close in time and space. And 'Master and Slave' further hints at a still more historically expansive meaning than this, because it might call to our mind – as it might have called to the mind of the educated reader of July 1889[4] – any number of the renderings across historical and philosophical writing of Hegel's infamous Master-Slave dialectic. More commonly now 'Lordship and Bondage', or sometimes 'Master and Servant', Hegel develops the dialectic during the discussion of self-consciousness in *The Phenomenology of Mind* (1807), where the relationship he posits between 'master' and 'slave' could, when read against Keppler's cartoon, rather complicate the satirical point. It is after all this master-slave/lord-bondsman dialectic that Susan Buck-Morss has argued 'provided [Hegel with] the key to the unfolding of freedom in world history' (Buck-Morss 2009: 48)[5] and describes a dynamic both universal and intimately historical. The 'master', Hegel says, 'is consciousness existing for itself which is mediated with itself through an *other* consciousness' (Hegel [1807] 2008: 113, italics in original) – which is to say that the master cannot be entirely free because his self-consciousness (and his existence) is only ever realisable through his slave, while the slave, through his labour and his fear of death, acquires what the master does not have, 'a mind of his own' (116). There is, we could say, an insistently if seemingly overbearing Hegelian reading of Keppler's cartoon that his 'Master and Slave' caption sets in motion and that might undermine or enrich its specific satirical commentary.

Particular explications of the Master-Slave dialectic and the notoriously opaque *Phenomenology of Spirit* aside, it is the aftershocks of Hegel's thought that resonate more insistently with our own object-formation of this issue of

Puck. I said before that the 'past' Keppler portrays could, if we read it purely symptomatically, appear as nothing more than a stage set for his contemporary satirical point. But 'Master and Slave', read within the full density of its multiple significations, in its *constellation*, will not quite allow us to partition history off from the present like this. Because if Keppler takes us to Hegel, where does Hegel's metanarrational metaphor take us? To the classical world already encountered, of course; to Aristotle especially. But also, Buck-Morss brilliantly shows, to that rather more urgent connection to the American nineteenth century, the Haitian Revolution. 'Hegel . . . knew about real slaves revolting successfully against real masters,' Buck-Morss says, pointing to the Atlantic world Hegel's Germany shared with Toussaint Louverture's insurrectional Caribbean, 'and he elaborated his dialectic of lordship and bondage deliberately within this contemporary context' (Buck-Morss 2009: 50). *The Phenomenology of Spirit*, she points out, was 'written in Jena in 1805–6 (the first year of the Haitian nation's existence) and published in 1807 (the year of the British abolition of the slave trade)' (48), events that she insists frame the Master-Slave dialectic as much as its more abstracted intellectual lineages. 'Context' again, but now nothing so synchronically neat as the date printed above Keppler's cartoon can contain.

And it is via this Hegelian-Haitian unfolding of the 'Master and Slave' caption that we reconnect with Chesnutt's ancient Roman slave. Because in the revolutionary scenes of eighteenth-century Haiti that the constellation connects us to, there is Toussaint himself, the leader and embodiment of the self-conscious slave that Hegel theorised; the man who, in another moment of modernity's analogical fusion with antiquity, they called the 'Black Spartacus'. It was a comparison – this modern Black Caribbean slave with that ancient white Thracian one – conjured even at the time of Toussaint's rise, as well as one that has sifted down through later accounts of his life. Sudhir Hazareesingh's recent biography takes this 'Black Spartacus' as its title,[6] but perhaps the most critically significant place where Spartacus and Toussaint find themselves in analogical recognition is in C. L. R. James's enduring classic *The Black Jacobins* (1938). Here – in a book that already models for us a more constellated historicism – James recounts the moment in 1796 when Étienne Laveaux, the French governor of Saint-Domingue, spoke to the gathered crowds in the northern town of Le Cap following a narrowly averted uprising and 'proclaimed Toussaint Assistant to the Governor' (James [1938] 1989: 171). In the speech, Laveaux called Toussaint 'the saviour of constituted authority, the black Spartacus, the Negro predicted by Raynal who would avenge the outrages done to his race' (171). Which demands its own further connection, of course, because 'Raynal' here is Guillaume-Thomas Raynal, the French priest and historian already lauded earlier in *The Black Jacobins* as a 'literary opponent of slavery' (24) and whose book *Histoire des deux Indes* had first appeared in 1771. In that book, Raynal – or possibly his co-contributor

Denis Diderot[7] – had pondered the whereabouts, across Europe's vast imperial spaces, of the 'great man' who will resist tyranny: 'Where is he, this new Spartacus?' Raynal asks (227). The *Histoire* was widely read in the period, not least by Hegel himself, a committed 'Raynalist' throughout his life (Buck-Morss 2009: 23). But across the Atlantic, as James notes, Raynal's influential treatise also came into the hands 'of the slave most fitted to make use of it' (James [1938] 1989: 25) – Toussaint. '[H]e came in the end to believe in himself as the black Spartacus,' James says, 'foretold by Raynal as predestined to achieve the emancipation of the blacks' (250).

The edge connecting all these nodes of the late eighteenth-century imperial world – Toussaint and Hegel and Raynal – is, it turns out, nothing modern at all, but the ancient figure of Spartacus, another slave of imperial antiquity summoned to the troubled spaces of modern empires. A gladiator by training, he lived (so Roman sources suggest) from around 111 to 71 BC, and following his escape from captivity in the mainland city of Capua became the figurehead of the slave uprising known as the Third Servile War – the largest of a series of slave uprisings during the period, and the only one to offer a serious threat to Roman power. Ever since, Spartacus has been a byword for righteous insurrection and unfinished revolutions. Indeed, so often does he appear in the cultural and political archives of the modern world that his presence could virtually stand as the paradigmatic example of what Benjamin (in 'On the Concept of History') would call 'now-time': the moment when past and present struggles recognise each other in a flash of temporal fusion. From the abolitionist thought of Enlightenment France to the revolutionary Caribbean of France's colonial possessions to the Black radicalism of James's 1930s, the ancient Roman slave insists that our model of historical time – and our 'context' that follows from them – reject the sequentialism and periodisation that have otherwise underpinned our literary categories. The constellation that we can assemble from and through this ancient Roman slave creates an overlapping space where Keppler's and Chesnutt's slaves meet. As we read that space, antiquity will not authorise modernity's break from it, and we instead encounter a field of cross-temporal oppression and inequality, one which contains figures and moments able to recognise each other across their vast historical distances. Antiquity and modernity find themselves pressed into an uneven simultaneity.

Which asks, by way of ending, that when we return to Chesnutt's scene in Washington Square, what 'context' does his ancient slave really demand? The Black Roman slave allegorises some of the nineteenth-century recuperations of classicism concretised in the ornate Washington arch, but he also asks to be read literally – read, as it were, in his own (ancient) time. In doing so, he fuses together two quite different slaves from two quite different temporal orders – the Roman and the American – into a space of mutual recognition and structural alignment. Antiquity here is, again, not just a stage set or wardrobe of costumes, but a coeval presence forcing us to recognise the historical ecology of an Atlantic slave system which bore within it the juridical and moral chromosome of the ancient Mediterranean. Roman law was not just a source of inspiration for American founders, but seeded deep within the formation of their slaveholding republicanism; a dialectical image, taken from Rome, of republic and empire that 'has exerted an immense influence . . . on those broadly imperial and specifically Atlantic discourses of sovereignty, exceptionality, and enmity' (Baucom 2009: 131) – in short, slavery itself. Robin Blackburn's sweeping account of New World slavery from the fifteenth to the eighteenth centuries is useful here, not only because he asserts that US slavery is both a part of and conditioned by a long history of intra-imperial rivalry across an epochal Atlantic system, but because he points out that it proceeds through a pluralistic (and often opportunistic) restoration of ancient philosophies and practices. Antiquity becomes present for modernity's imperial powers, Blackburn says, through a legacy of 'Greek philosophy, Roman law and Christian doctrine' which combine to underpin the 'legitimacy of enslavement' (Blackburn 1997: 34). Neo-Roman legal and constitutional writing in the eighteenth century could consider the dynamic of freedom and slavery without necessarily paying heed to the specifically racialised forms of slavery they engaged in – indeed, that formed part of the appeal of Roman jurisprudence – because, as Blackburn explains, Roman law was marked both by 'the thoroughness with which it codified slaves as private property or chattels' and 'its formal lack of interest in the slave's ethnic or racial provenance' (35). Chesnutt's sketch bears some of the weight of this long conditioning history, his slave coded both as American in his Blackness and Roman in his antiquity; a body in which these epochal times coalesce into a temporal and moral contiguity that conventional historiography separates into radically different periods. The constellation that Chesnutt's story opens us out to – connected as it is via Keppler's front cover – makes the appearance of Caesar's slave from the first century BC in the Washington Square of the nineteenth century AD not ironically anachronistic and misplaced, but entirely timely and at home.

'Master and Slave' is the textual wink this issue of *Puck* opens with; an image and a joke that its readers that day would have passed over soon enough. And yet a few pages later Chesnutt's sketch of ancient slavery in modern New York casts us back to the terms of that cover image once more, to histories both deeply felt and publicly unacknowledged: to the slave himself, whose conspicuous presence forces the day out of its calendrical moorings and into the constellation of history that these moments of satire half glimpse – into the connections between the postbellum US, the revolutionary Atlantic and the ancient Roman imperium, connections that demand from us a reading and a history that is hardly containable, and hardly explicable, within the pages of that issue of *Puck* magazine on 17 July 1889.

Works Cited

Barnard, John Levi (2017), *Empire of Ruin: Black Classicism and American Imperial Culture*, Oxford: Oxford University Press.

Baucom, Ian (2009), 'Cicero's Ghost: The Atlantic, the Enemy, and the Laws of War', in Russ Castronovo and Susan Gillman (eds), *States of Emergency: The Object of American Studies*, Chapel Hill: University of North Carolina Press, pp. 124–42.

Benjamin, Walter [1928] (1998), *The Origin of German Tragic Drama*, trans. John Osborne, London and New York: Verso.

— (1999), *The Arcades Project*, trans. Howard Eiland and Kevin McLaughlin, Cambridge and London: Belknap Press.

— [1940] (2003), 'On the Concept of History', in *Selected Writings, Volume 4: 1938–1940*, trans. Edmund Jephcott et al., ed. Howard Eiland and Michael W. Jennings, Cambridge, MA: Harvard University Press, pp. 389–411.

Blackburn, Robin (1997), *The Making of New World Slavery: From the Baroque to the Modern, 1492–1800*, London and New York: Verso.

Buck-Morss, Susan (2009), *Hegel, Haiti, and Universal History*, Pittsburgh: University of Pittsburgh Press.

Chesnutt, Charles W. (1889), 'A Roman Antique', *Puck*, 17 July, via Hathi Trust digital library: <https://babel.hathitrust.org/cgi/pt?id=mdp.39015075986987&view=1up &seq=337> (accessed 29 October 20210).

— (1993), *The Journals of Charles W. Chesnutt*, ed. Richard Brodhead, Durham, NC: Duke University Press.

Hegel, Georg Wilhelm Friedrich [1807] (2018), *The Phenomenology of Spirit*, trans. and ed. Terry Pinkard, Cambridge: Cambridge University Press.

James, C. L. R. [1938] (1989), *The Black Jacobins: Toussaint L'Ouverture and the San Domingo Revolution*, New York: Vintage Books.

Krauss, Andrea (2011), 'Constellations: A Brief Introduction', trans. James McFarland, *MLN*, 126(3): 439–45.

Palen, Marc-William (2016), *The 'Conspiracy' of Free Trade: The Anglo-American Struggle over Empire and Economic Globalisation, 1846–1896*, Cambridge: Cambridge University Press.

Notes

1. Between 1887 and 1889, Chesnutt would publish many of the short stories that his later critical reputation has tended to hang on: 'The Goophered Grapevine' (1887), 'Po' Sandy' (1888), 'Dave's Neckliss' (1899) and 'The Sheriff's Children' (1889) all appeared in literary magazines in the period around 'A Roman Antique' in July 1889.

2. 'I have just finished Merivale's General History of Rome,' Chesnutt announces in his journal on 12 March 1881 (Chesnutt 1993: 163), referring to Charles Merivale's *A General History of Rome*, published in 1875. It is only one instance of many readings in classical history that Chesnutt details in his journals of the 1880s.

3. For an account of Chesnutt's visit to Washington in these terms, see Barnard 2017: 107–14.

4. John Kaag and Kipton Jensen have traced the American reception of Hegel amidst a general Germanophilia in nineteenth-century intellectual circles, pointing to the widespread engagement with his philosophy especially from the 1860s onwards (679).

5. This is a simplified parsing of Hegel's notoriously opaque term; for a clarifying discussion of the Lordship-Bondage dialectic (and for a different historicisation than Buck-Morss's), see Andrew Cole's boldly titled 'What Hegel's Master/Slave Dialectic Really Means', *Journal of Medieval and Early Modern Studies*, 34.3 (Fall 2004): 577–610.

6. See Sudhir Hazareesingh, *Black Spartacus: The Epic Life of Toussaint Louverture* (Penguin, 2020).

7. Raynal's controversial and colossally ambitious book was widely read – in French, and also in its numerous translated editions – throughout the Enlightenment world. A complex, digressive work of geography, political philosophy, science and history, it is made up of eighteen books that tackle between them the global experiences of European colonialism in the eighteenth century. Its authorship is not a straightforward question, however, and by the time of the 1780 edition Diderot had substantially augmented and edited Raynal's original, often with philosophically opposing points – indeed, with a more polemical sense of antislavery sentiment than Raynal's earlier ambivalence, and possibly even the line about Spartacus. It isn't clear which edition Toussaint would have read, but given the tone of the changes Diderot made and James's connection between the book and Toussaint's radicalisation, it seems likely this later, collaborative work is what found its way into his hands. For more on the *Histoire des deux Indes* see Peter Jimack, ed., *A History of the Two Indies: A Translated Selection of Writings from Raynal's Histoire Philosophique et Politique des Etablissements des Europeens dans les Deux Indes*, Aldershot and Burlington, VT: Ashgate Publishing, 2006.

13

DEMOCRACY/STATE: JAMES FENIMORE COOPER ON THE FRONTIER, 1826/1757

CÉCILE ROUDEAU

The third day from the capture of the fort was drawing to a close, but the business of the narrative must still detain the reader on the shores of the 'holy lake'. When last seen, the environs of the works were filled with violence and uproar. They were now possessed by stillness and death. The blood-stained conquerors had departed; and their camp, which had so lately rung with the merry rejoicings of a victorious army, lay a silent and deserted city of huts. The fortress was a smoldering ruin; charred rafters, fragments of exploded artillery, and rent mason-work covering its earthen mounds in confused disorder.

The date is 6 August 1757 and the battle one of those historians retrospectively describe as turning points – the French army's siege of Fort William Henry during the Seven Years' War. The scene is familiar, and any reader ever so slightly versed in the American classics will need no more than this to identify the climactic juncture of James Fenimore Cooper's *The Last of the Mohicans*. At the heart of Cooper's frontier romance, the memorable heroes – the self-reliant Hawkeye, the ever-vanishing 'Indians' – have receded from the scene, yielding to the spectacle of global warfare. The paradox is worth pondering: the pivot of Cooper's tale of rugged individualism, a text that has repeatedly been read as the illustration of that American 'aversion to state authority' (Gustafson 2011: 168), is a grandiose conflagration between two European imperial state powers flexing their fiscal-military muscles on the other side of the Atlantic. Have we missed something?

The fort, or what remains thereof, looms large in the eighteenth chapter of Cooper's romance, imparting a sense of tragedy to the scene. No matter how eager we may be to learn what has happened to our travelling companions, the scout, the girls, the Mohicans and their British allies, we are detained, forced to contemplate the smoking ruins of a military edifice in the wilderness. The choice to plant such a formidable silhouette on the threshold of what used to be the second volume of the romance merits pause and, I'd like to suggest, should prompt us to revisit some of the assumptions we have carried into our reading of Cooper's text. What if the question left unanswered in 1757, and raised again by Cooper in 1826, when he wrote *The Last of the Mohicans* on the other side of the Revolutionary divide, did not concern the protection of individual liberty nor individual rights, as has been so repeatedly presumed since the middle of the twentieth century, so much as the kind of state that would govern once the bond with the metropolis had been overthrown? As our vision is obfuscated by the smoke and the mist and the gloom, we are left to wonder what will become of the fort's 'smoldering ruin', the 'fragments of exploded artillery' and 'rent mason-work'. Would they be left to moulder into ruins and later signify an American antiquity not unlike the Indian mounds or Native blockhouses that the text also commemorates? Or, would the military masonry be restored, new artillery be sent, a new empire be built? The question of state investment that overwhelmed the North Atlantic world in the aftermath of the Seven Years' War and in the chaotic years before and after the American War of Independence came rolling back in the 1820s, yet in a different guise and with different constraints attached to it. I propose to read *The Last of the Mohicans*, an 1826 romance that chose 6 August 1757 for its diegetic turning point, as Cooper's attempt to fictionally come to terms with the most burning issues of his day: that of state intervention in a self-appointed democracy.

Historically considered, the concepts of 'democracy' and 'the state' have hardly gone hand in glove. In fact, the state seems to have found its place as a foil to any meaningful democratic thrust: regarded by a postwar liberal tradition as a hindrance to individual freedom and individual rights, the state, in the two major responses to the liberal tradition, the Marxian and the Weberian/Foucaldian critiques, has been similarly opposed to popular power. For the one, as is well known, the withering away of the state is the desired horizon of emancipation; for the other, the state either checks popular power through bureaucratic expertise or by contributing to regimes of insidious surveillance. When spoken in these narratives, democracy is elsewhere. If it is regarded as a plausible or even a desirable cure, it is opposed to the bureaucracy, surveillance institutions and courts that serve to disempower and act against collective engagement.

We are therefore left with the dire perspective of having to turn away from the 'coldest of all cold monsters' (Nietzsche qtd in Brown 1995: 166), that is, the state, and from democracy, or, at the very least, to embrace a veneer of democracy understood at best as a naive illusion, at worst as a regime complicit with white supremacy and surveillance. Faced with this impasse, some have found new resources in the democratic political: a democracy sans liberalism inspired by the unlikely heritage of Carl Schmitt (Laclau and Mouffe 1985); or a democracy outside and contra institutions, a 'fugitive democracy' (Wolin 1994). In the latter instance, democracy is set against any prolonged or institutionalised set of practices or everyday politics, and perforce immune to anything state-like. Once again, the state and democracy emerge as binary opposites, or, to quote Wolin in his biography of Cooper's contemporary, Alexis de Tocqueville, 'the democratic state is a contradiction in terms' (Wolin 2001: 369). For Wolin, it was so in the age of Tocqueville; it remains so today. The payoffs of such a critical orientation are undeniable.

In the field of nineteenth-century US literature, Wolin's 'fugitive democracy' has paved the way for a number of important political readings (among others, Castronovo and Gillman 2006; Castiglia 2008) that have revisited decades of laudatory rhetoric emerging out of an exceptionalist America in which nineteenth-century US letters were synonymous with the very 'possibilities of [liberal] democracy' (Matthiessen [1941] 1968: ix). As important as this work has been, however, it has had the unfortunate side-effect of making the state a villain by default. This chapter suggests that a persistent turn away from the democratic potentialities of state power comes at our own risk.

Natty Bumppo's supposed Davy Crockett-like anti-statism may serve here as a starting point. Writing in the context of our overblown security apparatus, Russ Castronovo's 2016 article, eloquently titled 'James Fenimore Cooper and the NSA: Security, Property, Liberalism', investigates Cooper's resistance to the ineluctable progression of the state (the *federal* state) over a wilderness that had not been turned yet into a territorial grid. Cooper reveals – and thus provides grounds for a critique of – the Lockean conception of private property that serves as a justification for relentless state surveillance. In Castronovo's view, his tales are an early example of resistance to classical liberalism's complicity with terror and territory. The reading is perceptive and important. It is also revealing. The state is encroaching on the wilderness and will soon be everywhere, overseeing and dominating, and *therefore* democracy is nowhere to be found. The premise is clear: (liberal) democracy is always already tainted by its defence of private property – not only complicit with domination and terror, but somehow one with it.

Such logic of incommensurability between democracy and the state, however, has lately been called into question by empirical and theoretical work in sociology, political science and history (Balogh 2009; Clemens 2020; Edling 2008; Pincus 2016; Rao 2018; among others). A recent essay in *The Tocqueville Review* warns us about 'the myth of stateless democracy' pivoted on 'a zero-sum, hydraulic theory of the relation of democracy and state – *i.e.*, more democracy, less state; more state, less democracy' (Novak et al. 2015: 24). This hydraulic logic, they argue, is something that we need to reconsider. If such recent approaches have been central to the social sciences and instrumental to a rethinking of American political development more broadly, nineteenth-century US literature has remained isolated from these insights. With a few exceptions.

Dana Nelson, for one, in *Commons Democracy* (2015), has tried to recover these muddy entanglements between state and democracy in Cooper's 1820s and later. In line with Novak's denunciation of 'the myth of the "weak" American state' (2008), Nelson does bring the state back in her reading of Cooper and other early American writers. She retrieves in their pages the tradition of alternative systems of laws, the practice of a local decentralised regulated social order. But here too, as the democratic tide rises, the horizon of the state falls in turn. For Nelson, Cooper's novels are the loci where two versions of the democratic vie with each other – schematically, the vernacular democratic tradition of local processes of self-government (what she calls 'commons democracy') versus the constitutional representative system of federal law. Of course, such 'robustly participatory, insistently local, roughly equalitarian' democracy on the frontiers was exclusive in terms of race and gender and often violent (Nelson 2015: 10). Yet, we need to reread Cooper's tales, Nelson argues, precisely because they adumbrate utopian or dystopian futurities that it is valuable for us to confront or claim back as we try to get out of the impasse between the excesses of a state apparatus and the shortcomings of vernacular democratic practices. But while she invites us not to choose between 'the vernacular, daily ordinariness of commons democracy' (176) and 'the state-based democratic institutions of government' (Nelson 2015: 281), she insists that this tradition of 'local self-governing neither aims at nor requires state organization and administration' (177). Democracy and the state, yet again, are at odds with each other.

I have dwelt at length on Nelson and Castronovo's rereading of Cooper because both, however differently, attempt to retrieve the ideological instabilities of antebellum US literature that have been structurally erased by a Cold War liberal indoctrination. However, while they highlight how reluctant we have been to call into question a basic suspicion of 'the state', both ironically and unwittingly reinforce the very liberal – and neoliberal – distrust of the state to do anything but command, control and classify. In other words, they remain trapped in the 'hydraulic theory of the relation of democracy and state'. Escaping such a trap requires us to revisit the concept of the state *and* democracy together. And to do so, it is important to return once again to Cooper and his own difficulties with one of the most fundamental questions of his age: that of the everyday practice of what we may dare to call 'an American democratic state', in which the central question was not so much how to destroy the state as to democratise it. If only for some, sadly.

In Cooper's 1826 romance, the state is not only the forbidding, if spectral, fiscal-military power that conditioned the existence of a thriving overseas British empire – until the Seven Years' War, that is. Because it straddles two regimes of historicity – recounting the 1750s from the perspective of the 1820s – *The Last of the Mohicans* allows the romancer-historian to address the debates of his own democratic age through a genealogical perspective that goes back to the days of empire.

The question of state intervention, historians tell us, was harshly debated in the aftermath of the Seven Years' War. The increasing withdrawal of British investment from the American colonies, in an attempt to cope with a huge war debt, is now largely considered one of the main grievances that led to the Revolution. The War of Independence, it follows, is no longer held as the origin of an American commitment to small government. Until the very last moment, Steve Pincus insists, 'the authors of The Declaration of Independence made no anti-imperial or anti-government claim' (Pincus 2016: 23). What motivated the Patriots, instead, was the hope 'that a new British ministry would return to the pre-1760 policies of state supporting imperial development, promote economic development by opening up markets for American products' (150). That did not come to pass. But the question of state intervention certainly did not vanish from the new nation's agenda.

Ever present throughout an American 'revolution in favor of government' (Edling 2008), the question of American state-building resurfaced with a vengeance a few decades later in the 1820s when the expanding nation faced tremendous expenses on the frontiers that could not be met by available bullion. Who and what would guarantee the loans that were necessary to invest in the territories? Would it be a strong banking system supported by the federal state, as argued by Henry Clay, champion of the massive banking, regulatory and infrastructural project known as the American system? Or, after the panic of 1819 caused by the overextension of credit by the Second Bank of the United States, was it time to get rid of such illegal monopoly, as Andrew Jackson forcefully claimed?

The fact that the charter for the Second Bank of the United States was set to expire in 1826, the year, coincidentally, when *The Last of the Mohicans* was published, kindled vivid debates over the relevance of a regulatory federal organ and also about the new modes of value based upon paper and not on specie (gold and silver). Moves towards a more speculative economy were opposed by strong counterforces that insisted on traditional means of producing value, based on trade or farming.[1] In a replay of the battle that had opposed Jefferson and Hamilton, Andrew Jackson's war on Nicholas Biddle, then president of the Second Bank of America, was merciless.[2] A 'democratic', anti-bank populist fervour quickly grew, fed in particular by the Locofocos, who ferociously combatted the champions of a federal bank. Such is the usual narrative that puts democracy on the side of Jacksonian anti-bank, anti-regulation populism. This narrative, I argue, is complicated by Cooper's novel, which neither castigates an economy of debt nor enforces a strict 'mercantilist form of capitalism, in which value is thought of as stable and linked to local trade and secure sites of gold bullion' (Anthony 2009: 3).

Cooper, it is well known, was no speculator. A member of the landed gentry of Otsego County, the owner of a large estate that he had inherited from his father, Judge Cooper, James Fenimore was not in favour of the wild speculation that was rampant in his time. Neither was he exclusively attached to a Whig economy that spurned the importance of cash flow. A Hamiltonian at heart in the 1820s, he understood the advantages of cash investment *and* a strong national bank with money to be spent in the expansive territories of the new nation. Put differently, the 'American democrat' was not against state intervention. Not unlike many of his contemporaries, Cooper was working on new ways to articulate state and democracy. *The Last of the Mohicans* offered a fictional response to that urgent question.

In the remainder of this chapter, I want to highlight the ways in which the mutual alignment of state and democracy in Cooper's frontier romance plays out in the questioning of the currency of signs on the frontier at a transitional moment, the 1820s, when the era of 'hard money' morphed into the age of speculative capitalism. I argue that the novel can be understood as a meditation on the question of debt as it articulates interrogations about the formation of an early US state and democratic experiments with governance and monetary policy. Where many accounts of the novel emphasise Cooper's distrust of the state, this chapter instead insists on Cooper's interest in the correlated emergence of state and democracy not as oppositional but as compatible forms.

While the text speculates on signs that no longer stand for a stable material referent, Cooper's fictional hermeneutic of suspicion maps out onto the burning issue of trust that was itself at the heart of the broader question of state investment in a democratic regime. Displacing the double-barrelled debate of democracy vs the state/free-floating currency vs regulation to the realm of fiction, *The Last of the Mohicans* troubles what we think we know within the precincts of a genre, the frontier romance, that forcefully engages with the question of the emergent unreadability of signs on the frontier, the issue of referential bonds and the credit to be given to marks and indices.

As such, Cooper's romance stands for us today as a testimony to unactivated historical possibilities, in particular to alternatives latent in democratic statecraft that have become unreadable to us. Because the concepts of both 'democracy' and 'the state' have been confined within the narrow limits of classical liberalism, the story Cooper is telling, as Nelson rightly suggests, is a story that 'we can't actually remember how to tell' (Nelson 2015: 136). But this perspective, I would suggest, requires yet one more turn.

Democracy is not the only concept that needs to be put back to work. Rather, the oxymoronic relationship between democracy and the state is what deprives us of the possibility – and obliterates the urgency – of recovering for our times what has not yet in a sense come to pass: the co-agency of democratic regulation and state power. This co-agency is necessary to rescue the global commons from the relentless drive towards environmental, sanitary and financial deregulation for the benefit of the few. This challenge, I contend, was already one that Cooper's fiction took up.

That 'the paper money debate was concerned with symbolization in general, and hence not only with money but also with aesthetics' (Shell 1993: 6) is a staple of early American literature. I believe, however, that such an assessment requires taking another step into the wilderness. Implicit in this analogy is the little-addressed question of regulation that Cooper's text illuminates: What, or who, should regulate the circulation and meaning attached to signs on the frontiers? Regulation, when considered at all, has rarely been read as the lynchpin of Cooper's democracy; and yet, pace those who have loved in Natty Bumppo the lone libertarian hunter, the need for government and regulation is the blatant pivot of Cooper's politics, as illustrated in the very first sentence of the first chapter of *The American Democrat*, 'On Government': 'Man is known to exist in no part of the world, without certain rules for the regulation of his intercourse with those around him' (Cooper 1838: 9). In this later text, regulation mediates between government and democracy, not as what protects private property only, but as the guarantee of inflation and public debt when public debt means public investment in the public good. If debt and inflation are no panacea for Cooper, if they are a threat when they are left to escalate without proper – that is legal – safeguard, they are however necessary in times of crisis. Obliquely, yet powerfully, chapter XVIII of *The Last of the Mohicans* addresses this issue of debt, inflation and the need to regulate the very means – signs, paper money – on which public provision and democratic governance simply depend. Let us now go back to it.

With 'the ruined works' of the Anglo-American empire as its backdrop, the second volume of *The Last of the Mohicans* starts with a hermeneutic interlude that brings the illegibility of signs to a (playful) peak. As the 'forms of five men' emerge from 'the somber gloom' that hovers over the desolate spot, the narrator plays riddles with the reader, insisting on veiling the identity of those 'figure[s]' for two long, winding paragraphs. The scene depicted is one of 'deformity' and disfiguration; what is being perceived is no longer amenable to representation nor computation.

The book of nature itself, the only one Bumppo has been able to read and enjoy so far, lies open no longer. The waters of the Horican, described as 'limpid' on the first page of the novel, are now 'polluted', 'impure', and the reader finds relief in vain 'by attempting to pierce the illimitable void of heaven, which was shut to the gaze, by the dusky sheet of ragged and driving vapour'. We are entering a fallen world indeed, and what we can see is only observable 'through a glass, darkly'. As contours no longer hold, the charred remains of what used to be bodies are lumped pell-mell in a 'melancholy pile'. Not even the regular turn of season obtains. The sixth of August is swept by 'the blasts of a premature November'. Time, truly, is out of joint.

That the fall into the messiness of representation, mediation and the instability of any signifying medium should be made to coincide with the crumbling of a mighty state power, the British empire, is what interests me here – all the more so because, as we, and Cooper's readers at the time, know, the British, defeated in 1757, did in fact win the war and the right to reign over those territories. What is intriguing, then, is this forced coincidence between a military defeat that the text cunningly turns into a proleptic sign of Independence and the question of the proliferation of illegible, unreliable signs, forms, figures, whose convertibility into a referent is no longer guaranteed. In other words, the disinvestment of state power in the colonies, figured here by the loss of Fort William Henry, is made to concur with an increase in the volatility of signs, and soon with their proliferation. Why?

We need to be more precise. Not all the parties have trouble reading signs nor read them the same way. As the familiar cohort is looking for traces of the vanished sisters, Uncas, the Mohican, first uncovers a portion of a veil, then a 'tooting we'pon', and finally 'a shining bauble', all of which are easily identified as belonging to Cora, David and Alice, respectively. Being at one with nature, the Mohicans trace the uncongenial smear of the human animal. They have no difficulty detecting and interpreting signs of men in scenes of nature. When Duncan Heyward, however, comes across 'the palpable impression of the footstep of a man!', the question of the mutual relation between the print and the man, the sign and the body, is raised with renewed intensity. Duncan may well claim that 'the mark cannot be mistaken', the scout only half trusts him and asks him to 'try what you can make of the moccasin'. In the time after the fall (of the fort), the scout no longer reads nature as an open book but knows that the time for deciphering has come. For him, the sign is a 'tell-tale', it gives notice; and indeed, Uncas, appointed as translator, or mediator, brings light to the referent: 'Le Renard Subtil' is the body that made the mark, the body that the mark figures and betrays.

The episode could easily have stopped there with the evidence of the two daughters being held captive by Magua. The revelation, however, does not close the debate. At the most improbable, and highly Cooperian, moment, the text delays the closure of the deal and the final conjunction of sign and referent, print and body, or – to pick up the interpretive thread that the narrative itself is offering us – the contentious gap between paper money and specie. Turned into a human counterfeit detector,[3] a hint that Cooper's readers would not have missed, Uncas is said to 'examine [the print] with much of that sort of scrutiny, that a money-dealer, in *these* days of pecuniary doubts, would bestow on a suspected due-bill' (emphasis mine). The lengthy debate that ensues, then, is not only a proto-detective story à la Poe, or a nod to Daniel Defoe's *Robinson Crusoe*; it is Cooper's explicit reference to the 'pecuniary doubts' of *his* days. Mark Shell reminds us that a heated debate about coined and paper money 'dominated American political discourse after 1825' (Shell 1993: 6), most notably after the panic of 1819, when wildcat banks over the territory were unable to meet their obligations and many frontier borrowers defaulted on their loan and mortgage payments – Cooper being one of them.[4] Chapter XVIII is also, and maybe above all, concerned about the crisis of credit and trust – the foundational questions for the construction of a nineteenth-century fiscal and infrastructural state. Replete with phantom-like figures reminiscent of the phantom bank notes that circulated and could pass for solid specie when not examined closely, narration and dialogues raise the question of the value of money and the validity of inflation.[5]

When the print has been authenticated by Uncas as being Magua's, Heyward remains unsure: 'One moccasin is so much like another, it is probable there is some mistake.' Heyward, who had been the one to believe he could read into the mark, now refuses to give credit to Uncas's authentication and bets on the interchangeability of (foot)prints – if in a lukewarm way that hardly hides his reluctance to do so. 'A young gentleman of vast riches, from one of the provinces far south', as he is introduced earlier on in the novel (chapter 4), Duncan Heyward is a hard-money man who does not bank on signs, prints and other marks. Throughout the passage, he insists on finding 'Alice', and when old Munro sheds a fatherly tear on the 'nearly obliterated impression' of Cora's footprint, he urges the group to move on to find the corresponding bodies. As to Alice, he will only be convinced of her presence when he sees the little shining trinket that was hers in Uncas's hands. A footprint would not do, but a 'palpable' precious metal object dispels his suspicions. Read in the context of the 1820s, and the debates on the renewal of the charter of the Second Bank of the US, the reaction of the 'southern gentleman' is hardly surprising. Duncan, not unlike a majority of his fellow white Southerners, is opposed to an inflation of paper money and a widespread circulation of worthless bank notes that were the perverse effect, in the view of Jacksonians, of central banking. Duncan's reaction, in a sense, prefigures 1830s critiques of finance capitalism that resented the disembodying capacity of the speculative economy and emphasised instead the power of labour in producing actual material value. For Duncan the Southerner, bodies are what matter, contra the abstraction of money that allows for speculative flights unrelated to the value of land.

But as the spectre of slavery hovers over the western frontier of Cooper's tale, the dialogue takes another sharp turn, when Duncan's addressee, Natty himself, signs on to a very different relation to the signifier. 'One moccasin like another! you may as well say that one foot is like another; though we all know that some are long, and others short; some broad and others narrow; some with high, and some with low insteps; some intoed, and some out.' Hawkeye may no longer live up to his name, but he knows his prints yet, and knows above all how to tell one from another. Belying Duncan's disillusioned belief in the universal treacherousness of the signifier, or, to take up the fiduciary language of the day, in the unreliability of paper money, the scout proves an exacting reader, and, more surprisingly, he knows how to appreciate the fluctuating value of the pedestrian currency of the wilderness. 'One moccasin is no more like another than one book is like another,' he adds. 'Let me get down to it, Uncas; neither book nor moccasin is the worse for having two opinions, instead of one.' Unexpectedly perhaps for one who pretended earlier to read only one book – the book of nature – Natty, here, admits that the signs of the wilderness no longer are transparent. More important still, they can no longer be backed up with bodies in a one-to-one infallible correspondence. Even if finding the body that matches the sign remains the ultimate goal, the scout here acknowledges the extrication of the sign from its material backing, and Cooper's narrative takes pleasure in deferring the moment of correspondence.

Hardly has Uncas matched the print and the body – 'Le Renard Subtil!' – when the party launches into the aforementioned digressive analogical interlude between books and moccasins, only to be closed when the older Native, Chingachgook, has himself authenticated the mark: 'Magua!' One print, one body, two names. Or rather, a double name, pronounced the first time in translation; the second time, in the language of the tribe. Retrospectively, the time between, the interval, just before the final pronouncement, leaves the name that betrays the body some poetic latitude, still. 'Subtil' (from the Latin *subtela,* under the woof) is itself duplicitous – meaning both 'deceitful, treacherous' and 'refined, fine, acute', as Webster's 1828 dictionary avers. While the cohort debates about the relevance of interpretation, the name, or the translation thereof (Le Renard Subtil), is left to fork, and maintain its ambivalence until the Indian appellation (Magua) settles the deal, and brings the parenthesis to a close. The poetic interval – the moment of *poiesis* – holds to yet another mediation, or translation; the print needs to be glossed, translated and then labelled unequivocally to designate the body it refers to, the material backing of the sign. This in-between moment, where meaning fluctuates, is a communal deliberative interlude, and, as such, it functions as a mise-en-abyme of the whole episode.

The larger part of chapter XVIII relishes indeed in discussions and deliberations around the meaning and value of prints. Are they what they look like?

How accurate the measurements? How reliable the conclusions regarding the backing of those signs with the substance of bodies? With the scout leading the search, the natives busily work to offer interpretations that Hawkeye translates and eventually substantiates under the watchful eye of Heyward. The print has no value outside these communal debates. Put differently, its value as sign, and ultimately its meaning, is determined not so much by the object represented, nor by an external law, but by the exchanges around it – an episode that could be reclaimed, in line with Nelson's argument, as a moment of 'vernacular democracy'. Participatory, local, immune from institutionalisation, these democratic practices on the frontier, she insists, had not yet been captured by formal modes of representative government nor a state-sponsored standardised modus operandi. On this, Duncan and Hawkeye would seem to agree, however opposite their premises might be: Heyward, attached as he is to the one-to-one correspondence of body and print, would not favour the semantic inflation and poetic fluctuation embraced by Hawkeye; both, nonetheless, would resist the principle of a strict standardisation implemented, or so we have been accustomed to believe, at the expense of grassroot vernacular practices. I argue that the story Cooper is telling, however, defies such binary logic. If he lauds the ambivalence of print, and acknowledges the pliability of signs, Hawkeye is no extravagant poet like David Gamut, nor a vain speculator as there were so many of in the 1820s. To the contrary, he proves an exacting surveyor, praising the accuracy of measurements and demanding from his cohort the right amount of effort that should be rewarded by a just return on investment. If he's not afraid of a certain pliability of signs, those prints that tend to multiply on the frontiers as the result of the fall of the British fort, if he indeed 'wagers' on a certain inflation of their semantic ambit, he also, as a *scout*, embodies the need of governance. As a democratic frontiersman, he is Cooper's unexpected spokesman for regulation.

Against the grain of many classic readings of his work, Cooper was neither anti-commerce nor anti-debt nor anti-paper money. In his chapter 'On the Circulating Medium' in *The American Democrat*, Cooper exposes at length the necessity, 'for practical reasons' 'in a country like America' where 'a purely specie currency is utterly impracticable' to resort to the fabrication of paper money, and he was no exception among the literati of his days (Cooper 1838: 172). In *Securing the Commonwealth: Debt, Speculation, and Writing in the Making of Early America*, Jennifer Baker goes a step further and shows how the literature of colonial British America and the early United States 'saw the representative and unstable nature of paper currency as precisely its greatest asset' (Baker 2005: 2). In these texts, public debt figures 'a catalyst for sympathetic social interaction' 'binding people to their government as well as individuals to one another' (2). 'Paper credit schemes', she explains, 'defined the boundaries of a community – quite literally because, unlike metal, paper was not universally accepted and often could only circulate where it was originally issued – but they also defined a community by soliciting, and even exacting, commitment' (17). By going back to the Seven Years' War, Cooper, I propose, reclaims this tradition across and against the Revolutionary divide, and doing so, he speaks to his own time and to ours. Baker is right when insisting on the communal bonding resulting from deliberation and compromise, themselves the outcome of a debt economy. Cooper's 1826 romance has indeed been read as 'the great American deliberative novel' (Gustafson 2011: 181), and the lengthy dispute to assess the nature of the (foot)prints in this episode is one example among many of the ways in which deliberations, in this famously verbose novel, perform Cooper's democracy. And yet, such emphasis on *deliberative* democracy on the frontiers does only partial justice to Cooper's lifetime entanglements with the *practical*, state-like dimensions of the democratic. In Cooper's vision of democracy, deliberation cannot abide without its twin attendants of governance and regulation. It has ceased to be fugitive.

Cooper's European writings, right after the publication of *The Last of the Mohicans*, are a vibrant defence and illustration of an American democracy that, unlike the dispendious French monarchical regime, can boast a virtuous management of public money.[6] The nation was able, his American democrat lauds, to support the veterans, the poor, to build public transportation and public post services, encourage public schooling, pay for public servants, all with 'the utmost deference to the public will' (71). It is beyond the scope of this essay to review Cooper's adamant vindication of the dual need for federal investment *and* proper regulation so as to eschew the ultimate evil that awaits democratic regimes – a corrupted and improvident governance. His cautious betting on the fluidity of abstract money is not a way out of a highly substantive notion of political action. In other words, his being tempted by the potentialities of paper money does not in fact put him on the side of the deregulating speculators of his day. To the contrary, the unhinging of paper from value was, and so he well knew, the very condition for the production of debt as public investment – provided that it was democratically regulated. In that sense, *The Last of the Mohicans* is less an elegiac consolation to, and compensation for, the emergence of a market economy, as critics such as David Anthony and others, have labelled antebellum literature: if there is nostalgia in Cooper's romance, it is not for an earlier pre-capitalist world, but for the very age of empire that was the age of state intervention and investment, the age of a controlled public debt. A final mention of *The American Democrat* will suffice to illustrate Cooper's position as a political pragmatist avant la lettre. In 'On the Circulating Medium', Cooper indeed agreed with the need for inflation and public debt, but only 'in the interest of society', not in those of 'money dealers' (Cooper 1838: 173). Cautious as ever, Cooper does not cut the Gordian knot; still, his precepts are clear: laws and regulations, if democratically passed, are the sine qua non for public provision that will serve the many (however constricted this notion remained) instead of gratifying the few.

Have we strayed too far away from Hawkeye and the smouldering ruins of Fort William Henry? Not as far as we might think. On the backdrop of a crumbling, yet provident, British empire, signs and prints proliferate and deliberation ensues to determine the value and meaning of the semantic currency in circulation. This moment of deliberative democracy, in which Mohicans, British gentlemen and American hunters have their say, is productive of a fictional interval that is only so gratuitous. At the close of the parenthesis, the print has spoken, or rather, it has been made to speak at the intersection of imagination and hermeneutics – the latter obeying rules that are all but vernacular and, as such, guarantee the validity of the communal pronouncement. Put differently, the poetic and martial interval ushers us from one form of state (the aristocratic state of the British empire) to another – a yet-to-come (in 1757) but already born, if thoroughly imperfect (in 1826), democratic state that must still be articulated on the imperative of freedom and right for all *and* the need for public provision. That Hawkeye be our guide in this episode, and more largely in Cooper's 1826 romance, is no accident. Leading the little cohort and the reader away from a maze of babbling signs into a space of legibility where signs can be relied on, from bewilderment to action in the interest of all, Hawkeye, alias 'the scout', is not the solitary wolf, jealous of his inalienable liberty and opposed to the rules that make public provision possible. Reaching the end of a long and eventful career in *The Prairie*, the novel Cooper began immediately upon completing *The Last of the Mohicans*, Natty emphatically states precisely this. To Ellen Wade, 'venturing in a place where none but the strong should come', he asks: 'Did you not know that, when you crossed the big river, you left a friend behind you that is always bound to look to the young and feeble, like yourself.' And promptly solving the riddle, he adds: 'yes, the law is needed, when such as have not the gifts of strength and wisdom are to be taken care of' (chapter 2). For the aged and the weak, for women without fathers or brothers, the law, however faulty, however exclusive, is the only provision. This is the lesson of a life on the frontier, and of a saga that ends – it is worth noting – with the grandson of Duncan Heyward and Paul Hover, the impetuous bee-hunter, going to serve the state and federal governments.

If the collapsing of the British empire, and the ensuing depletion of state provision in the colonies as of 1757, haunts *The Last of the Mohicans* and exposes the limited agency of a deliberative vernacular democracy absent the state, *The Prairie*, set in the time of the Louisiana Purchase, asks a different question. As an American state was fast developing, the problem facing Cooper's characters then becomes how to democratise that state in the making, or, more accurately, how to invent the state as democratic – a state that would provision the poor, the aged, and construct a public good at the scale of an expanding nation. Pace Nelson, Cooper's *Leatherstocking Tales* do not so much confront us with the double bind between vernacular practices of deliberative democracy and state-sponsored governance of the public good, as allow us to retrieve forms and practices of vernacular democracy that, however defective, challenge our inherited (liberal) definitions of democracy and the state. We are asked to go beyond the hydraulic logic of democracy vs the state, and embrace them as historical and literary practices to be grasped in and as relations. Reading *The Last of the Mohicans* as part of a genealogy of an American democratic state suggests that literature is one of the places and modes of representation that can give shape and voice to these alternative practices of statecraft as public provision. Risking it opens the possibility to tell a story that we haven't so far remembered how to tell, that of the co-evalness of the regulatory power of the state, debt and democracy, their crossings and their intertwined histories.

WORKS CITED

Anthony, David (2009), *Paper Money Men: Commerce, Manhood, and the Sensational Public Sphere in Antebellum America*, Columbus: The Ohio State Press.

Baker, Jennifer J. (2005), *Securing the Commonwealth: Debt, Speculation, and Writing in the Making of Early America*, Baltimore: Johns Hopkins University Press.

Balogh, Brian (2009), *A Government Out of Sight: The Mystery of National Authority in Nineteenth-Century America*, Cambridge: Cambridge University Press.

Beard, James Franklin (1985), 'Cooper, Lafayette, and the French National Budget: A Postscript', *Proceedings of the American Antiquarian Society* 95(1): 81–99.

Brown, Wendy (1995), *States of Injury: Power and Freedom in Late Modernity*, Princeton: Princeton University Press.

Castiglia, Christopher (2008), *Interior States: Institutional Consciousness and the Inner Life of Democracy in the Antebellum United States*, Durham, NC: Duke University Press.

Castronovo, Russ (2016), 'James Fenimore Cooper and the NSA: Security, Property, Liberalism', *American Literary History* 28(4): 677–701.

Castronovo, Russ, and Susan Gillman, eds (2006), *States of Emergency: The Object of American Studies*, Chapel Hill: University of North Carolina Press.

Clemens, Elizabeth (2020), *Civic Gifts: Voluntarism and the Making of the American Nation-State*, Chicago: University of Chicago Press.

Cooper, James Fenimore (1826), *The Last of the Mohicans*, www.gutenberg.org.

— (1827), *The Prairie*, www.gutenberg.org.

— (1828), *Notions of the Americans, Picked up by a Travelling Bachelor*, Philadelphia: Carey.

— (1838), *The American Democrat, or Hints on the Social and Civic Relations of the United States of America*, Cooperstown, NY: H. & E. Phinney, 1838.

Dillistin, William H. (1949), *Bank Note Reporters and Counterfeit Detectors, 1826–1866, with a Discourse on Wildcat Banks and Wildcat Bank Notes*, New York: American Numismatic Society.

Edling, Max (2008), *A Revolution in Favor of Government: Origins of the US Constitution and the Making of the American State*, New York: Oxford University Press.

Franklin, Wayne (2007), *James Fenimore Cooper: The Early Years*, New Haven: Yale University Press.

Gustafson, Sandra M. (2011), *Imagining Deliberative Democracy in the Early American Republic*, Chicago: University of Chicago Press.

Laclau, Ernesto, and Chantal Mouffe (1985), *Hegemony and Socialist Strategy: Towards a Radical Democratic Politics*, London: Verso.

Matthiessen, F. O. [1941] (1968), *The American Renaissance: Art and Expression in the Age of Emerson and Whitman*, Oxford: Oxford University Press.

Mihm, Stephen (2007), *A Nation of Counterfeiters: Capitalists, Con Men, and the Making of the United States*, Cambridge, MA: Harvard University Press.

Nelson, Dana (2015), *Commons Democracy: Reading the Politics of Participation in the Early United States*, New York: Fordham University Press.

Novak, William J. (2008), 'The Myth of the "Weak" American State', *The American Historical Review*, 113(3): 752–72.

Novak, William J., James T. Sparrow and Stephen W. Sawyer (2015), 'Beyond Stateless Democracy', *The Tocqueville Review*, 36(1): 21–41.

Pincus, Steve (2016), *The Heart of the Declaration: The Founders' Case for an Activist Government*, New Haven: Yale University Press.

Rao, Gautham (2018), 'Taking Stock of the State in Nineteenth-Century America', *Journal of the Early Republic* 38(1): 61–7.

Sellers, Charles (1991), *The Market Revolution: Jacksonian America 1815–1846*, New York: Oxford University Press.

Shell, Marc (1993), *Money, Language, and Thought: Literary and Philosophic Economies from the Medieval to the Modern Era*, Baltimore: Johns Hopkins University Press.

Skocpol, Theda (2010), 'Bringing the State Back In: Strategies of Analysis in Current Research', in Peter B. Evans, Dietrich Rueschemeyer and Theda Skocpol, eds, *Bringing the State Back In*, Cambridge: Cambridge University Press, pp. 3–38.

Sugden, Edward (2019), 'The Speculative Economies of Sheppard Lee', *Nineteenth-Century Literature* 74(2): 141–66.

Wolin, Sheldon S. (1994), 'Fugitive Democracy', *Constellations* 1(1): 11–25.

NOTES

1. On the clash between the rise of a market economy and the conservative forces of a landed gentry, see Sellers. I want to thank Edward Sugden for pointing to me this reference, and others, on these questions. His essay 'The Speculative Economies of *Sheppard Lee*' takes up the question of a material vs a speculative capitalism as reflected in a later antebellum novel (*Sheppard Lee*, 1837), this time in the context of Jacksonian America, and offers an interesting counterpoint to Cooper's inquiry into the matter of debt and speculation in the 1820s.

2. In the debate Hamilton vs Jefferson, Hamilton championed a national bank so as to fund a national debt. Creating cash was necessary in order to compete on the world stage, he maintained. The Jeffersonian opposition, on the other hand, insisted that 'real material value inhered only in actual specie (gold and silver), while paper money and banknotes not backed by specie offered the mere illusion of value'.

'Such arguments were echoed by a range of critics in the years before and after the Panic of 1819, [. . .] and persisted in the policy begun during the War of 1812 of refusing specie payment "on demand"' (Anthony 12).

3. On the prevalence of counterfeiting in early America and on the multiplication of bank note reporters and counterfeit detectors, see Dillistin. On the circulation and use of the word 'mark', see for example the following excerpt from the *Commercial Advertiser of New York*, 10 January 1800: 'We stopped the press to insert a piece of information which must be esteemed eminently important to the Public. It is discovered that the Twenty Dollar *Albany Bank Bills*, have been counterfeited, and many of them are in circulation. [. . .] Not having received the specific marks that distinguish the counterfeit from the genuine, we can only mention it generally, to induce greater caution' (Dillistin 13). Two decades or so later, *Niles's Register* (26 January 1822) sounded the same note of caution: 'The public should be exceedingly cautious in the receipt of bank notes, generally, unless well acquainted with them, just now. The counterfeiters who have been secretly busy for a long time have sent a flood of spurious paper abroad, some of which so nearly represents the genuine bills, that it is exceedingly difficult to detect them' (Dillistin 15).

4. As his biographer explains, Cooper did not resent contracting 'sizable loans' (217) in the 1810s and 1820s. The leasehold properties assigned to him in his father's will, however valuable, could not cover his expenses after his marriage. The 'dramatic fall in land value' during the 1812 war left him scrambling for new funds. He therefore had to launch himself in diverse commercial enterprises – a retail outlet on a frontier area that only increased his debt; a whaleship that failed to solve his financial troubles. In the 1820s, Cooper found himself always short of cash and desperately trying to assign his debts to portions of land as a compensation for his lack of money. Even if he found himself a victim of 'the new and unstable paper economy in the period from 1819' (Anthony 3), Cooper knew that if he wanted to invest, he needed cash, and that his interests therefore depended to some extent on the circulation of a currency that could not immediately be redeemed in gold, or land.

5. On the distrust of paper money as 'paper promises dependent on yet more paper promises', see Mihm 2007: 13.

6. See Cooper's 1831 response to Louis Sébastien Saulnier, spokesman for the royalist majority of the French Chamber of Deputies, who had attempted to prove statistically that the cost of government in the US was 'greater than it was in France' and that 'a republic, in the nature of things, must be a more expensive form of government than a monarchy'. In his *Letter of J. Fenimore Cooper, to Gen. Lafayette*, Cooper defended a virtuous American democracy that invested in public infrastructures as a duty to the public and as expected of a new country in which 'pavements, and sewers, and wells and pumps, and fire engines, and market-houses and many other conveniences' were 'necessary' (Beard 1985: 83, 91).

14

ULSTER, 1785/PENNSYLVANIA, 1817/ ULSTER, 1845: JAMES MCHENRY'S PALIMPSEST OF ANGLO SETTLER COLONIALISM

JARED HICKMAN

The literal and literary Atlantic crossings of the man billed as the first 'Irish-American' novelist (Fanning 1999: 43), James McHenry, provide a perhaps unique window on a long history of the 'plantation' of Anglo-Reform culture. That is, the going-on-a-millennium experiment in the exogenous installation of a culture projecting itself as the smartest form of Christian civilisation and thus both the worthiest of and tidiest at replication. That experiment began with the twelfth-century Anglo-Norman attempt to make over the Indigenous Irish way of life – of which an idiosyncratic Catholicism was an organic part but to which it is not reducible – with cutting-edge religious orders and agricultural schemes (Elliott 2001: 3–56; Gillingham 2000; Gillingham 2001: 27–9, 117–18; Montaño 2011); resumed in the sixteenth century with the freshly Protestant English (re)conquest of Ireland that presaged the colonisation of North America (Beers 1985; Canny 1988; Canny 2001; Ellis 1998; Horning 2013); and culminated in the nineteenth-century genesis of nothing less than a world – an 'Anglo-World' – through (1) 'the settler revolution', an unprecedented period of 'explosive colonization' (Belich 2009) predicated on the 'elimination' of Indigenous peoples (Kauanui 2016; Wolfe 2006) in what are now consequently known as Australia, Canada, the United States, and beyond; and (2) the first full subsumption of the original Anglo settler colony, Ireland, within the British empire under the 1800 Act of Union, a legacy that persists – for now – in the political subdivision of the island.

McHenry's cultural biography gave him a unique perspective on and stake in this centuries-long development of Anglo settler colonialism. He was a particular sort of 'Irish-American' – a tail-end participant in 'the earliest example of European *mass* migration overseas' (Belich 2009: 60): the relocation of Scots Presbyterians across a 'long' eighteenth century from one Anglo settler colony – the northern Irish province of Ulster – to another: North America, Pennsylvania in particular (Dolan 2008: 3–63; Griffin 2001; Ridner 2018). Isolated by rocky shores and a band of drumlins, Ulster has served as a cradle of Native Irish civilisation (Bardon 1992: 1–24). It was comparatively unaffected by the medieval Anglo-Norman adventurers (Bardon 1992: 34–49; Bardon 2011: 7–12); and it became 'the despair of the Tudors' by fuelling the resistance to their early-modern attempts to reconquer Ireland by revamping the so-called Pale around Dublin, which had dwindled over centuries due to the Gaelicisation of the 'Old English' descendants of the original Anglo-Norman lords, and 'planting' 'New English' colonists in the southern province of Munster (Bardon 2011: 18–48; Canny 2001; Ellis 1998). Hence, it was the bitterest retribution that Ulster was not only eventually made the most successful site of Anglo-Protestant plantation in Ireland, with settler majorities being created in Counties Antrim and Down (Bardon 2011; Clayton 2005), but made so through a mechanism that 'dr[ove] a wedge' in a long-standing Gaelic world spanning the Irish Sea (Calloway 2008: 25): the mass settlement of Lowland Scots, primarily of the Presbyterian persuasion – McHenry's ancestors among them – on the 'promise of obtaining land that had been confiscated from Irish natives' as a consequence of the Nine Years' War (1594–1603), the Cromwellian conquest (1649–53) and the Williamite War (1688–91) (Ridner 2018: 11, 14; cf. Bardon 2011).

The quality that made these Scots Presbyterians crucial to the subordination of Ulster to the Crown (comprising the kingdoms of both England and Scotland with James I's 1603 coronation) also made them dangerous to the Anglican church-state created by Henry VIII – leading to their second-class treatment by the so-called Protestant Ascendancy in Ireland and, in turn, the emigration of at least 250,000 of these Scots Presbyterians from Ulster to North America between 1700 and 1820, 'the heyday of the Scots Irish' in the US (Ridner 2018: 6). That quality was their zealous sense of themselves as a covenant people – which, on the one hand, promised to power the dirty work of aggrandising the Anglican church-state if enough common cause against Catholic Gaels in Ireland and the Scottish Highlands could be found; and, on the other, threatened the disestablishment of that church-state and even an establishment alternative to it (Brooke 1987; McBride 1998). Scots Presbyterians were determined to become the modern Israelites they imagined themselves to be – if this style was cramped in Ulster, on to North America they would go to 'destroy-and-replace' other 'Canaanites' (Akenson 1992; Horne 2018: 177; Kenny 2009: 138, 146). The seventeenth-century evidence that Ulster Scots were effective agents of Indigenous elimination in Ireland emboldened Ulster Scots themselves to hop a much bigger pond than their forebears had just a century earlier to take on another set of heathenish Indigenes in North America and even made them the object of recruitment by settler-colonial forces already there. Most famously, the Ulster-born James Logan recommended to the Penn family that Scots-Irish could prove really useful in protecting their colony's nonviolent Quaker elite from Native peoples on the frontier (Kenny 2009: 3–4, 26–30; Ridner 2018: 23–4). Scots Presbyterians were thus 'shock troops' of Anglo settler colonialism both in Ireland and North America (Belich 2009: 42).

Born in 1785 to a Scots-Presbyterian settler family[1] in the port town of Larne on the Antrim coast, McHenry launched both a medical and literary career in Belfast before emigrating with his family to rural Pennsylvania around 1817. By 1823 he had moved to Philadelphia where, alongside Lydia Maria Child, James Fenimore Cooper and Catharine Maria Sedgwick, he pioneered 'the American historical romance' (Dekker 1983; Dekker 1987: 149–50)[2] as well as a pointedly 'Ulsterized' version of the related Irish 'national tale' (Beiner 2018: 185–201; Dornan 2009; Ferris 2002: 135–6; Trumpener 1997: 128–57); before returning to Ulster in 1843 as US Consul in Derry and dying on a jaunt back to his natal place in 1845 (Blanc 1939; Clarke-Robinson 1908; *Poems of the Pleasures* (1841): 273–82).[3]

McHenry's personal there-and-back-again is reflected in his toggling between settler Ireland and settler North America in his first four novels. His first American and Irish novels, respectively – *The Wilderness; or Braddock's Times* (1823) and *O'Halloran; or, the Insurgent Chief* (1824) – centre on Scots-Irish settlers at different sorts of *proto*-'revolutionary' moments: the prefiguration of the American Revolution by the strain of the Seven Years' War on the North American frontier; and the abortion of the 1798 United Irishmen Rebellion in Ulster and consequent precipitation of the 1800 Act of Union. In both cases, the potentiality of 'revolution' is exhausted in that which best serves the local success of settler colonialism – Independence and Union being merely superficial opposites insofar as both outcomes are revealed to be driven by the same calculus of how best to eliminate the Native and thereby showcase the settler's self-divinising worldmaking power (Hickman 2020; Hickman 2022). McHenry's second transatlantic novelistic pair – *The Spectre of the Forest; or Annals of the Housatonic* (1823); and *Hearts of Steel: An Irish Historical Tale of the Last Century* (1825) – regress in time towards what for McHenry is the *ur*-'revolutionary' moment: the 'Glorious' Revolution of 1688 that stabilised the British empire as an Anglo-Reform project after a century and a half of turmoil in both the metropole and the settler colonies. The universal enlightenment that McHenry wants us to see as liberated by William and Mary's constitutional modulation of a troublemaking monarchical Anglican church-state into a proficient parliamentary Protestant church-state is exposed in these novels as sheep-and-goat-separating eschaton – what historian Gerald Horne has called the 'dawn' of 'the apocalypse of settler colonialism', wherein the sheltered sheep are 'white' capitalists and the slaughtered goats expropriated Native Americans and enslaved African Americans (Horne 2018: 28, 179–92).

McHenry's deepening palimpsest of Anglo settler colonialism turns out to be the handiest of devices for both tracking the dynamic evolution of the temporally and spatially extensive project of Anglo-Reform plantation and discerning its abiding logic. What is revealed is that the world that many people today feel themselves to inhabit – a more or less 'secular' world of more or less 'rational actors' more or less responsibly pursuing 'private' fulfilment in a 'resource' milieu so abstract it encompasses human beings, the vague 'profitability' of which is the effective definition of the public good – is actually a product of the cumulative realisation of Anglo settlers' destructive worldmaking fantasies at the expense of Indigenous worlds in Ireland, North America and Australasia over centuries. This arrogant and arduous striving for apotheosis is, at certain thresholds of apparent achievement, widely normalised as just the way of the world. McHenry's historically obscure corpus thus shows us something of the greatest historical significance – that secularism and capitalism are tenets of a faith in and of settlerism.

THE COLONIALISM OF REVOLUTION IN THE ANGLO-WORLD:
THE WILDERNESS (1823) AND *O'HALLORAN* (1824)

Both McHenry's first American and first Irish novel anoint the Ulster Scot as the practical instigator of the historical 'revolution' towards enlightened modernity by virtue of being the ur-settler, the boots on the ground at the frontline of civilisation. In *The Wilderness*, the meaning of 'revolution' – the American Revolution in particular – is messianically subsumed by the 'settler revolution' that would only be triggered by the unprecedented outcome of US independence. McHenry deliberately situates the action at one of the lowest ebbs of Anglo settler colonialism in North America – the 1755 defeat of General Edward Braddock's army of imperial regulars and colonial militia by a Native confederacy allied with the French near Fort Duquesne (now Pittsburgh) – in order to find even there the signs of its irresistible crash across the continent (Preston 2015; McHenry 1823a, 1: 5–7). To wit, that field of defeat is preemptively made a field of victory by the narrator's interjection – *before* the military debacle is recounted – that it is 'now changed by the hand of industry to one more rural and more gratifying to the eye of the philanthropist' (McHenry 1823a, 2: 157–8). This prolepsis is not just a predictable narrative strategy from the convenience of retrospect; it is the essence of the 'fake-it-till-you-make-it' antics of settler colonialism (Hickman 2022). The sure sign of this triumph is what Charles Fanning deems 'the first Ulster Protestant immigrant family in American fiction' (Fanning 1999: 44):[4] the pious Presbyterian Fraziers of County Derry – most pertinently, patriarch and matriarch Gilbert and Nelly, their adopted daughter, Maria, and the man who marries her at novel's end, another Ulster Scot named Charles Adderly (McHenry 1823a, 1: 16; 2: 46).

McHenry's characterisation of the Frazier/Adderly clan reveals a great deal about how he inhabited his Scots-Irish identity both in Ireland and Pennsylvania. McHenry's Ulster Scots are the vanguard of civilisation not because they are rough-and-ready Indigene-haters and -killers, like the notorious Paxton Boys who would emerge at the other end of the Seven Years' War (Kenny 2009: 3–4, 118–20, 150). The novel has a critique of Anglo settlers as bringing disaster upon themselves to some extent by failing to 'soothe and conciliate a people whose heritage they were . . . gradually, but rapidly engrossing to themselves' (McHenry 1823a, 1: 28); something the Fraziers conspicuously do through their friendship with the fictional Native prophet Tonnaleuka and the fictionalised historical personage Queen Alliquippa, an Ohio Iroquois (or Mingo) leader who entered into strategic alliance with the English in the years leading up to the Seven Years' War (Preston 2015: 113, 167, 185–6). Like the Frazier/Adderly clan, McHenry seems to have distanced himself from more nakedly aggressive elements of Anglo settler colonialism: the publication of *The Wilderness* more or less coincides with his move to Philadelphia from the Scots-Irish stronghold of rural Butler County as a result of a felt dearth of 'the pleasures of friendship', the title of the first book McHenry published in the US – an 1822 poetry collection (*Poems of the Pleasures* 1841: 277–9). By the same token, the book of poems that had commenced McHenry's literary career in Belfast, *The Bard of Erin, and Other Poems Mostly National* (1808), suggests a subtler and more self-deceived – and thus perhaps all the more pernicious – version of settler ideology: one that feels itself inclined towards and also permitted to appropriate Native traditions, enabling McHenry to blithely project himself as 'the bard of Erin' – that is, a signal member of the venerable Indigenous Irish class of scholars and poets that had been systematically extirpated by Anglo-Protestant plantation; to conceive his poems as 'national' in their thrust even though he endorsed the 1800 Act of Union that severed Ireland's last shred of formal autonomy; and to dedicate those poems to the Society for the Revival of the Irish Harp, the revival of which was of course necessary only because colonialism had pushed this Native practice to the brink.

McHenry's conceit for making the Ulster Scot a more palatable vanguard of civilisation in *The Wilderness* is ingenious, it has to be said: Before they are jilted from their frontier home by warfare they try but fail to forestall, the Frazier/Adderly clan nurtures the most famous participant in Braddock's Defeat, none other than twenty-three-year-old George Washington – who falls in love with Maria but graciously withdraws his suit when he realises she loves Adderly, the fellow 'Briton' who saved him on that ignominious battlefield (McHenry 1823a, 2: 89, 174). Hence, even though the novel demands the Fraziers' abandonment of their fruitful farm on Turtle Creek (McHenry 1823a, 1: 27; 2: 287), their cultivation of young Washington portends that this wilderness will ultimately 'blossom as a rose' in good millenarian fashion (McHenry 1823a, 1: 251; 2: 12). The fictional alliance that McHenry forms between Ulster Scots and the future father of the republic highlights that the primary causes and effects of the American Revolution were settler-colonial: impatience with British-imperial restrictions on trans-Appalachian settlement – restrictions put in place in no small part because of the memory of Braddock's Defeat – animated visions of independence, the achievement of which immediately unleashed a tide of humanity of western European descent into what the British empire had designated as Indian Territory. *The Wilderness* puts a point on this by bringing the fictional Adderly into the action as an expeditionary for the actual Ohio Company, a land speculation agency in which the Washingtons invested (McHenry 1823a, 1: 51–2, 270; 2: 8; Greer 2018: 384, 392; Preston 2015: 20–1; Weaver 2003: 101–5). Doing his own kind of speculation, then, McHenry suggests that the first family of the American Revolution may have gotten a head start on the settler revolution on a stock tip, as it were, from an Ulster Scot.

The immediate setting of McHenry's historical fiction, as well as his plying of a gentler version of Scots-Irish vanguardism, mean that the crudest forms of Indigenous elimination are not showcased in *The Wilderness* – the Natives win the battle, after all, if not the war, and the protagonists are kept out of the worst of it. But the novel nonetheless kills its main Native characters in creatively gratuitous ways. For one, it creates an extravagant counterfactual for those characters based on real Indigenous persons: the Western Lenape (or Delaware) leader 'Shingiss' [Shingas], made the lover of the aforementioned Queen Alliquippa, is killed fighting alongside the British even though the actual Shingas raided Pennsylvania settlements for the full extent of the Seven Years' War (McHenry 1823a, 2: 8; cf. Dowd 2002: 129–30; Kenny 2009: 118; Preston 2015: 114–15, 302); and then this invented death is made the cause of Alliquippa's pathetic expiration from heartbreak (McHenry 1823a, 2: 63–4). But, most spectacularly, the novel's most developed Native character, the prophet Tonnaleuka – who throughout has walked a confusing line between voicing Indigenous calls for justice (albeit often in the idiom of the Judeo-Christian Bible) and protecting 'good' settlers like the Fraziers, Adderly and Washington from violence – is breathtakingly (and breathlessly) revealed at novel's end to in fact be . . . Mackintosh, a royalist 'laird' of the Scottish Highlands who escaped prosecution for his participation in the 1715 Jacobite Rising on behalf of the Catholic Stuarts by enlisting in the French army in North America, where he married the aristocratic Quebec garrison commander's heiress, upon whose death he went mad, leaving his infant daughter – none other than Maria, of course – to the Fraziers in order to live with Indians, among whom he cultivated the figure of the prophet 'in order to tame their manners, and restrain their barbarous practices toward their enemies' (McHenry 1823a, 2: 273–80)!

Tonnaleuka's unveiling as a displaced denizen of England's Catholic 'Celtic fringe' captures the full craft of Anglo settler colonialism's 'elimination of the Native *as Native*' – to quote J. Kēhaulani Kauanui's crucial emendation of Patrick Wolfe's now-famous thesis (Kauanui 2016). Its significance is amplified by the related trajectory of a comparatively minor character, Adderly's Native Catholic Irish servant, Peter M'Fell. His brogue deliberately made to clash with the meticulously rendered Scots dialect of the elder Fraziers, M'Fell at first seems just to be comic (high) relief vis-à-vis the Fraziers – the silly, superstitious simpleton McHenry insists his Scots-Irish frontierspeople are not (McHenry 1823a, 2: 29–34). But despite having been relegated to a distant farm for fear that his stereotypical 'rashness' would imperil his master's high-stakes diplomacy and espionage, Peter returns at a crucial moment to rescue Adderly from an ambush, shouting 'Huzza for old Ireland' when he dispatches a French officer (McHenry 1823a, 2: 107–9). As a result, the novel accords Peter a final place in its settler world: after saving Adderly, he attempts to return to Ireland, we're told, but 'no sooner [had] he reached . . . port' in Cork, he is impressed by the British navy and dragged back into the Seven Years' War, after distinguished service in which he returns to Adderly's employ in Philadelphia and marries the girl he fell for during his exile from the frontline (McHenry 1823a, 2: 288–9). In both these cases, sectarianism is overcome by evidence of the meaningful collaboration of these Catholic 'Celtic' characters in the settler worldmaking/destroying spearheaded by Ulster Scot characters. The novel finds in the North American settler colony a place where the Catholic M'Fell can greet the Presbyterian Maria as a fellow 'christian in the Wilderness'; and the Presbyterian patriarch Gilbert can even resign himself to the exigency of his daughter Nancy's marriage by the French army chaplain, that is, 'one of the priests of the Antichrist' (McHenry 1823a, 1: 273; 2: 48). As happens in the better-known but subsequent historical romances by Lydia Maria Child and Catharine Maria Sedgwick (*Hobomok*, 1824, and *Hope Leslie*, 1827), something like the mutual toleration ascribed to secularism is approached in *The Wilderness* only through a shared experience of settler realisation – among the diverse settler characters on the diegetic plane, but also between the narrative world and the world of the settler reader (Shreve 2017). In the case of *The Wilderness*, a 'secular' world in which various kinds of people can mutually 'make a living' while respectively – and respectfully – 'just living their lives' is constituted by an eliminative relay of the Anglo-World's Indigenes: the Anglo-World's original Indigenes – its dubiously Christian 'Celtic fringe', represented by Mackintosh and M'Fell, is eliminated by transforming them into settlers who eliminate Indigenes in North America. Hence, any catholicity achieved by this American reconciliation of Anglo settlers with their original Indigenes not only constitutively excludes Indigenous Americans; it augments and consolidates the eliminative force arrayed against them. In these details a now-familiar story of the Gaelic Irish and Scottish becoming 'white' by becoming settlers over and against both Indigenes and Black exogenes[5] is thrown into high relief by a story of the Scots-Irish as primally white because they were 'always already' settlers (Allen 2012; Calloway 2008: 234–7; Ignatiev 1995; Mullen 2016). The American Revolution McHenry means us to see brewing in the spectacle of Ulster Scots and Anglo-American Protestants and Highland Scots and Native Irish Catholics all finding a way to get over their Old-World hang-ups in the New is one and the same as the boiling-over that is the settler revolution. McHenry's liberalism has no place for the Native *as Native*: American Indigenes are precluded; 'Celtic' Indigenes are included to the extent they become settlers; and the ur-settlers, the Scots-Irish, are the exemplary subjects.

If *The Wilderness* affirms republican revolution to the extent that it subtends the settler revolution, *O'Halloran* negates republican revolution to the extent that it might subserve decolonisation, which becomes evident once the 1798 United Irishmen Rebellion hatched by Scots-Presbyterian liberals such as the title character is perceived to have gone south, figuratively speaking, by literally going south (Bardon 1992: 183–239; Clayton 2005; McBride 1998: 207–31; Stewart 1995: 257–64). This variance can be chalked up to a demographic difference – the persistence of Indigenous majorities across Ireland except for in its north-east corner and the decimation of Indigenous populations across North America by an unparalleled influx of settlers in the wake of the American Revolution. But *O'Halloran*'s problem of the very accessibility of republican revolution to Indigenes in Ireland can also be traced to a sort of Anglo settler-colonial uroboros effect that McHenry is ever keen to heighten. The very promise of alliance between Ulster Scot United Irishmen and Native Catholic Defenders was to some extent suggested precisely by what *The Wilderness* dramatises – the tentative racialisation of 'Celtic' peoples as white *through* their demonstrable collaboration with Anglo settlers in eliminating unambiguously non-white Indigenes in North America. At the same time, the Ulster-Scot United Irishmen's very conception of revolution was influenced – often quite directly in the form of transatlantic relatives – by the precedent of the exclusively settler anticolonialism of the American Revolution (Clayton 2005: 240; Kenny 2009: 226–33). As McHenry points out in the epilogue to the posthumous Belfast edition of *Hearts of Steel*, 'the most turbulent and obnoxious' of the eponymous Scots-Presbyterian direct-action group of the 1760s 'emigrated to America, where their exasperated feelings . . . soon broke out in open defiance of European authority. The Hearts of Steel refugees eagerly enrolled themselves under the standard of Independence, and formed a large portion of that celebrated division of the American army, the Pennsylvania line' (McHenry 1846: 497–8). And when O'Halloran is, for a hot minute, a fugitive, he immediately schemes to escape to America, as many United Irishmen did (McHenry 1824a, 2: 62, 66).

Hence, when 'Celtic' peoples occupy the subject position of the Indigene rather than the settler, republican revolution is not an option. On the contrary, the solution that materialises within the presumptively enlightened horizon of the Ulster Scot is an unprecedented Union of Ireland with Britain arising from the mutual recognition between the English Protestant Ascendancy and Scots-Presbyterian settlers of their organic alliance against any decolonisation of Ireland that would restore the Native Catholic Irish as a self-determining polity. McHenry effects this solution, as a few scholars have noted, through an explicit and pointed rewriting of the quintessential Irish 'national tale', Sydney Owenson's *The Wild Irish Girl* (1806) (McHenry 1824a: xii–xiii; McHenry 1825: iii–x; cf. Beiner 2018: 185–201; Dornan 2009: 152–3). In the place of Owenson's deliberately suspended marriage plot between an Anglo-Protestant man and a Native Catholic Irish woman, which, with counterfactual wilfulness, makes the actual consummation of the Union literally conditional on the demonstration of an adequate English love of Native Irish civilisation (Dougherty 2012; Rezek 2015: 62–84; Trumpener 1997: 128–57), McHenry brings to completion an intra-Protestant-settler marriage plot: scion of the English Protestant Ascendancy, Edward Barrymore, makes a wife of the Scots-Presbyterian paragon, Ellen Hamilton, O'Halloran's granddaughter. Any liberalism these novels countenance is one under which the metropole forgives settler animus in order to retain a stake in the settler colony, and settlers forgive metropolitan oppression in order to maintain a crucial source of support against Native resistance – a resolution that applies both to Ulster, where Union with Britain was reaffirmed, and to the US, where independence was achieved but friendly relations with the former metropole swiftly resumed (Belich 2009: 50–1, 479–82). All that such liberalism can offer Native peoples is a gentler form of elimination: a frankly insulting 'recognition' as another set of minoritised subjects enhancing the multicultural tapestry woven by the settler state (Byrd 2011: xxiii–xxiv; Coulthard 2014; Simpson 2014).

O'Halloran chronicles the subsidence of a *settler* anticolonialism – that is, a settler bid for independence from the imperial metropole – in the face of a *Native* anticolonialism whose primary animus is against the settler. McHenry's representation of the almost instant disillusionment of the Presbyterian settler radicals in Ulster when Native Catholic Irish militants seize the occasion of the 1798 Rebellion to initiate the expulsion of all settlers is perfectly frank. Indeed, the revolution in the north is more or less over before it begins due to incoming reports of the infamous Scullabogue barn massacre in County Wexford, in which 'insurgents of the Catholic persuasion' were perceived to have indiscriminately targeted Protestants (McHenry 1824a, 2: 43–56; cf. McBride 1998: 208–9; Stewart 1995: 257–64). This event is made evidence for O'Halloran and his 'radical' Scots-Presbyterian settler cohort that their tense coalition with the Catholic Defenders is an 'unnatural confederacy', because the latter will not be 'confined to the acquirement of some civil or political right' (the so-called Catholic emancipation that many United Irishmen patted themselves on the backs for supporting) but will rather lapse into 'religious warfare' (McHenry 1824a, 2: 43). What McHenry himself perhaps can't see but nonetheless helps us to see is that the very terms of this dichotomy – a noble fight for 'civil or political right' versus a despicable 'religious warfare' – constitute the spoils of Protestant settlers' 'religious warfare' against the Native Catholic Irish. By narrowly interpreting 'religious warfare' as a bid for 'the establishment of Catholic supremacy and intolerance in the island', McHenry occludes the fact that the presumptively enlightened framing of the struggle in terms of an equalisation of all current inhabitants of the island, regardless of creed, is arguably the coup de grâce in the establishment of *settler* supremacy and intolerance on the island. For this delimitation of the field of political possibility presupposes the legitimacy of the Protestant settler presence in the first place – it both presumptuously indigenises Protestant settlers to Ireland and placidly immanentises the world imposed by their creative destruction as 'the world' as such.

This is played out in a remarkable way in the conclusion of *O'Halloran*. Once the Catholic insurgents 'go decolonial' and the rebellion in Ulster consequently dies on the vine because the Scots-Presbyterian cohort recognises that their 'natural confederacy' is with their English fellow Protestants, a Unionist party literally breaks out. The exonerated O'Halloran, Barrymore, and their train embark on a pleasure cruise around the Islandmagee peninsula that transacts a quite shameless erasure of the Native Catholic Irish. When they spy from their boat 'one of those ancient monuments of superstition, called the Rocking Stones', the ceremonial site of 'druidical priests', Francis Hamilton, the Scots-Presbyterian father of our heroine, Ellen, doesn't hesitate to attribute them to '*our* ancestors' (McHenry 1824a, 2: 157). En voyage, Ellen makes 'a deep impression on all present' by singing a ditty composed by a local Scots-Presbyterian rhymer about the sense of 'home', 'the domestic contentment and tranquillity expressed in the verses . . . contrast[ing] with the political exasperation and disasters of the times' (McHenry 1824a, 2: 159–60). Most egregiously, O'Halloran hastens to dismiss the Native Catholic Irish lore attaching to a particular stretch of coast. Known as 'Catholic Leap', at this spot in the 1640s, 'the Presbyterians of the neighborhood' – in retaliation for Catholic depredations to the south in Armagh – are alleged to have marched 'fifteen hundred Catholics of both sexes' over the edge of 'limestone cliffs soaring upwards of two thousand feet above the surface of the sea' (McHenry 1824a, 2: 160–1). But in this, O'Halloran blithely condescends, the Catholic locals are surely 'mistaken . . . There are, indeed, at the top of the cliffs some veins of a reddish ochry substance, which, in wet weather, is apt to be washed down the precipice, and, at a distance, may be mistaken for blood, and has, no doubt given origin to this absurd story' (McHenry 1824a, 2: 161). Whereas the first report of Catholic massacre of Protestants in distant Wexford was enough to entirely deflate the United Irishmen in Ulster, a time-honored local Catholic memory of Protestant settler violence is rejected out of hand as just another instance of the Catholic refusal of every 'opportunity of being undeceived' (McHenry 1824a, 2: 161).

As though on cue, the novel's only two Catholic characters (McHenry 1824a, 2: 45) – the fugitive rebels Daragh and M'Cauley – suddenly materialise on the beach of Portmuck, the island to which the daytrippers are bound. They are in vindictive pursuit of a local Protestant bigwig who had cynically courted the rebels for the purpose of landing Ellen and then betrayed them. McHenry gives M'Cauley a monologue that distinguishes the stakes of the rebellion for the Native Catholic Irish and Protestant settlers: 'Be joyous – Follow your revels,' M'Cauley declaims, for 'Why should you be sad! The desolation, the ravaging, the destructions, the burnings, the bayonetings, the shootings, the hangings, the gibbetings, cannot reach you. They are destined for us, an unpitied, execrated, persecuted, proclaimed, outlawed, miserable race; whose homes are ruined, whose families are scattered, and whose heads are sold for a price' (McHenry 1824a, 2: 166). But any sting in this shout is taken out by the assurance McHenry preposterously puts in M'Cauley's mouth that he intends no 'reproach' and just can't help wanting 'sweet revenge' and by O'Halloran's condescending pity: 'Poor fellow ... his whole soul is devoted to an unfortunate cause; but a cause which he conscientiously believes to be just' (McHenry 1824a, 2: 167). However 'conscientious' M'Cauley's cry on behalf of decolonisation may be, it clearly does not fall within the acceptable range of the 'liberty of conscience' sacralised by the Anglo-Protestant order – an order thereby exposed as far from approaching the perfect neutrality ascribed to the secular. For when we next encounter M'Cauley alongside French republican allies on a battlefield in County Mayo, he is swiftly dispatched by Barrymore and made to confess that he may have 'flattered [him]self' that 'an instinctive perception', an 'impulse of feeling', was 'the dictate of conscience' (McHenry 1824a, 2: 201–2). A righteous pursuit of decolonisation on the basis of legitimate grievance is thus systematically precluded from McHenry's Ireland.

The Protestantism of Secularism in the Anglo-World: *The Spectre of the Forest* (1823) and *The Hearts of Steel* (1825)

McHenry doubles down when he doubles up his corpus of American and Irish historical romances. *The Spectre of the Forest* and *The Hearts of Steel* both replay with greater amplitude and intensity the plots of their respective predecessors but in chronologically remoter settings – *Spectre of the Forest* recedes from the last 'French and Indian War' to the first; and *Hearts of Steel* plumbs the prehistory of United Irishmen in the 1760s. The net effect is to suggest a profounder source for McHenry's circumscription of 'revolution' by settler imperatives in *The Wilderness* and *O'Halloran*. Namely, what is for McHenry the once-and-for-all revolution after which any subsequent revolution is by definition counterrevolutionary: the 1688 'Glorious' Revolution under which the Catholic James II was deposed and the Protestant William and Mary installed. Deemed 'glorious' in part because it was largely 'bloodless' in England, this sectarian revolution was anything but in Ireland and North America. In the former, it culminated in the infamous Battle of the Boyne (1690) in which William himself decisively defeated the largely Native Irish Catholic forces of James II, a flashpoint to this day in what is now Northern Ireland; in the latter, where it is known as 'King William's War' (1688–97), it was the beginning of the end for the French-supported Wabanaki Confederacy in the face of the Anglo settler-colonial onslaught (McHenry 1823b, 1: 111–21). For these reasons, among others, Horne, with devastating irony, rebrands the 'Glorious' Revolution as the 'dawn' of the 'apocalypse of settler colonialism'.

Spectre of the Forest and *Hearts of Steel* are cost-benefit analyses that frankly determine to pay this 'apocalyptic price tag' as a kind of investment in a settler millennium whose first seal, as it were, was perceived to have been opened by the Williamite order of things (Horne 2018: 179). In other words, McHenry, in these two novels, owns that the 'personal life' beneath and beyond theopolitical struggles that he has striven to conjure and valorise as the locus of significance in all his work is in fact a privilege secured by a very particular Protestant theopolitical arrangement. For McHenry, William and Mary oversee what is in effect the establishment of a radical Protestant belief in the sanctity of individual conscience, which may seem to behave like a disestablishment that liberates everyone to cultivate the integrity of their subjectivity, but in fact preempts any form of collectivism perceived to disrupt this idealised status quo of happily self-actualising individuals. The Williamite establishment is, for McHenry, a historical universal destined to replace any Indigenous establishment that preexists and persists against it. In the preface to *Hearts of Steel*, McHenry stated his intention to complete his Irish trilogy by resorting to 'that critical period of Irish history, when the long-vacillating views and wavering fortunes of millions were finally settled by the decisive battle of the Boyne' (McHenry 1825: x). McHenry never wrote this novel of the Williamite triumph in Ireland, but he didn't have to, I'm going to suggest, because he'd already 1) told that story in the North American settler-colonial context in *Spectre of the Forest* – the climax of which, we shall see, occurs in the court of William and Mary; and 2) fleshed out a Williamite eschatology in *Hearts of Steel* itself.

McHenry comes by this Anglo-Protestant triumphalism in *Spectre* through a conceit arguably as nifty though perhaps not as accessible as attributing the formation of the young George Washington to the example and care of Ulster Scot immigrants. More elaborately than Walter Scott had done the year before in a tale within a tale in *Peveril of the Peak* (1822) and also much earlier than either of Scott's American emulators, James Fenimore Cooper in *The Wept of Wept-Ton-Wish* (1829) and Nathaniel Hawthorne in 'The Grey Champion' (1835) (Dekker 1983; Orians 1932), McHenry dilates on the local settler legend of 'the Angel of Hadley' – robustly fictionalising it by temporally transplanting it. Documented as early as Thomas Hutchinson's 1764 *History of the Colony of Massachusets-Bay*, the legend tells that the Puritan regicide, William Goffe, who did indeed live in hiding in New England for an indeterminate period of time after the Stuart Restoration in 1660, 'suddenly' materialised before a congregation in Hadley, Massachusetts in order to save them from a Native attack during King Philip's War (1675–6), 'not only encourag[ing] them to defend themselves but put[ting] himself at their head, rall[ying], instruct[ing], and le[ading] them on to encounter the enemy, who by this means were repulsed', and then 'as suddenly . . . disappeared' (Hutchinson 1764: 219n). Although evidence suggests Goffe died shortly after these alleged events, McHenry suggestively extends the legend into 'King William's War' (1688–97).

McHenry has Goffe live on to meaningfully intervene in this watershed moment for Anglo-Reform culture – as in *The Wilderness*, not necessarily to do the dirty work of Indigenous elimination (as he is supposed to have done in Hadley in 1675) but to accomplish that end nonetheless. The entire thrust of Goffe's spectral appearances, which notably take place in the valley occupied by the unrepentant Indian-hunter Hugh Bradley (McHenry 1823b, 1: 166), is to incite the social reproduction of a durable and equable Anglo-Reform culture after the theopolitical convulsions of the seventeenth century. Goffe first appears in spectral form to save the pregnant Olivia Parnell, kidnapped by the pirate Henry Morgan after rebuffing him to marry – not coincidentally – 'the son of a large landed proprietor in Queen's County, Ireland', by directing her to the Stratford, Connecticut home of the Presbyterian reverend Devenart, the novel's paragon of Protestant piety (McHenry 1823b, 1: 33). When Olivia tragically drowns, her infant son George Parnell is cared for by Devenart's sister until she mysteriously disappears, because, we only learn much later, she has joined herself to the fugitive Goffe, the fruit of which union is Esther, who comes to live with her reverend uncle when Miss Devenart passes away. At his next spectral apparition, Goffe decrees to the adolescent George Parnell the fulfilment of his beloved wife's wish that he, her adopted son, and her biological daughter, Esther, be united to inaugurate an ideal Anglo-Protestant line (McHenry 1823b, 1: 102–4). The inside joke of McHenry's whole oeuvre might be said to be that History trails after the skirts of mouth-wateringly virtuous Presbyterian women – in addition to Miss and Esther Devenart, Maria Frazier and Ellen Hamilton from *The Wilderness* and *O'Halloran*, respectively, and, in *Hearts of Steel* alone, the unnamed Mrs M'Manus, Eliza McCulloch and Isabella M'Manus. Scots-Presbyterian women seem to multiply exponentially across these novels, reminding us of the centrality of the reproductive capacity and unwaged domestic labour of women to settler colonialism (Meissner and Whyte 2017; Morgensen 2012).

But George is waylaid from this commission by his participation in King William's War, which leads to George's capture by the Huron, a chief of whom – in the fashion of the 'mourning war' – adopts George to replace his dead son. Three years in the wilderness, so to speak, George is about to be subjected to 'the discipline of the huskanaw', which McHenry glosses as a 'Lethean process' whereby Iroquoian young men are pharmacologically brainwashed in a ceremonial context in order to 'be the more effectually liberalized into patriots' (McHenry 1823b, 1: 134). The religious and political functions combined in the huskanaw, not to mention its potential application to George, suggest the existence of something like a Huron church-state bent on enforcing its sovereignty over those in its territory. Settler-Native conflict is cast in sectarian terms. But George narrowly evades this Native ritual of replacement-to-replenish the Indigene by engaging as never before in the settler-colonial business of destruction-to-replace the Indigene. The Indian-hunter Bradley, on the track of his son Ephraim, George's fellow captive, shows up in the nick of time, and together they gun down and stab Indians left and right. In the battle's aftermath, when Hugh Bradley crows his full-blown 'metaphysics of Indian-hating' – expressed and experienced in terms of the Israelites' righteous extirpation of the Canaanites, George initially demurs, as he has before; but he ultimately concedes the exigency of the Indian-killing Bradley does with such relish: 'perceiving that moralizing to such an auditor would be literally to cast pearls before swine, and *not wishing to disturb the harmony which was so necessary for their mutual safety*, [George] shook the hand which Bradley held out to him' (McHenry 1823b, 1: 95–6, 142–3, my italics). Hugh's son Ephraim subsequently undergoes a similar transformation. When Hugh justifies his 'Canaanite-smiting' on the basis of Native murder of his wife and children, Ephraim suggests his father has taken sufficient 'vengeance' and might now turn or at least allow his son to turn to more respectable settler endeavours; but Ephraim's own quest to be a more reputable and monied member of settler society, he acknowledges in his suit to Rachel Wilkins, is predicated on his father's work: 'The scripture saith, "God made man male and female, that they might multiply and replenish the earth", and thou knowest that *since the Indians have been driven away from our land*, which is goodly and wide, it requireth to be replenished' (McHenry 1823b, 1: 155–6; 2: 25, my italics).

Having been ushered from the Huron village back to Goffe's haunt in Bradley's valley, George is duly accosted by the spectre and reminded of the command to multiply and replenish the earth with Esther, but this time he is waylaid by witch-hunting rather than Indian-hunting – his linkage of the New England witch trials and King William's War anticipating contemporary historians such as Mary Beth Norton. 'The witch-mania' first targets Marian Settle, the infirm mother of one of Bradley's Indian-hunting crew, George's attempted rescue of whom draws suspicion and so leads him to flee to England, during which absence both Reverend Devenart and Esther are targeted, George returning just in time at novel's end to save his promised wife and prosper in the promised land. The second volume's focal shift from Indian-hunting to witch-hunting is instructive. Whereas the Indian-hunting of Hugh Bradley is ambivalently admitted as a necessary evil of Anglo-Protestant plantation, witch-hunting is unambiguously condemned as a self-defeating aberration from it insofar as it internally divides and diminishes the settler collective, who need to be as broad a front as possible to defeat the Indigene. This settler realpolitik is neatly enacted by making the dubious Indian-hunt-ers into the heroic witch-hunter-*hunters*: it is Bradley and company, including George, who bravely defy the witch-hunt and ultimately bring it down. The excesses of Indian-hunting are thus not only pardoned in their own right but sublimated into a commonsensical aversion to 'fanaticism' that manifestly imperils the settler colony. By the same token, McHenry's Goffe saves his most spectacular apparition for the purposes of frightening a Puritan con-gregation into abandoning their witch-hunting rather than leading them in Indian-hunting – a pointed reworking of the original 'Angel of Hadley' leg-end (McHenry 1823b, 2: 98–100); but all the while tacitly endorses Indian-hunting – appearing as he does in Bradley's valley and provoking George for his lack of urgency in initiating settler social reproduction with Esther by disdainfully asking if he has become 'a worshipper of the new-moon' as a result of his time among 'the wild prowlers of the forest' (McHenry 1823b, 1: 167–78). The message is clear: Indigenous elimination is the increasingly unworried premise of the worrying primary task of fine-tuning an Anglo-Protestant order of things presumed to be ascendant.

This bloodless backgrounding of Indigenous elimination is made possible by the focusing of the 'Glorious' Revolution in the novel's foreground. Goffe sends the hunted George to England with a cache of documents that turn out to be so consequential as to bring him to the court of William and Mary – a wonderfully ludicrous contrivance to showcase the new Williamite order as the agency of the (re)establishment of a proper transatlantic Protestant church-state that heals the wounds of the English Civil War even as it inflicts a new level of hurt on Indigenous peoples in its settler colonies. A set piece in the cosmopolitan parlour of Earl of Dorset Charles Sackville, William's Lord Chamberlain, has George rub shoulders with English literary greats who had polemicised on opposite sides over the course of the preceding fifty years. In particular, the royalist and Catholic convert John Dryden so that McHenry can highlight the temperateness and compassion evident in Sackville's private patronage of the poet and dramatist after he lost the poet laureateship due to his theopolitical commitments. Here an enlightened 'secularism' manifests as an objective appreciation of aesthetic merit untainted by sectarian judgements – a point to which we shall return (McHenry 1823b, 2: 162–76).

When William and Mary themselves peruse the documents prepared by Goffe and presented by George, they resolve (1) to quash the witch-craze in New England, which is thereby relegated to the dustbin of a previous 'bad' Protestant history; and (2) to grant a pardon to Goffe on the condition that he accept what McHenry wants us to see as the eminently rational 'new order of things' they embody of a monarchy and church-state subjected to constitutional limitations in response to the lessons of the preceding royalist-republican furore (McHenry 1823b, 2: 178–94, 241–2). McHenry's nineteenth-century Unionism is irrepressible in his reverential portrait of William and Mary, the latter praised for her magnanimity in granting amnesty to the man who killed her granddad, and the former lionised as the man 'whose actions have had a greater influence upon the affairs of mankind than, perhaps, those of any other individual of modern times' (McHenry 1823b, 2: 186). The narrator clearly intends this as a compliment, but the 'military costume' William wears is a reminder that his 'influence' was far from salutary from the perspective of the Native Catholic Irish he crushed at the Battle of the Boyne (McHenry 1823b, 2: 186). Indeed, we are invited to play out the implications of McHenry's counterfactual: If Goffe had indeed survived to be pardoned by William and Mary, would he have stayed in the North American settler colony, as McHenry's Goffe does, to foresee the fruition of his fictional descendants in the 'dawnland' of the Wabanaki? Or would he have occupied the lands granted him by Richard Cromwell in Counties Waterford and Wexford, as his actual son did and descendants continue to do?[6] In either case, the Williamite revolution is located in Britain's settler colonies, where it was unambiguously bloody in its violence against Native peoples. *The Spectre of the Forest* doesn't anxiously repress Indigenous elimination; it frankly accepts it as the collateral damage of the social reproduction of an Anglo-Protestant culture. At its conclusion, the novel doesn't afford readers blissful ignorance by immersing them in the happy insularities of either the Williamite metropole or settler colony after warfare paused in 1697; instead, it commemorates that 'Hugh Bradley died in the year 1698, as he wished to die, fighting with Indians' and reminds us of the preface's lost-manuscript conceit – that what we have just read is based on papers compiled by Barnabas Bradley, grandson of the Indian-hunter (McHenry 1823b, 2: 244).

If *Spectre of the Forest* hails the Williamite revolution to end all revolutions as auguring in North America a settler millennium in which the only people socially reproduced are those properly Reformed into full, right-feeling persons – neither supercilious Anglicans, irascible Presbyterians nor of course Indigenous peoples who would contest such Reformation, *Hearts of Steel* goes so far as to enact in cameo that millennium in Ireland – beyond

Ulster, even. Upping the ante of *O'Halloran*, the novel is structured by an intra-Protestant-settler marriage plot between Isabella M'Manus, the pious daughter of Bernard M'Manus, a Native Catholic Irish *convert* to Presbyterianism as a result of two other impeccable specimens of Presbyterian womanhood, his mother, Mrs M'Manus (a long-suffering crypto-Presbyterian amidst Catholic firebrands), and his wife (Isabella's mother), Eliza M'Culloch; and Frederick Rosendale, occupant of and heir to the M'Manus lands in County Meath because of an Ascendancy ancestor's exploits in – you guessed it – the 'revolution' effected by 'King William' (McHenry 1825, 1: 5–6). The novel even has a set piece of Williamite pageantry on the expropriated M'Manus lands in which Rosendale's lordly father 'marche[s] to the music of the "Boyne Water" with the British standard waving in the air before them' and the local Anglican rector 'dr[aws] a striking picture of . . . the happy state of both religious and civil liberty which they then enjoyed, under the protection of a popular constitution, and a benign and virtuous race of monarchs' (McHenry 1825, 1: 173–85).

Not coincidentally, amidst that same pageantry comes one of the highlights of the novel's most compelling character, the Native Catholic Irish rebel, Edmund 'Munn' M'Manus, who is in disguise on a reconnaissance mission to strategise how to take back his traditional lands. When the local wrestling champ, Skipdale, a self-proclaimed 'true protestant, and . . . soldier of King George', is inflamed to bluster by the sectarian festivities, Munn challenges him, and Skipdale 'find[s] that he might as well have attempted to shake the pedestal of King William's statue in Dublin from its stand, as to move his antagonist' (McHenry 1825, 1: 181). The stakes couldn't be higher, then, as attested by Skipdale's attempt, in short order, to murder Munn. But Munn is saved by none other than his nemesis, the young Rosedale, who by so doing demonstrates what McHenry wants us to believe is the impartiality that makes the Williamite order both unshakeable and world-historically moving-and-shaking. Munn's ideology of Catholic Defenderism is certainly shaken by Frederick's act (McHenry 1825, 1: 194).

The Indigenist monologue of M'Cauley that McHenry muffles in *O'Halloran* is amplified into the fully rendered subjectivity of a major character in *Hearts of Steel*, then; and so the diminutive end McHenry scripts for Munn is commensurately devastating in its implications for Indigenous peoples in settler colonies. M'Manus is depicted as a Native Catholic antihero and super-villain who schemes 'to turn the hand of heresy against itself' by 'lead[ing] the heretical peasantry of the North', the Scots-Presbyterian tenant farmers of Ulster, 'against the heretical aristocracy of the South', the English Protestant Ascendancy in his home territory of Meath in particular, as we've seen (McHenry 1825, 1: 205, 161; 2: 321). Hence, the Hearts of Steel organisation, which prefigures the United Irishmen who feature in *O'Halloran*, are here represented as the creature of a canny Native Catholic Irishman whose endgame is the extirpation of all Protestant settlers. The chaos these machinations unleash, Munn reasons, 'are but a just retribution for those which their ancestors inflicted on thousands of the ancient and rightful owners of the land' (McHenry 1825, 1: 160). Although Munn has greater sympathy for the Scots-Presbyterian working class who have been 'the mean instruments' rather than 'artificers' of 'the ruin of my name and race', identifying with them to some extent as 'children of the soil' bilked out of their lands, his political arithmetic is nonetheless bracingly exact: 'What are their injuries compared with ours? As the drop is to the ocean! – as the sparkle of the flint is to the flame of the sun! Not one family of these boors, who now make such an outcry for their lost patrimony, has been in possession of it more than two or three generations back; but our forefathers were robbed by theirs of what they had enjoyed for countless ages!' (McHenry 1825, 1: 141, 160–1).

The political arithmetic by which McHenry attempts to balance the Irish equation is not nearly as compelling, so he rather transparently makes it so by arbitrary authorial fiat. McHenry forces decolonisation outside of the frame after perhaps too vividly picturing it through that most foolproof device: a self-generated and thus self-fulfilling prophecy. That is, the author McHenry outright invents at the novel's outset a prophecy from a Scots-Presbyterian soothsayer that predetermines the action that follows: 'M'Manus in Rosendale ever shall find/An invincible foe, or a friend that is kind; –/And M'Manus from Rosendale's power may depend,/As his sorrows began, so his sorrows shall end' (McHenry 1825, 1: 36; 2: 336–7, 411). The Scots-Presbyterian soothsayer is McHenry's inside woman, so to speak, realising in the narrative world the Anglo-Protestant settler's fantasy of a world in which the settler is to the Native both 'invincible foe' and sole recourse, in a word, the alpha and omega of a universe of his own creation. Munn is predestined, then – in good Presbyterian fashion – to find whatever abatement of 'sorrow' he can only in his oppressor. Finally caught by the authorities, Munn is sentenced to 'transportation' – presumably to North America, which, he despairs, will be 'a living death' insofar as he 'shall be dead to Ireland', his body unable to 'moulder and mingle with [his] native soil' (McHenry 1825, 2: 399–400). But the benevolent settler Rosendale of course intervenes, albeit in a way that brings North America to Ireland, as it were, for what he arranges is something like an Indian reservation. Munn is brought to Rosendale's estate to 'spen[d] the remainder of his days in the venerated castle of his ancestors', where, we're told, 'he kept a generous table in the true style of Irish hospitality, at which all wanderers of Milesian extraction were gladly welcomed and joyously entertained' (McHenry 1825, 2: 411). The Native is thus granted a tiny fraction of his traditional land within the effectually sovereign domain of the settler where he can harmlessly practise his Native way of life in a kind of museum, receiving fellow Natives who are no doubt 'wandering', as Munn himself once did, as a result of their displacement by settlers.

Munn's end mutually translates otherwise discrete stories about secularisation and settler colonialism. Rosendale's toleration of Munn's Indigenous way of life under a specific condition of quarantine highlights how so-called 'Catholic emancipation' in Ireland is on the same continuum as 'Indian removal' in the US. Both preempt the Native as a worldmaking subject by projecting the world made by Protestant settlers as (God-)given. Native peoples can continue to exist – insofar as they give in to the givenness of this world of recent, violent vintage. Hence, McHenry's participation in Philadelphia's celebrations of the Catholic Emancipation Act and publication of a tribute to fellow Scots-Irish Andrew Jackson's Indian-fighting exploits in the same year – 1829 – were not at all contradictory but perfectly of a piece. The ostensibly enlightened 'secularism' of the former and embarrassingly benighted 'settlerism' of the other are two sides of the same Anglo-Protestant coin.

CONCLUSION

McHenry's blatant exercise in *Hearts of Steel* of what Jonathan Culler has called authorial 'omnipotence' (Culler 2004) underlines the extent to which settler colonialism is a faith – a fragile and fervid faith in the right to and feasibility of realising a worldmaking fantasy that becomes complacently secularised into a 'fait accompli' once realisation apparently occurs (Hickman 2022; Wolfe 2006: 392–3). As McHenry's work shows time and again, this faith turns on a construction of Indigeneity, whether Irish or American, as a problematic embeddedness in networks of being that span the species divide and animacy spectrum often shorthanded as 'land' (Estes 2019: 89–91; Simpson 2017: 71–82), the dissolution of which furnishes a stage for evincing the worldmaking power of humans as such by 'improving' said 'land' (Montaño 2011; Wood 2017: 106–15). In this Anglo settler-colonial exhibition of the divine image exceptionally stamped upon human beings through their (re-)creation of something out of the 'nothing' they would make of what are in fact incredibly rich Indigenous 'ontologies of land' (Moreton-Robinson 2015: 3–18), we might find a sorely needed postsecularist history and critique of capitalism. Ellen Wood traces 'the origins of capitalist imperialism' – which is to say, the first evidence of capitalism's intrinsic need to expand in order to outrun the crisis its 'imperatives of competitive production and capital accumulation' inevitably induce – to the late-sixteenth-century attempt to 're-create' in Ireland 'the conditions of south-east England', where the agrarian transition to capitalism first occurred, by 'planting' settlers who knew the properly profitable way to plant (Wood 2017: 147–65; Wood 2005: 73–88). More than that, an uncharacteristic rhetorical flourish makes clear that Wood glimpses in this moment at which capitalism – *through settler colonialism* – comes to self-consciousness – and self-congratulation – something too many

Marxists fail to fathom: the advent of 'a new religion' under which 'human beings engaged in improvement' feel themselves to have 'assumed God's role as creators of value' (Wood 2017: 165). In sum, Anglo settler colonialism-*cum*-capitalism proceeds through a brazenly self-divinising fantasy of realisation predicated on an Indigenous dispossession that Robert Nichols rightly insists amounts not just to deprivation of direct access to the means of production but 'something like deracination or desecration' (Nichols 2020: 28–30, 71).

All this might remind us of Colin Jager's point that the English word 'secularisation' originally referred to Henry VIII's expropriation of property owned by the Roman Catholic Church in order to enrich his insurgent Anglican church-state, not only materially but spiritually (Jager 2015: 7–11). This seizure of church lands enacted the sovereignty of the new church-state and, in so doing, suggested its alignment with divine sovereignty, which in short order incited its extension to Catholic Ireland and heathen North America. If we start the story here, 'secularization', in the Anglo-World at least, comes into view not as a presumptively liberatory progress towards disestablishment and disenchantment but rather as the eschatological establishment of an Anglo-Reform culture in the place of Indigenous establishments through the desecrating dispossession of otherwise consecrated lands and the consecrating repossession of those lands as a godmaking platform. As it becomes ever clearer how these activities have imperilled planetary life as never before, it becomes increasingly possible and direly necessary to relativise the world made by Anglo-Reform and make a new one. Here it may be useful to recognise that McHenry's author-God flex also suggests that because this faith in/of settlerism is unmoored from the infrastructure of a specific ecclesiastical denomination, imaginative literature, with its worlding effects, has been an indispensable technology in this faith's establishment; and, consequently, that criticism of that literature may be a decisive tool in that faith's disestablishment.

WORKS CITED

Akenson, Donald Harman (1992), *God's Peoples: Covenant and Land in South Africa, Israel, and Ulster*, Ithaca: Cornell University Press.

Allen, Theodore W. (2012), *The Invention of the White Race*, 2nd ed., 2 vols, New York: Verso.

Bardon, Jonathan (1992), *A History of Ulster*, Belfast: Blackstaff Press.

— (2012), *The Plantation of Ulster: The British Colonisation of the North of Ireland in the Seventeenth Century*, Dublin: Gill Books.

Beers, David Quinn (1985), *Set Fair for Roanoke: Voyages and Colonies, 1584–1606*, Chapel Hill: University of North Carolina Press.

Beiner, Guy (2018), *Forgetful Remembrance: Social Forgetting and Vernacular Historiography of a Rebellion in Ulster*, New York: Oxford University Press.

Belich, James (2009), *Replenishing the Earth: The Settler Revolution and the Rise of the Anglo-World, 1783–1939*, New York: Oxford University Press.

Blanc, Robert E. (1939), *James McHenry (1785–1845): Playwright and Novelist*, Philadelphia: University of Pennsylvania.

Brooke, Peter (1987), *Ulster Presbyterianism: The Historical Perspective, 1610–1970*, Dublin: Gill and Macmillan.

Calloway, Colin G. (2008), *White People, Indians, and Highlanders: Tribal Peoples and Colonial Encounters in Scotland and America*, New York: Oxford University Press.

Canny, Nicholas (1988), *Kingdom and Colony: Ireland in the Atlantic World, 1560–1800*, Baltimore: Johns Hopkins University Press.

— (2001), *Making Ireland British, 1580–1650*, New York: Oxford University Press.

Clarke-Robinson, W. (1908), 'James MacHenry, Author of "O'Halloran," "Hearts of Steel," etc., etc.', *Ulster Journal of Archaeology* 14(2/3): 127–32.

Clayton, Pamela M. (2005), 'Two Kinds of Colony: "Rebel Ireland" and the "Imperial Province"', in Terrence McDonough (ed.), *Was Ireland a Colony? Economics, Politics, and Culture in Nineteenth-Century Ireland*, Dublin: Irish Academic Press.

Coulthard, Glen Sean (2014), *Red Skin, White Masks: Rejecting the Colonial Politics of Recognition*, Minneapolis: University of Minnesota Press.

Culler, Jonathan (2004), 'Omniscience', *Narrative* 12(1): 22–34.

Dekker, George (1983), 'Sir Walter Scott, the Angel of Hadley, and American Historical Fiction', *Journal of American Studies* 17(2): 211–27.

— (1987), *The American Historical Romance*, New York: Cambridge University Press.

Dolan, Jay P. (2008), *The Irish Americans: A History*, New York: Bloomsbury Press.

Dornan, Stephen (2009), 'Irish and American Frontiers in the Novels of James McHenry', *Journal of Scottish and Irish Studies* 3(1): 139–56.

Dougherty, Jane Elizabeth (2012), 'The Last of the Milesians: The 1801 Anglo-Irish Marriage Contract and *The Wild Irish Girl*', *Journal of Eighteenth-Century Studies* 35(3): 391–405.

Dowd, Gregory Evans (2002), *War under Heaven: Pontiac, the Indian Nations, and the British Empire*, Baltimore: Johns Hopkins University Press.

Elliott, Marianne (2001), *The Catholics of Ulster: A History*, New York: Basic Books.

Ellis, Steven G. (1998), *Ireland in the Age of the Tudors, 1447–1603: English Expansion and the End of Gaelic Rule*, 2nd ed., New York: Routledge.

Estes, Nick (2019), *Our History Is the Future: Standing Rock versus the Dakota Pipeline, and the Long Tradition of Indigenous Resistance*, New York: Verso.

Fanning, Charles (1999), *The Irish Voice in America: 250 Years of Irish-American Fiction*, 2nd ed., Lexington: University Press of Kentucky.

Ferris, Ina (2002), *The Romantic National Tale and the Question of Ireland*, New York: Cambridge University Press.

Gardenmore Presbyterian Church (1894), *Historical Sketch of the Gardenmore Presbyterian Church, Larne: 1769–1894*, Belfast: M'Caw, Stevenson, & Orr.

Gillingham, John (2000), *The English in the Twelfth Century: Imperialism, National Identity and Political Values*, Woodbridge: Boydell Press.

— (2001), *The Angevin Empire*, London: Arnold.

Greer, Allan (2018), *Property and Dispossession: Natives, Empires, and Land in Early Modern North America*, Cambridge: Cambridge University Press.

Griffin, Patrick (2001), *The People with No Name: Ireland's Ulster Scots, America's Scots-Irish, and the Creation of a British Atlantic World, 1689–1764*, Princeton: Princeton University Press.

Hickman, Jared (2020), 'The Apocalypse of Settler Colonialism and the Case for the Americocene', in John Hay (ed.), *Apocalypse in American Literature and Culture*, New York: Cambridge University Press, pp. 17–29.

— (2022, forthcoming), 'Africa', in Robert Morrison (ed.), *The Oxford Handbook of Romantic Prose*, Oxford: Oxford University Press.

Horne, Gerald (2018), *The Apocalypse of Settler Colonialism: The Roots of Slavery, White Supremacy, and Capitalism in Seventeenth-Century North America and the Caribbean*, New York: Monthly Review Press.

Horning, Audrey (2013), *Ireland in the Virginian Sea: Colonialism in the British Atlantic*, Chapel Hill: University of North Carolina Press.

Hutchinson, Thomas (1764), *The History of the Colony of Massachusetts-Bay . . .*, London: Thomas & John Fleet.

Ignatiev, Noel (1995), *How the Irish Became White*, New York: Routledge.

Jager, Colin (2015), *Unquiet Things: Secularism in a Romantic Age*, Philadelphia: University of Pennsylvania Press.

Kauanui, J. Kēhaulani (2016), '"A Structure, Not an Event": Settler Colonialism and Enduring Indigeneity', *Lateral* 5(1).

Kenny, Kevin (2009), *Peaceable Kingdom Lost: The Paxton Boys and the Destruction of William Penn's Holy Experiment*, New York: Oxford University Press.

McBride, I. R. (1998), *Scripture Politics: Ulster Presbyterians and Irish Radicalism in the Late Eighteenth Century*, Oxford: Clarendon Press.

McHenry, James (1808), *The Bard of Erin, and Other Poems Mostly National*, Belfast: Smyth and Lyons.

— (1823a), *The Wilderness; or Braddock's Times: A Tale of the West*, 2 vols, New York: E. Bliss and E. White.

— (1823b), *The Spectre of the Forest, or, Annals of the Housatonic: A New-England Romance*, 2 vols, New York: E. Bliss and E. White.

— (1824a), *O'Halloran; or, the Insurgent Chief: An Irish Historical Tale of 1798*, 2 vols, Philadelphia: H. C. Carey and I. Lea.

— (1824b), 'A Review of *Wieland*, and Other Novels, By Charles Brockden Brown, of Philadelphia', *American Monthly Magazine* 1(1): 42.

— (1825), *The Hearts of Steel: An Irish Historical Tale of the Last Century*, 2 vols, Philadelphia: A. R. Poole.

— (1846), *The Hearts of Steel: An Irish Historical Tale of the Eighteenth Century*, Belfast: John Henderson.

McNeilly, David J., David Esler and Robert Victor Alexander Lynas (1953), *Gardenmore: A Record of the History and Tradition of Gardenmore Presbyterian Church, Larne*, n.p.p.: n.p.

Meissner, Shelbi Nahwilet, and Kyle Whyte (2017), 'Theorizing Indigeneity, Gender and Settler Colonialism', in Paul C. Taylor, Linda Martín Alcoff and Luvell Anderson (eds), *The Routledge Companion to Philosophy of Race*, New York: Routledge.

Montaño, John Patrick (2011), *The Roots of English Colonialism in Ireland*, Cambridge: Cambridge University Press.

Moreton-Robinson, Aileen (2015), *The White Possessive: Property, Power, and Indigenous Sovereignty*, Minneapolis: University of Minnesota Press.

Morgensen, Scott Lauria (2012), 'Theorising Gender, Sexuality and Settler Colonialism: An Introduction', *Settler Colonial Studies* 2(2): 2–22.

Mullen, Mary L. (2016), 'How the Irish Became Settlers: Metaphors of Indigeneity and the Erasure of Indigenous Peoples', *New Hibernia Review* 20(3): 81–96.

Nichols, Robert (2020), *Theft Is Property! Dispossession and Critical Theory*, Durham, NC: Duke University Press.

Orians, G. Harrison (1932), 'The Angel of Hadley in Fiction: A Study of Hawthorne's "The Grey Champion"', *American Literature* 4(3): 257–69.

The Poems of the Pleasures . . . (1841), Philadelphia: J. B. Lippincott, Grambo.

Preston, David L. (2015), *Braddock's Defeat: The Battle of the Monogahela and the Road to Revolution*, New York: Oxford University Press.

Rezek, Joseph (2015), *London and the Making of Provincial Literature: Aesthetics and the Transatlantic Book Trade, 1800–1850*, Philadelphia: University of Pennsylvania Press.

Ridner, Judith (2018), *A Varied People: The Scots Irish of Early Pennsylvania*, Philadelphia: Pennsylvania Historical Association.

Shreve, Grant (2017), *Fragile Belief: Secularity and the Antebellum American Novel*, PhD dissertation, Johns Hopkins University.

Simpson, Audra (2014), *Mohawk Interruptus: Political Life across the Borders of Settler States*, Durham, NC: Duke University Press.

Simpson, Leanne Betasamosake (2017), *As We Have Always Done: Indigenous Freedom through Radical Resistance*, Minneapolis: University of Minnesota Press.

Stewart, A. T. Q. (1995), *The Summer Soldiers: The 1798 Rebellion in Antrim and Down*, Belfast: Blackstaff Press.

Trumpener, Katie (1997), *Bardic Nationalism: The Romantic Novel and the British Empire*, Princeton: Princeton University Press.

Weaver, John C. (2003), *The Great Land Rush and the Making of the Modern World, 1650–1900*, Montreal and Kingston: McGill-Queen's University Press.

Wolfe, Patrick (2006), 'Settler Colonialism and the Elimination of the Native', *Journal of Genocide Research* 8(4): 387–409.

Wood, Ellen Meiksins (2005), *Empire of Capital*, New York: Verso.

— (2017), *The Origin of Capitalism: A Longer View*, New York: Verso.

Notes

1. McHenry's maternal grandfather, Samuel Smiley, was one of the select gentlemen granted the 1769 lease for Gardenmore Presbyterian Church in McHenry's natal place of Larne (Public Record Office of Northern Ireland T502/13). This was an Antiburgher Seceder congregation (Minute Book of the Antiburgher Seceders, Public Record Office of Northern Ireland D3815/D/4; cf. Gardenmore Presbyterian Church 1894: 6–20, 35–47; McNeilly, Esler and Lynas 1953: 8–33, 250–1) whose first minister was McHenry's mentor, James Nicholson, a critic of the most radical

elements of late eighteenth-century Ulster Scots society and moderate supporter of the Union, as most Antiburgher Seceders tended to be according to I. R. McBride (McBride 1998: 84–110).

2. For an unfavourable period rating of McHenry vis-à-vis these other historical romancers, see Sumner Lincoln Fairfield, 'Four Months in Europe. No. IX', *New-York Literary Gazette and American Athenaeum* 3.4 (30 September 1826): 37–9; for a celebration of McHenry of the sort lamented by Fairfield, see 'Irish-American Literature', *New-England Magazine* (1 June 1832): 490–9.

3. Besides his publications, many of the major movements of McHenry's life register in the archival record on both sides of the Atlantic: his practice as a doctor in Philadelphia as of late 1823 (3 November 1823, *National Gazette*, p. 3); his setting up shop as an importer of Irish linens (14 December 1826, *National Gazette*, p. 3; 10 September 1829, *National Gazette*, p. 2; 13 March 1834, *National Gazette*, p. 1; 17 April 1834, *National Gazette*, p. 2); the literary tributes to him upon his triumphant return to Larne ('Doctor James McHenry', 23 September 1839, *Belfast Commercial Chronicle*, pp. 1–2; 8 February 1840, *National Gazette*, p. 2); his heading up of a US Consulate in Derry as of 1843 (17 March 1843, *Londonderry Standard*, p. 2); and his death in Larne (29 November 1845, *Northern Whig*, p. 1).

4. The unsavoury Selbys of another fiction of the Pennsylvania frontier, Charles Brockden's *Edgar Huntly* (1799), are arguably an earlier Scots-Irish immigrant family in literature. In his own review of this novel, McHenry himself didn't make the connection, although he did question the plausibility of the name of another Irish character, Clithero (McHenry 1824b).

5. Elsewhere I have argued that the logic of the Anglo settler revolution is to eliminate both the Indigene and what I call the Black exogene, who is deemed inassimilable to the settler collective (Hickman 2022). In *The Wilderness* this is suggested by Gilbert's refusal of Washington's grant of Virginian land in part because of his disinclination to 'sae mony black-a-moors, the very sicht of wham wad gar my flesh creep to look at' (McHenry 1823a, 2: 287).

6. See *Burke's Peerage* for the details: <http://www.thepeerage.com/p34521.htm#i 345201> (accessed 29 October 2021). Horetown House in County Wexford remains the home base of the Davis-Goff baronetcy, created in 1905.

INDEX

1904 Louisiana Purchase Exposition, 82

abolitionism, 24–5, 95, 158–69
Act of Union (1800), 222, 224, 230–2
Alliquippa (Ohio Iroquois leader), 226–7
American Revolution, 224–9
American Studies Association, 35, 39n1
Anzaldúa, Gloria, 39n1, 64
Arendt, Hannah, 119n2
Armistead, Wilson, 158–62, 164–6, 168
Augustine, Saint, 103

Barbata, Laura Anderson, 124–5, 126, 134–6
Barr, Roseanne, 125
Battle of the Boyne (1690), 233, 237
Benezet, Anthony, 159
Benjamin, Walter, 39n5, 199
Bennett, Jane, 109, 111, 120n3
Bernier, Celeste-Marie, 22
Birch, Carol, 132–4, 144n7

Bird, Robert Montgomery, 88–100
    Adventures of Robin Day, The, 88–98
    City Looking Glass, The, 92
    Gladiator, The, 92, 99–100n1
    journals and letters, 97, 99–100n1, 100n3
    Nick of the Woods, 89
    'Night on Terrapin Rocks, A,' 96
    Sheppard Lee, 89, 92, 95, 100n2
    theatre career, 91–2, 99–100n1
Blackness, 89, 93; see also race
Black Americans, 89, 95, 97, 100n3
blackface minstrelsy, 89, 92, 95
Blum, Hester 30
body, 42–3, 46–8, 50, 213, 215–16
Bourne, George, 95
    Picture of Slavery in the United States of America, 95
Brexit, 130
British Friend, The, 158, 164, 169
Bromell, Nick, 23
Brooks, Maria Gowan, 146–57
    Zóphiël, 146–8, 150–1, 153–4

Brown, John, 32, 107, 114, 115
Brown, William Wells, 159
Buford, Henry 60–7
Butler, Judith 61

Caesar, Julius, 197, 203
capitalist reproduction, 183–5,
    188
caste, 89, 93–4
Castiglia, Christopher 30, 36–7
Catholic emancipation, 231, 240
census, 159
Channing, William Ellery, 21
Chesnutt, Charles, 195, 197–8,
    201, 203
citizenship, 79, 83
Civil War (US), 33, 34, 59–68
Clark, Jane, 35
Cold War, 35
Colectivo el Pozo, 144n7
coloniality, 131, 133
Colored American Magazine, 78
Collier's Weekly, 71, 75–6, 78, 82
Colson, Daniel, 115
Combahee, South Carolina, 35
Confederacy 59–68
Continental Congress, 29, 34, 37
constellation, 29, 30–4, 36–7
Constellation, USS [ship] 29
Cooper James Fenimore, 206–21
Craft, Ellen and William, 159
credit, 210–11, 214, 216
crisis, 177, 180–1, 184–6,
    188–91
critical Whiteness studies, 90–1,
    98
cross-racial identification, 95
Cuba, 59–61, 65, 146–7, 154, 156

Darwin, Charles, 114
debt, 210–12, 216–17, 219–21
Delany, Martin, Blake; or the Huts of
    America 32
Deleuze, Gilles, 110, 111, 120n4

democracy, 207–9, 211–12, 216,
    218–19
    deliberative democracy, 217–19
Diderot, Denis, 202
Dorantes, Raúl, 144n7
Douglass, Frederick, 19–26, 30–7, 177,
    181, 190
    'Composite Nation,' 33–4,
        36, 37
    My Bondage and My Freedom, 22–5,
        31, 190
    reading habits, 20–5
    'What to a Slave is the Fourth of
        July?' 33
Duane, Anna Mae, 31
Du Bois, W. E. B., 73–4, 77

Ellis, Cristin, 114
Emerson, Ralph Waldo, 105–6
epic poetry, 147–54
Equiano, Olaudah, 133, 134,
    145n12
Esquer, Rafael, 135

Farias, Larissa, 144n7
Fichte, Johann Gottlieb, 23
Finley, James, 113
Fishkin, Shelley Fisher, 30, 39n1
Fitzhugh, George, 177–80, 183,
    185, 188
Forrest, Edwin, 92
Fourier, Charles, 101
freedom, 23
Fugitive Slave Law, 178, 180–1

Gandhi, Mahatma, 102
Garland, Rosie, 132–4, 144n7
Garrison, William Lloyd, 23, 32
gender, 59–69
gingival hyperplasia, 123
'Glorious Revolution', 224–5, 233,
    236–8
Goffe, Richard, 234–7
Great Comet of 1843, 32

Griggs, Sutton E., 79
Gros, Frederic, 101, 120n5
Guattari, Felix, 110

Haitian Revolution, 201
Harper's Ferry, 32
Harrison, Benjamin, 197, 198
Hawthorne, Nathaniel, 234
Hearts of Steel (Ulster-Scot direct-action
    group), 229–30, 238–9
Hegel, G. W. F., 200–1, 202
Heidegger, Martin, 103
Hernandez, Mari, 134–7
Hicks, Elias, 41–6, 48–50
Hicks, Granville, 30, 36–7
Hicksite Quakers, 41–3, 45–8
'Hindoo', 93, 97
Hoggart, Richard, 36
Hughes, Henry, 183–6, 188
human
    and anthropocene, 108–11, 116
    as abstract standard, 134
    as category of democratic rights, 126,
        136
    as grounding of citizenship, 127
    as means of occluding racial
        difference, 128
    boundaries between human and
        non-human, 135, 136
hypertrichosis, 123, 144n2,
    145n9

Igorot, 81–2
India, 89, 92–4
indigeneity, 129, 130, 131
infrastructure, 210, 214
Inner Light, 42–3, 47, 56
Inward Light, 43, 45–6, 50, 56
Ireland, 222–3, 229–33,
    237–40

Jacobite Rebellion (1715), 227–8
Jacobs, Harriet, 30, 33–4, 36–7
James, C. L. R., 201

Jarrett, Valerie, 125
Jones, Thomas, 158–69
Junior [ship], 35

Kaplan, Amy, *Cultures of United States
    Imperialism*, 35
Keppler, Joseph, 195–7, 200–1,
    203
King Jr, Martin Luther, 102
King William's War (1689–97),
    232–7
Klein, Naomi, 112
Kodak camera, 195

Laing, Daniel J., 161–2
Laveaux, Étienne, 201
Leeds, 158–9
Lemke, Thomas, 111–12
Lent, Theodore, 124, 125, 126, 129,
    131, 134
Leonid Meteor Shower, 31–2
LePage, Paul, 98
Lepore, Jill 29, 30
less-than-White, 90, 91, 94
Levine, Robert S., 22, 31
liberalism, 208
Liberator, The, 32
Light Within, 45, 50, 56
local colour, 72, 75–6, 81
Lodge, Henry Cabot, 75–6
London, 126, 132
    Royal College of Surgeons, 123,
        136
Louverture, Toussaint, 201, 202

McHenry, James, 222–41
Mark, Gospel of, 31–2, 35
Marx, Karl, 47, 56, 112, 177, 181,
    184, 188
Marx, Leo, 35–6, 40n6
Marxism, permanent revolution 30,
    39 n2
materialism, 19–21
Matthiessen, F. O., 39n3

Melville, Herman, 177, 180–1,
    186–90
'Bartleby, the Scrivener', 180–1,
    186–90
meteor shower, 31, 32, 35
Mexico
    and Loreta Janeta Velazquez,
        59–60
    birthplace of Julia Pastrana, 123
    in the Victorian, British imagination,
        127
    Island of the Dolls, 134
    repatriation of Julia Pastrana's
        remains to, 124, 125, 126
    trade with Britain, 130
    trade with the US, 129
Miller, William, 32
Moore, Mary, 160
Morton, Samuel George, 93–4
    Crania Americana, 93–4
Moscow, Russia, 123
Munby, Arthur, 144n4

nation-state, 29, 36
n-gram, 124, 126, 144n5
Northern Lights, 32

Orientalism, 88, 92
Oskan, May, 123, 144n7
Oslo, Norway, 124, 126
    Office of Contemporary Art, 135
Owenson, Sydney, 230

Page, Walter Hines, 75–6
Paley, William, 21
Parker, Captain Gideon, 35
Pastrana, Julia
    as antinomy of citizenship, 127
    as engine of informal empire, 128
    as sign of contemporary racism, 129
    cast of teeth, 123, 126, 131, 136
    display after death, 124
    physical deformities, 123
Plessy v Ferguson, 83

Poe, Edgar Allan, 'The Conversation of
    Eiros and Charmion' 32
poetess tradition, 148–157
political economy, 177, 182–6
politics
    and Civil War, 59–69
    and labour, 41–54, 177–91
    and nation, 29–35
    and race, 71–84, 88–98,
        158–69
    democracy, 206–19
    environmentalism, 101–18
    of empire, 123–37, 223–41
    of reading, 21–2
    see also abolitionism, democracy,
        freedom, settler colonialism, slavery
precarity, 89, 95–7, 98
Prendergast, Shaun, 124, 126, 128,
    132, 134
    The True History, 124, 126, 128
print, 213–16, 218
public provision, 217–19

Quakerism, 41–50, 55
Queer Theory, 65–6

race
    race science, 89, 93–4
    racial performance, 88, 92–3,
        95, 97
    racial transformation, 88–90, 91,
        92–5, 97
    racial uplift discourse, 74, 82
    see also Blackness, slavery, Whiteness
Radway, Janice 36
Raynal, Guillaume-Thomas, 201–2
Reader, Charles, 144n4
realism, 75
regulation 211–12, 216–17
Republicanism, 203
Romanticism, 146–55
Rose, Wendy, 144n6
Ruiz de Burton, Maria Amparo,
    67–8

Salem witch trials, 235–6
Scott, Walter, 234
Scullabogue Barn Massacre, 230
Second World War, 36
sectionalism, 178–82
segregation, 97, 100n3
self
  and (dis)embodiment, 41–54
  and gender, 59–69
  and labour, 177–91
  and multilingualism, 146–55
  and the state, 206–19
  as relational, 101–18
  categorisation of, 2–4
  fluidity of, 22–6, 59–69
  race and nation, 71–84, 88–98
  see also Blackness, body, citzenship,
    gender, human, indigeneity, race,
    Whiteness
Senchyne, Jonathan, 20
settler colonialism
  and capitalism, 240–1
  and secularism, 225, 239–41
  in Ireland, 222–3, 229–33,
    237–40
  in North America, 223–9,
    232–7
Seven Years' War, 225–9
Shingas (Western Lenape leader),
  227
signs, 213, 215–6
slavery, 21, 23, 147, 198,
  200, 203
  in *Sheppard Lee*, 89, 92, 95,
    100n2
  in *Adventures of Robin Day, The*, 90,
    94–6, 97
  pro-slavery positions, 177–9, 182–3,
    185–7, 189–90
  slave narratives, 94–6
Socrates, 119n2
soul, 45, 47–50, 54
Southey, Robert, 146–56

space
  Caribbean, 146–55
  cosmic, 29–37
  immaterial, 19–28
  natural, 101–18
  transamerican, 59–69, 123–37
  transatlantic, 123–37, 146–55, 223–41
  transpacific, 71–84
Spartacus, 201, 202
state, 206–14, 216–19
State Department, 35
strike, 177, 179–80, 185–90

Temple-Tuttle, Comet, 31, 34
Thoreau, Henry David, 101–20
time
  and liberal historiography, 177–91,
    206–19
  apocalyptic time, 31–3
  periodisation, 195–203
  serendipity, 158–69
Tolstoy, Leo, 144n4
transnational turn in American Studies,
  29, 30, 35, 39n1
Trump, Donald, 5, 98, 129
Turner, Nat, 32–3

United Irishmen Rebellion (1798), 224,
  229–32
United States of America
  decline of, 5
  flag 29, 33–4, 37

'Vanishing Indian', 98
Velazquez, Loreta Janeta, 59–70

Wabanaki Confederacy, 232–7
wage slavery, 96, 177–91
Washington, George, 226–32
Washington Square, 197, 198,
  202
Webster, Daniel, 33
Wharton, Edith, 71, 75

White, William Allen, 75–6
White, Stanford, 198
Whitehead, Alfred North, 110
Whiteness, 89–91, 93, 95–8, 133, 134, 145n14
  white anxiety, 90, 95–8
  White privilege, 96, 97, 134
  white slavery, 95, 96
  white supremacy, 98
  white victimhood, 98
  see also less-than-White, race

Whitman, Walt, 39n3
  'Elias Hicks, Notes (Such as They Are),' 41–2, 44–5, 48, 51
  'Father Taylor (and Oratory),' 42, 56
  Leaves of Grass, 42
  'Song of Occupations,' 42–3, 46–9, 51–3, 56
  November Boughs, 41, 44
William and Mary, 224–5, 233, 236–8

Yancy, George, 90